FORGOTTEN
FAYETTEVILLE
AND WASHINGTON COUNTY

also by

J.B. HOGAN

Tin Hollow
Fallen: A Short Story Collection
Bar Harbor: A Short Story Collection
The Rubicon: A Poetry Collection
Losing Cotton
Living Behind Time
Angels in the Ozarks

FORGOTTEN FAYETTEVILLE

AND WASHINGTON COUNTY

J.B. HOGAN

Otterford

Otterford

An Imprint of Roan & Weatherford Publishing Associates, LLC
Bentonville, Arkansas
www.roanweatherford.com

Copyright © 2023 by J.B. Hogan

Library of Congress Cataloging-in-Publication Data
Names: Hogan, J.B., author
Title: Forgotten Fayetteville and Washington County | J.B. Hogan
Description: First Edition | Bentonville: Otterford, 2023
Identifiers: | ISBN: 978-1-63373-638-2(trade paperback) |
ISBN: 978-1-63373-639-9 (eBook)
BISAC: HISTORY/United States/State & Local/South |
HISTORY/United States/State & Local/General

Otterford River trade paperback edition September, 2023

Cover & Interior Design by Casey W. Cowan
Editing by Gordon Bonnet & Jessica Crowder
Indexing by T. Scott Cowan

This book is dedicated to Phydella Hogan:
mother, teacher, musician, poet and more.
Without her there is no me—in any manner whatsoever.

TABLE OF CONTENTS

ACKNOWLEDGEMENTS

I WISH TO thank Susan Parks-Spencer, Ellen Compton, Gretchen Gearhart, Tony Wappel, Tim Nutt, Charlie Alison, Tom Dillard, Washington County Historical Society, University of Arkansas Libraries Special Collections (especially Geoffery Stark and Joshua Youngblood), Fayetteville (AR) Public Library (especially Mickey Clement), John Paul Davis, Fayetteville (AR) Mayor Lioneld Jordan, the late Fayetteville (AR) City Clerk Sondra Smith, Sgt. Craig Stout of the Fayetteville (AR) Police Department, Deputy Bobby McDonald of the Washington County (AR) Sheriff's Office, Trisha Beland, the late Jimmy Fletcher and the Fletcher Family of Baldwin/Fayetteville, Arkansas, Robert Crawford and the Crawford family of Rhea's Mill/Lincoln, Arkansas, Charles Clinehens, Bill Mayo, Mel Collier and the Collier Drug Store Family, the late Professor Jim Chase, Bob Besom, my late brother-in-law Kirby L. Estes and my sister Martha Hogan Estes.

All of the articles in this collection appeared, though in slightly different form, in *Flashback,* the journal of the Washington County Historical Society.

AUTHOR'S NOTE

THE CHAPTERS OF this book are essentially laid out in chronological order from oldest to newest. Each chapter was originally an historical essay.

EARLY HISTORIANS OF FAYETTEVILLE
& WASHINGTON COUNTY[1]

OVER OUR NEARLY 200-year existence, Fayetteville and Washington County have had a number of historians record the events, places, and people that came before and have made us who we are today. Names like W. S. Campbell, Kent Brown, and Walter J. Lemke immediately come to mind. Their contributions, as well as that of so many others, have helped preserve much of our past. Lesser known, though, are the first historians, the ones who recorded our early years—they deserve to be remembered as well.

A. W. Arrington

One of the first local historians, and certainly one of the most entertaining if not always the most reliable, was A. W. Arrington. Arrington came to Fayetteville around 1832 from Missouri where he had recently been expelled from the Methodist ministry. Born on September 17, 1810, in North Carolina[2], Arrington's story is remarkable in and of itself, independent of his legacy as a local historian.

A youthful prodigy of sorts, he took to the pulpit early and was a highly regarded and charismatic evangelist in the American heartland, being ordained a Methodist minister in 1831 at Indianapolis, Indiana. But his passion for the Word shortly shifted towards women and strong drink and by the following year he had done a spiritual flip-flop, renouncing his faith and "becoming a militant infidel."[3] Arrington's lust for alcohol and ladies would color most perceptions of the man throughout the rest of his life.

In 1832, the year he denounced his faith, he temporarily relocated to Little Rock then moved north to Fayetteville. The following year he requested and was allowed back into the ministry but by 1834 had once again been expelled by the Methodist leadership. Also that year, Arrington married Sarah Connor, daughter of a respectable Fayetteville family.[4]

With his preaching days behind him, Arrington read the law and was admitted to the bar in Fayetteville.[5] He quickly rose to prominence and was "noted for the brilliancy of his imagination and the success which attended his practice in the courts."[6] Despite his success, his reputation suffered because he was said to be "erratic in his manner of living" and "frequently indulged in fits of dissipation"[7]—elsewhere described as "he liked his corn whiskey."[8]

The year 1839 was a momentous one for Fayetteville and Washington County and Arrington was an active participant and observer of the events in that dramatic time. Three acts of violence that year had a great impact on the area. First was the Trail of Tears detachment led by John Benge which passed through Fayetteville in January and resulted in the killing of Cherokee Nelson Orr. Then on June 15, members of the Wright family near Cane Hill were murdered, putting the young county into a state of fear and paranoia. One week later to the day, June 22, members of the Cherokee Treaty Party, Major Ridge, John Ridge and Elias Boudinot, were killed in retaliation for their role in the relocation of the tribe from its ancestral homes in the east.

When the man who stabbed Nelson Orr to death, Willis Wallace, was acquitted of the killing in May of 1839, Arrington was incensed at what he perceived to be an injustice—so much so that the conflict between the two men, although no shots were fired, became known as the Arrington-Wallace War.

Arrington also felt that the men accused and then hung for the Wright family murders in Cane Hill were innocent. He railed against the thirty-six men known as the Cane Hill Regulators who conducted the investigation and interrogation of the purported murderers. Ar-

A.W. Arrington
Uncredited, Arkansas Historical Quartlerly, Winter 1955

rington did not recognize the legitimacy of the Regulators and was appalled by the actual hangings of the accused men.[9]

Despite his controversial stand on these cases, Arrington continued to have a successful law practice. By 1842, he was popular enough to campaign for and win a seat in the Arkansas Legislature, running on the Whig Party ticket.

In May 1843, he led the defense team that helped Cherokee Stand Watie, brother of the late Elias Boudinot and later a Confederate General and war hero, get acquitted for the killing of James C. Foreman, who was allegedly involved in the death of Major Ridge. Arrington's defense summation was so strong that the jury returned a Not Guilty verdict for Watie in five minutes."[10]

In the 1844 election, however, things began to go bad for the eloquent, dynamic Arrington. Although he campaigned as a Whig candidate for a presidential elector position, he ended up voting almost a straight Democratic ticket. His shifting political allegiance and wild behavior—he had challenged two men to duels, including Alfred M. Wilson who had prosecuted Stand Watie, but both men refused—made Arrington a pariah in Arkansas politics and in the pages of its leading newspapers.[11]

That same year, he chose to leave Arkansas, forever abandoning his wife Sarah and family and heading south to Texas with a mistress in tow. From 1844 until the mid-1850s, Arrington spent most of his time in Texas, but he also lived briefly in New York. He then went back to Texas for several years, where he first became a judge, and finally in 1855 moved to Madison, Wisconsin.

As far back as 1832, Arrington had stated that his goal was to earn "his living writing poetry and novels"[12] and while in Texas he ended up writing several books under the pseudonym Charles Summerfield. In 1847, while he was in New York, he married once again and found a publisher for his books. His first book was *The Desperadoes of the South-West,* followed in short order by *Duelists and Duelling in the South-West.*"[13]

These two books were combined and reissued as one in 1849 by publishers in both New York and Philadelphia. The New York version was titled *The Lives and Adventures of the Desperadoes of the South-West* while the Philadelphia book was called *Illustrated Lives and Adventures of the Desperadoes of the New World.*

Even though both of these books at times may be seen as "highly imaginative"[14] accounts of the Wright Family murders and Willis Wallace affair, Arrington's stories are based on actual Arkansas history. If we can get past the fact that he often wrote "with more than poetic license,"[15] there is a foundation of historical accuracy in his works that is and has been invaluable to subsequent historians for nearly 170 years.

Arrington's writings as Charles Summerfield brought him some level of "national fame"[16] and after his brief sojourn in Madison, in 1857 he moved to Chicago, Illinois. His writing from this point on was mostly limited to poetry but as a lawyer and judge his success was described as being "without parallel in the history of the profession."[17] Once again, he married "a lady of refinement" and settled into a life wherein it was said he "lived like a hermit and worked like a horse."[18]

In the fall of 1867, perhaps due in part to his heavy workload, Arrington suffered a "paralytic stroke."[19] On December 31, 1867, he died. His success in Chicago had been so great that upon his death the Chicago Bar issued a lengthy *Memorial of Alfred W. Arrington,* filled with encomiums to the fallen judge. Alfred W. Arrington, the man who had the ability "to electrify an audience beyond all living men"[20] and whose written work is, despite its frequent flights of fancy, of enduring significance to our local history, was no more.

James H. Van Hoose

James H. Van Hoose, especially when compared to someone like A. W. Arrington, was a solid beacon of rationality and stability. He was born in Kentucky on January 8, 1830, and came to Arkansas with his family in May of 1839.[21] The family settled near the Middle Fork of the White River in the White River Township.[22]

He worked for his father until he was 21 years old when he walked to the Ozark Institute in Mt. Comfort northwest of Fayetteville[23] to further his education. There he was under the tutelage of school president Reverend Robert Mecklin, noted Methodist minister and early Washington County educator. Van Hoose spent some fifteen months at the institute where he paid for his schooling by working for Reverend Mecklin for $13 a month.[24]

On March 12, 1852,[25] Van Hoose moved to Fayetteville and began working as a clerk in the general store of James Sutton.[26] In November 1855 Sutton went out of business, selling his store to William McIlroy, Van Hoose's new father-in-law. Just three months earlier, on August 9, 1855, he had married Melinda Ann, McIlroy's only daughter. In 1864,

Melinda died and in 1869 Van Hoose married Martha W. Skelton, daughter of William Skelton.[27]

Throughout this time, even after the death of his first wife, Van Hoose continued to work for and then partnered with William McIlroy in both the mercantile and banking businesses. Finally, in 1881-1882, he severed his connection to the McIlroy businesses and went into life insurance which he followed for the "rest of his life."[28] Actively involved in local politics as well as business, he was elected Mayor of Fayetteville twice, serving from 1880-1881 and again from 1888-1890.[29] In 1897, he also served one term in the Arkansas General Assembly.[30]

Van Hoose was a very prominent Mason as well, joining the organization in 1853 and over the years serving as Grand Master, Grand High Priest and Grand Commander.[31] He was friends with Albert Pike, the well-known poet, adventurer, soldier and Mason himself. Pike "was a central figure in the development of Masonry"[32] in the State of Arkansas and as Grand Commander signed Van Hoose's 32nd degree certificate for the group.[33]

Van Hoose also thought of himself as a poet but is remembered today for his "many sketches" of our early history, "graphically" portraying "scenes of pioneer life in Arkansas."[34] He was a correspondent for several papers outside Fayetteville,[35] writing for Little Rock and eastern newspapers.[36]

One of the more interesting stories about Van Hoose, rather than written by him, concerned an early 1865 trip he took to Washington, D. C. His first wife Melinda had died in the fall of 1864 and his brothers Peter and Zach, captured Confederate soldiers, were confined by the Union to the Springfield, Missouri area. While visiting them in Springfield, he learned that another brother, George, also a Confederate soldier, was doing poorly in the Union Prison Camp at Johnson's Island, Ohio.[37]

Setting off from Fayetteville in mid-winter, he went to Washington by way of St. Louis, Indianapolis and Philadelphia. He arrived in the capitol on February 17 and after enduring long waits and assurances he could not see the president finally met Abraham Lincoln in person on February 20, 1865. After some discussion and delicate negotiations on his part, he was able to get a note from the president allowing a visit with George Van Hoose. Lincoln's note indicated "contraband" was not allowed but Van Hoose was able to provide his brother with clothing, blankets, food and the like.[38]

Peter Van Hoose died in March 1865 and was brought home for burial in the family plot in Fayetteville.[39] Zach and George survived the war to return home. They died in 1887 and 1909, respectively

In early 1882, Van Hoose wrote two very important local history articles. The first of these was printed in the March 15 issue of the *Fayetteville Sentinel,* founded by veteran newsman James R. Pettigrew in 1875.[40] Entitled "Fayetteville Thirty Years Ago," the article commemorated Van Hoose's thirtieth year in town. In it, he described what things were like on March 8, 1852, when he came to stay in the "pretty little village of about 600 inhabitants."[41]

He describes Robert Graham's Ozark College and Sophia Sawyer's Female Seminary and lists Fayetteville having two hotels, two wagon shops, two groceries/saloons, and many lawyers. He gives us the cost of foodstuffs, potatoes were ten cents per bushel and corn twenty cents, and the cost of soda drinks at the new James Stevenson drug store: "two glasses for 10c."[42]

In the May 25, 1882 issue of the weekly *Fayetteville Democrat,* Van Hoose wrote about the town's "Early History." In this article he presented a "sketch" of Fayetteville from March of 1829 through December of 1830 based on records found in the "vaults" of the County Clerk's office. He gives us court officials and grand jurors, and tells of the building of the first courthouse—including the amount allocated for its construction: $49.75.[43]

On April 19, 1889, he wrote a reminiscence of the California gold mine expedition that left Fayetteville in April 1849—forty years before. He tells us that "snow was falling all day," that the adventurers left in ox-pulled wagons, and that the expedition was led by Lewis Evans, first sheriff of Washington County.[44]

Van Hoose then recalls many of the men who made the trip and

James H. Van Hoose
Washington County Historical Society, Flashback, February 1974

the few who still remain in 1889. "Mr. S. K. Stone," he wrote, "is the only one living who was then engaged here selling goods." Among the lawyers, he tells us, were A. M. Wilson, W. D. Reagan, and Judge David Walker. In closing, he comments about how much Fayetteville had changed over those forty years and that he expects more change to come in the next forty. "If I am here April 15, 1929," he promised in referring to the expected changes, "I will write them up for you."[45] It's no doubt the town's loss that he did not get that chance.

On Saturday, May 6, 1899, while hunting, Van Hoose's rifle accidentally discharged. The recoil hit him "with such force that an internal injury was inflicted, resulting in his death soon afterward."[46] An "unfortunate accident"[47] had extinguished the life of one of Fayetteville's most prominent citizens and in the opinion of many, the town's "first important historian."[48]

Unknown "Saunterer"

In the early 1870s, an anonymous writer took "saunters" around the Square, describing the stores and people he met in his leisurely walks. They were breezy, light tours, enjoyable not just for the running descriptions but for the specific details about the Square as it was 145 years ago, giving us the written equivalent of a time capsule.

The following brief excerpt is from the December 1871 "saunter" and gives a fair notion of how each of the articles was presented in the *Democrat*:

> *The snow having disappeared, the weather having somewhat moderated, ye local ventured on a little saunter round town this week to "see what could be seen."*
>
> *We first peep in at Blackwell's (on the North Side), find all hands busy with country customers, notwithstanding the bad state of the roads, inclemency of the weather, &c. The next house on our route is the stove, tin and hardware house of*
> *"Uncle Joe" Kimbrough. Calling in at Peacock & Pendleton's Drug Store we found everything as neat as a new pin, and the gentlemanly proprietors busy with a host of cash customers....*[49]

Each visit ends back at "the office." Because the columns appear in the *Fayetteville Democrat*, which was put out by brothers E. B. and W. B. Moore, it seems reasonable to assume that one of these men was the "saunterer."

E. B. Moore had sustained a serious wound to his hip at the Battle of Oak Hills, better known by its Union-labeled name of Wilson's Creek, in Missouri. Because of this severe injury and the difficulty it gave E. B. Moore the rest of his life, the best guess as to the identity of

the anonymous "saunterer" is that it was his brother, W. B. Moore—
but there's no direct evidence available to confirm this.

Uncle Gus Lewis

Another contributor to Fayetteville history from this era was Augustus B. "Uncle Gus" Lewis. Born in Hempstead County in 1835, Lewis came to Fayetteville with his family in 1844. He attended Reverend Robert Graham's Arkansas College in the early 1850s and had a store on the Square at the outbreak of the Civil War. He enlisted in the Confederate Army and served the full four years of the war, seeing action at the Battle of Wilson Creek.[50]

After the war, with his store burned to the ground and himself heavily in debt, he worked for several years as a clerk at Baum & Brothers, a long-running store on the East Side of the Fayetteville Square. The south end of the Baum & Brothers store stood where Lewis' store had prior to the war.[51]

Around 1875, Lewis "established the first known Dickson Street business." His mercantile was located approximately where George's Majestic Lounge is today.[52] In the early 1900s, he served as a commissioner on the Dickson Street Improvement District.[53] In 1922, he joined a group of residents who successfully defeated an attempt to rename Dickson Street to Main Street.[54]

Lewis was said to be a "mine of information for those seeking stories of former days" and "was willing to talk of the past."[55] His recollections had appeared after World War I in local papers like the *Fayetteville Sentinel* and the *Fayetteville Daily Democrat*. They were reprinted in a series of 1960 issues of *Flashback*, the journal of the Washington County Historical Society.

The "Civil War Reminiscences of A. B. 'Uncle Gus' Lewis" appeared in the January 1960 *Flashback* and consisted of three stories about treachery, combat, and graft.[56] "'Uncle Gus' Lewis Tells of Old Saloon Days in Fayetteville" was in the April 1960 *Flashback* and told the humorous story of how a local saloon-keeper who sold whiskey at 10 cents by the horn was duped by a traveling man who got the better of the deal

Uncle Gus Lewis
Washington County Historical Society, Flashback, July, 1960

by producing an oxen horn three feet long to be filled with whiskey. The locals enjoyed the joke so much they and the traveler pulled it on two other unsuspecting barkeeps before the man "returned to his wagon, replaced his horn, and like the wild goose, returned north to his old haunts." The horn, it turned out, could hold three quarts of whiskey—a great deal for the drinker but not so much for the saloon.[57]

In "Chasing Guerrillas in Arkansas," Lewis tells of being part of a Confederate unit that pursued and defeated a guerrilla band, hanging its two vicious leaders. As it turned out, in 1867, back home in Washington County after the war, Lewis met Nelson Hewitt, who had been

captured by the same guerrilla group but managed to safely escape.
The following year, Lewis met Hewitt's daughter Rebecca and they
married in 1869.[58]

"Uncle Gus" Lewis remained in Fayetteville for the rest of his life,
running his mercantile business and serving two years as Washington
County Treasurer in 1872-1874. After retiring, he was known for his
knowledge of local history and his ability to predict the weather.[59] He
passed in 1928.

James P. Neal

James Preston Neal (1820-1896) was an early settler of Washington County, a lawyer, businessman, military veteran, philanthropist,
local historian, and the founder of Prairie Grove, Arkansas. In 1829,
the nine-year-old Kentucky native arrived in Prairie Grove with his
stepfather and mother, Andrew and Sinai Buchanan, younger brother,
William Neal, and Mary Woods, a "young lady" the Buchanan's had
adopted while in Kentucky.[60]

After studying law in Fayetteville at Judge David Walker's office,
Neal was admitted to the Arkansas bar and then became Walker's part-
ner. A year after the outbreak of the Mexican-American War in 1846,
Neal joined the Arkansas Mounted Volunteers where he became a first
lieutenant and fought in Mexico.

During his military service, he met two future presidents: Jefferson
Davis, who led the Confederate States of America during the Civil
War, and Ulysses S. Grant, the 18th President of the United States.
After the war ended in 1848, First Lieutenant Neal returned to Fay-
etteville and his previous occupation as a lawyer.[61]

In 1849, Neal married Adaline Bean,[62] the daughter of wealthy
Cane Hill businessman Mark Bean. Three years later, Neal won a position on the Fayetteville Town Council and was appointed its "chief
alderman or mayor."[63] After Neal had served two years, he and his wife
moved from Fayetteville to Austin, Texas, due to Adaline's ill health.[64]
During their time in Austin, the couple had six children with only two
surviving, Sam and Eleanora.[65]

Neal became an active supporter of the Confederacy during the Civil War by donating money to help supply their forces. He was also a presidential elector and cast his vote for Jefferson Davis to serve a second term as President of the Confederate States. His financial and political support of the Confederacy eventually earned him a military appointment of Colonel.[66]

In 1864, Neal received word that his brother, William, who was also a Colonel in the Confederate Army, had been killed by Union soldiers near Clarksville, Arkansas. Several local women buried William after the battle, but in 1884, Neal had his brother's body exhumed and laid to rest in the Prairie Grove Cemetery.[67]

Adaline's health declined further in the early years of the Civil War and she passed away in 1863. Five years later, Neal moved from Austin back to Fayetteville, where he and fellow lawyer, James M. Pitman, set up the law practice of Neal & Pitman.[68] In 1869, he married his brother William's widow, Lucy Jane Tinin Neal, and the couple had two sons, James Preston II and Jay Dudley, and one daughter, Sinai Belle.[69]

Neal moved the family back to his childhood home in Prairie Grove in 1871 so he could focus on increasing the town's population and developing a business district.[70] He was installed as Prairie Grove's second postmaster in 1872, replacing J.H. Addison, who had been appointed two years earlier.[71]

Neal was active in the local Democrat Party and in 1872 was elected as a delegate to the Democratic State Convention in Little Rock.[72] He was a Mason, a member of the Methodist Church, and a Justice of the Peace in the 1870s for Mountain Township.[73] Neal also organized a Mexican War veterans group that met in Fayetteville and sometimes Prairie Grove, where the Colonel would host his fellow veterans "in handsome style."[74]

In 1877, Neal asked Washington County surveyor, J.A. Buchanan to map out Prairie Grove's main street area. Buchanan used "stones and stone coal" to mark certain sections of town. There were five roads recorded on the plat: Garrison Avenue and Buchanan, Kate Smith, Mock, and Neal streets.[75]

It appears that Neal's historical writings began in the 1880s with articles that chronicled his childhood experiences in Prairie Grove and other early 19th century Washington County incidents. Several of his stories were published or reprinted in the *Fayetteville Democrat* in 1885, the *Prairie Grove Enterprise* in 1938, and the most detailed of these remembrances appeared in 1955 in three editions of *Flashback*. In these accounts, Neal described his family's journey from Kentucky in early 1829 and their arrival in Cane Hill on September 3rd of that year, where they stayed with his stepfather's brother, James Buchanan.

In the *Flashback* article, Neal described arriving at their new home:

> We reached the spring; the older portion of the company com-
> menced unloading the wagons; the younger ones to explore the
> surroundings. The spring and branch were alive with small fish,
> and the surrounding country abounded with birds and prairie
> chickens…At night the camp-lamp in front of the house was
> lighted, giving light for a hundred and fifty or two hundred yards
> around, astonishing the screech-owl, the night-owl, other forest
> birds and the smaller animals. About 10 o'clock the family re-
> tired; the young ones to sleep; the older ones to think.

Neal recalled an incident one night in 1833 that created such panic and fear "Women swooned and strong men trembled" as stars continuously fell from the sky. During the event, some of the locals blew horns and fired guns to alert the rest of the settlers, who then assembled at Andrew Buchanan's home. Neal's stepfather was an ordained Cumberland Presbyterian minister and the townspeople most likely turned to him for guidance in what appeared to be the end of the world.[76]

Neal also shared a story about an unplanned gathering at his house when a group of horsemen rode into town around the fall of 1834. At that time, fourteen-year-old Neal and the other youngsters in town were being educated in a "log schoolhouse" near the present-day corner of Buchanan and Kate Smith streets in Prairie Grove.

One day while Neal and his classmates were outside taking a break from their lessons, they were approached by several "servants" with packhorses, along with "five or six gentlemen, gorgeously dressed and finely mounted." The riders stopped and asked for directions to the spring so they could rest and water their horses.

As the men received directions, one of the students asked a servant who the men were. To their surprise, they were informed that two of the party included former Tennessee governor Sam Houston and Resin [Rezin] Bowie, who Neal credited as the inventor of the Bowie knife. Houston and the others were on their way to Archibald Yell's law office in Fayetteville in order to pick up documents and letters sent to them from President Andrew Jackson.[77]

In 1888, the *Fayetteville Democrat* printed Neal's account of the beginning of the Battle of Prairie Grove on December 7, 1862. His widowed mother, Sinai Buchanan, still lived at their home near the spring and possibly told Neal of the events since he was still living in Austin at the time.

At dawn on the day of the battle before the first shots were fired, four men on horseback, presumably Confederates, rode up to the house and asked one of the Buchanan slaves, Beck, if she knew of any Union soldiers that were inside. Minutes later, several of the boys in blue were seen running from the house headed west toward the Federal camp. The riders wheeled their horses back towards their own encampment and the battle soon began.[78]

In the same article, Neal tells the story of John Sharp, a private in the Confederate army who fought at the Battle of Prairie Grove. As Sharp and his fellow soldiers marched into Prairie Grove, he told them the landscape reminded him of a dream he'd had the previous week.

In it, he and his regiment had passed through mountains and then arrived at a valley where they engaged Union troops in a battle. In the dream, a soldier next to him was shot in the face above an eye and immediately fell to the ground. When Sharp ran over to assist him, he saw the face of the soldier and realized he was looking at himself. A short time later during the actual battle, Sharp was killed instantly when he was shot in the head, right above an eye.[79]

Health issues prompted Neal's retirement as postmaster in 1887, but he continued to write articles about the early history of Prairie Grove and Washington County for the next several years.[80] His wife, Lucy, died in 1893 and Neal passed away in 1896. Both are buried in the Prairie Grove Cemetery near Neal's first wife, Adaline, and his brother, William.[81]

THE FLETCHER FAMILY
OF BALDWIN

THE FLETCHER FAMILY of the Baldwin community in Washington County has a long and storied history. Tracing their ancestry to colonial America, present-day descendants count Revolutionary War, War of 1812, and Civil War veterans among their predecessors.

Reaching Northwest Arkansas by way of Virginia and Kentucky in the early 1820s,[82] the family settled in the Baldwin area. The stones and monuments dedicated to them in the Hester Cemetery in Baldwin as well as the King Cemetery in Harris (Elkins) bear witness to the Fletcher's impact on the county.

From the recently deceased Jimmy Fletcher,[83] late of rural Fayetteville, the genealogical path leads back to Robert Fletcher, Sr., who served two tours of military duty with Virginia Regiments during the American Revolution.[84]

The youngest son of John Fletcher, Chester County, Pennsylvania and Eleanor Hindman Fletcher, born in Londonderry County, Ireland, Robert Fletcher, Sr. was born sometime between 1738 and 1745 in Chester County, Pennsylvania. By no later than 1749, the Fletcher family had moved to Augusta County, Virginia.[85]

On June 12, 1777, Robert Fletcher, Sr. enlisted for three years as a Private in Captain Richard Stevens' Company of the 10th Virginia Regiment, which was actually commanded by Colonel Edward Stevens. Family genealogical records indicate that Robert Fletcher, Sr. was hospitalized (no reasons given) from July 1777 until March 1778.

After leaving hospital in 1778, Robert Fletcher, Sr. enlisted again for a term of about three months, this time to replace his brother John Fletcher. Robert Fletcher, Sr. served in Captain Samuel Haw's Company of the 1st Virginia Regiment commanded by a Colonel Woodford.[86]

Robert Fletcher, Sr. had two older brothers: Jobe and John, Jr. Jobe moved from Virginia to Kentucky in 1779 and John, Jr. did the same in 1800.[87]

Prior to the war, around 1763, Robert Fletcher, Sr. married Christian Febiger in Virginia. They had two sons: John and Robert Fletcher, Jr. Little is known of John Fletcher, but Robert Fletcher, Jr. was born July 19, 1788 in Rockbridge County, Virginia. On June 25 or 26, 1811, he married Mary "Polly" Wilson in Christian County, Kentucky. Polly Wilson Fletcher was born November 3, 1795 in Harden County, Kentucky.[88]

Robert Fletcher, Jr. and Polly Wilson Fletcher had eleven children, the first four born in Kentucky. The oldest, John was born in 1811, followed by Timothy Henry, 1813, Jobe, 1815, Eliza, 1818, and Elizabeth, known as Betty, 1820.[89]

On June 18, 1812 war broke out between the United States and Great Britain. On August 23, 1812, Robert Fletcher, Jr. enlisted in the Kentucky Militia for a six-month tour of duty. He served in Captain John W. Shirley's Company, Barbee's Regiment in the Kentucky Militia.[90] After the war, around 1820-1821,[91] Robert Fletcher, Jr. moved his family to Baldwin, Arkansas. Five more children were born in Baldwin beginning with James Alexander, 1822, Andrew Jackson, 1824, Jesse L., 1829, Mary Ann, 1832, Robert III, 1833 and Nancy A. 1834.[92]

During the Civil War, other Fletchers continued the tradition of serving in the military. On October 26, 1861, John C. Fletcher enlisted as a private in Company E, 1st Battalion, Arkansas Cavalry (Confederate). On December 6, 1861, Robert and William F. Fletcher also enlisted as privates in the same Company E.[93]

At the time, Company E was commanded by Captain William H. Brooks. Among the company officers was 2nd Lieutenant E. I. "Ras" Stirman who later became the youngest Colonel in the Confederacy and after the Civil War served as mayor of Fayetteville.[94]

COMMONWEALTH OF KENTUCKY
DEPARTMENT OF MILITARY AFFAIRS
OFFICE OF THE ADJUTANT GENERAL
FRANKFORT 40601

24 August 1964

STATEMENT OF SERVICE: FLETCHER, Robert
                         War of 1812

Rank: Private

Date of Appointment or Enlistment: August 23, 1812

To what time Engaged or Enlisted: Six months

From Roll of Capt John W. Shirley's Co., Barbee's Regiment, Kentucky Militia.

* * * * * * * * * * *

"I certify that the above is a true and correct statement of service for the above mentioned person as found on file in the office of The Adjutant General, Commonwealth of Kentucky, Frankfort, Kentucky."

FOR THE ADJUTANT GENERAL:

EUGENE P. REYNOLDS
Major, AUS (Ret)
Records Custodian

War of 1812 Statement of Service—Robert Fletcher
Courtesy of Jimmy Fletcher

John C. Fletcher was mustered out of the military in January or February of 1863 because he was "Left sick in Arkansas."[95] William F. Fletcher became a prisoner of war after being captured July 4, 1863 at Vicksburg, Mississippi.[96] Robert Fletcher died February 19, 1863, at Grenada, Mississippi.[97]

Jobe Fletcher, older brother of Robert Fletcher, III, was born December 4, 1815 in Kentucky. Settling with his family in Baldwin, Arkansas, Jobe became a farmer and a wagon maker and on January 23, 1840 married Sarah Ann Williford who was born December 5, 1821 in Tennessee. Jobe and Sarah Fletcher had thirteen children, only eight of whom reached adulthood.[98]

Jobe Fletcher Gravestone, Harris (Elkins), Arkansas
Courtesy of Jimmy Fletcher

The fourth oldest surviving child, John Franklin Fletcher, born at Baldwin, Arkansas on March 4, 1849, married Sarah Ellen Enyart of Fayetteville, Arkansas on October 8, 1877. This union produced five children who reached adulthood, including Charles Clifford Fletcher who was born April 20, 1887 in Baldwin, Arkansas.[99]

On June 17, 1908 Charles Clifford Fletcher married Lou Emma Eacret,[100] born March 26, 1886, in Red Star, Madison County, Arkansas. They had two children: Thelma Ruth, born October 2, 1910, and John Howard, born February 3, 1909.

Jimmy Fletcher, U.S. Army, 1958
Courtesy of Jimmy Fletcher

On July 21, 1928, John Howard Fletcher married Audra Beatrice Phillips,[101] born December 24, 1908 in Wyman, Washington County, Arkansas. This union produced two children: Audra Marie, born May 28, 1929 and Jimmy Lee, born February 10, 1940.[102]

The following family tree begins prior to the Revolutionary War with prime progenitor John Fletcher of Pennsylvania and Virginia and ends seven generations later with Audra Marie Fletcher Chandler and Jimmy Lee Fletcher of Baldwin and Fayetteville, Arkansas.[103]

FLETCHER FAMILY GENEALOGY[104]

John Fletcher (1717-1758)
m. (ca. 1735-1739) **Eleanor Hindman** (1719-1790)
Jobe
John
Robert

Robert Fletcher, Sr. (ca. 1738-1745-1796)
m. (1762) **Christian Febiger** (ca. 1746-1800)
John
Robert, Jr.

Robert Fletcher, Jr. (1788-1856)
m. (1811) **Mary "Polly" Wilson** (1795-1875)
John
Timothy Henry
Jobe
Eliza
Elizabeth (Betty)
James Alexander
Andrew Jackson
Jesse L.
Mary Ann
Robert III
Nancy A.

Jobe Fletcher (1815-1875)
m. (1840) **Sarah Ann Williford** (1821-1888)
Mary Jane
James W.
Lorana
Martha (twin)
Margaret (twin)

John Franklin
Sarah Elizabeth
Robert Jobe
Analiza
Francis A.
Thomas M.
Alice Magdaline
Amanda B.

John Franklin Fletcher (1849-1898)
m. (1877) **Sarah Ellen Enyart** (1858-1942)
Leland Alonzo
Bessie Leonara
James Franklin
Charles Clifford
Thomas E.
Martin Edward
Gertrude

Charles Clifford Franklin (1887-1967)
m. (1908) **Lou Emma Eacret** (1886-1952)
Thelma Ruth
John Howard

John Howard Fletcher (1909-2001)
m. (1928) **Audra Beatrice Phillips** (1908-1997)
Audra Marie
Jimmy Lee

THE CRAWFORD FAMILY
OF RHEA'S MILL

ROBERT CRAWFORD, LIKE countless young men before him, was raised on a family farm. In the fertile, rolling plains of western Washington County this is hardly an unusual situation. What makes Robert's case different, however, is that his family has lived on and worked the same land on which he grew up since well before the Civil War.

His fourth great-grandfather, James Crawford, came to Washington County in 1830 only two years after its creation in October 1828,[105] when the state-to-be was still the Arkansas Territory.[106] Arriving here from Tennessee with his wife Nancy Ann Sawyers Crawford and a brood of children, James Crawford was one of the earliest settlers in Northwest Arkansas.

James Crawford was the son of William and Rachel Sawyers Crawford of Augusta County, Virginia. William Crawford was a veteran of the American Revolution and is described in the Roster of Revolutionary Ancestors, as a "Private and Patriot, manufacturing and supplying arms to Continental Army, Augusta County, Virginia."[107] He is listed as Ancestor #A027666 by the Daughters of the American Revolution.[108]

William Crawford's parents, Alexander and Mary McPhetters Crawford were of Scottish ancestry but migrated from Ireland and "were among the earliest settlers in Augusta County, Virginia.[109] Alexander and Mary Crawford met a terrible end in the fall of 1764 when they were besieged and killed by Native Americans.[110] William Crawford was only twenty years old when he lost his parents in the gruesome attack. He was only forty-eight years old when he died himself.

His son, James Crawford, the early Washington County settler, bought land[111] in the Rhea's Mill area and established the family farm which still exists today. James and wife Nancy had a large family including the next to youngest child Robert Donald Crawford.

Robert Donald, known as "Uncle Bob" Crawford, was about fourteen years old when the family moved to Arkansas from his birth state of Tennessee. He remained on the Crawford family homestead until he died after a tragic Christmas Day 1899 fire accident.

The *Fayetteville Democrat* (Weekly) obituary said that the "very

James Crawford Gravestone, Lincoln, Arkansas
J.B. Hogan

highly respected" man had climbed into "a chair to wind a clock, and losing his balance fell into the fireplace and remained in the fire" until an unnamed child "gave the alarm" and the "old man" was pulled out of the flames. Robert Donald Crawford clung to life from Christmas Day, a Monday, until the following Saturday, December 30, 1899,[112] when he succumbed to his injuries.

Uncle Bob Crawford's son Leonidas E. Crawford was born in Washington County in 1850. By the latter part of the nineteenth century, Leonidas had done well enough in life to warrant a biographical sketch in the 1889 *Goodspeed's History of Washington County.*[113]

Leonidas Crawford is said to deserve "honorable mention as a successful farmer and stock raiser." In earlier times, he had been "captain of a company of militia for five years" and he and his wife Sallie E. Woodruff Crawford were members of the Cumberland Presbyterian Church.[114] The Cumberland Presbyterians were among the first Anglo-Europeans to arrive in Northwest Arkansas, a group of which settled in and founded the community of Cane Hill around 1826 and were also instrumental in locating and naming Fayetteville, the county seat.

In 1879, ten years before the *Goodspeed* biography, Leonidas Crawford and some of his brothers spent a year cattle ranching in western Texas. While in Texas, Leonidas married Sallie Elizabeth Woodruff, who also hailed from Washington County, Arkansas.[115] The couple returned to Arkansas in 1880 and raised their family on the original Crawford farmstead.

Clyde Woodruff Crawford, the youngest son of Leonidas and Sallie Woodruff Crawford was born at Rhea in 1887. In keeping with family tradition, he was a lifelong farmer, but in July of 1918 at the age of 31 he entered the military in Fayetteville and served during the latter part of World War I.[116] Five years later, in 1923, he married Ola "Granny" Hulett, a union that lasted almost fifty years.

Leon G., born George Leon, Crawford, son of Clyde Woodruff and Ola "Granny" Hulett Crawford, was born at Rhea's Mill in 1927. At the age of eighteen, Leon was drafted into the U. S. Army but requested and was assigned to serve in the U. S. Navy during World War II.

Crawford Family Cemetery, Lincoln, Arkansas
J.B. Hogan

After the war, he returned to the family farm, continuing the long-standing Crawford tradition. In 1955, Leon married Myrna Lou Patton, a native Oklahoman, and they raised three children on the same land just as generations of Crawfords had done before them.

In August 1990, the Leon Crawford family was chosen as the Washington County Pioneer Farm Family. The award was co-sponsored by the Fayetteville Chamber of Commerce, Washington County Fair and Washington County Farm Bureau. Criteria for the Pioneer Farm Family award included continuous ownership of farmland for at least one-hundred years "with a descendant of the original owner still living on the land."[117]

Steve Crawford, the eldest son of Leon G. and Myrna Crawford was born in 1956 at Olathe, Kansas where the family temporarily had moved to find work and where Leon's brother Wayne was already living. The family later returned to Washington County and now, five generations removed from first settler James, Steve Crawford actively farms the same property that has been in the family for over one-hundred and seventy-five years.

Today, with his descendants still homesteading and farming the land James Crawford purchased going on two centuries ago, the Craw-

Crawford Family, Four Generations
(From Left) R.J., Steve, Myrna, and Robert
Courtesy of Ryan Crawford

ford family remains firmly rooted in the soil of the Lincoln and Rhea's Mill area of western Washington County.

With Robert and Ryan Estes Crawford's three young sons, R. J., Calvin, and Mason and little daughter Abby growing up in the same area, the Crawford family name and tradition seems certain to continue well into a third century on Northwest Arkansas land.

CRAWFORD FAMILY GENEALOGY[118]

Alexander Crawford (Unknown-1764)
m. (ca. 1740) **Mary McPhetters** (Unknown-1764)
Margaret
John
Edward
William
Alexander
Rebecca
Elizabeth "Bettie"
Martha
Robert
Samuel
Mary
James

William Crawford
(1744-1792, Augusta County, VA)
m. **Rachel Sawyers** (*b.* April 30, 1750, Augusta County, VA,
d. September 4, 1821, Howell, Lincoln County, TN), about 1768
Alexander
George
Mary "Polly"
Nancy
James
John
Jane "Jenny"
Rachel
William

James Crawford
b. February 29, 1772, Augusta County, VA
d. October 10, 1854, Viney Grove, AR,

m. **Nancy Ann Sawyers,** about 1795
William
Lucinda
John Irbin
Rachel
Hannah
James Sawyers
Mary Armstrong
George Alexander
Robert Donald "Uncle Bob" Crawford
Edward Mclinn (Mack)

Robert Donald "Uncle Bob" Crawford,
b. August 01, 1816, TN,
d. December 31, 1899 Crawford Cemetery, Rhea's Mill, Arkansas,
m. **Elizabeth Henderson** (*b.* 1826, d. 1871), August 17, 1848
Lycurgis
Leonidas E. Crawford
Sardenia
Clomia
Adolphus D.
F. Oscar

Leonidas E. Crawford,
b. November 11, 1850, Washington County, AR,
d. 1919,
m. **Sallie Elizabeth Woodruff**
(*b.* 1862, *d.* 1930) November 15, 1880.
Francis R. "Frank."
Clifford P.
Clyde Woodruff
Harvey Oscar
J. T. (James Tilley)
Mamie

Ina
Vivian
Celia
Geneva

Clyde Woodruff Crawford,
b. January 2, 1887, *d.* January 15, 1971, Prairie Grove, AR,
m. **Ola "Granny" Hulett** *(b.* July 27, 1899, *d.* May 30, 1988),
October 17, 1923
Joe Woodruff
Leon George (b. George Leon)
Clyde Wayne
Donna Lee
Johnny

George Leon Crawford,
b. April 23, 1927, Rhea's Mill, AR,
d. August 9, 2001, Fayetteville, AR,
m. Myrna Lou Patton (*b.* May 27, 1936, Sand Springs, OK),
October 14, 1955
Steven Leon, *b.* August 21, 1956, Olathe, KS
Joe Wayne, *b.* November 19, 1957, Prairie Grove, AR
Denise, *b.* October 4, 1960, Prairie Grove AR

Steven Leon Crawford,
b. August 21, 1956, Olathe, KS,
m. **Sherry Sue Burkett** (*b.* March 24, 1956, Melburn, AR),
January 16, 1975

Nancy Leann,
b. May 3, 1978, Fayetteville, AR,
m. **Matthew Steven Boydstun** (*b.* January 7, 1977, Fayetteville, AR),
July 17, 1999
Kevin Mathew, *b.* October 6, 2002, Johnson, AR

Alexander Leon, *b.* May 30, 2006, Fayetteville, AR
Joshua Leon, *b.* December 15, 1979, Fayetteville, AR

Robert Anthony Crawford,
b. September 17, 1981, Fayetteville, AR,
m. **Ryan Estes** (*b.* April 14, 1984, Fayetteville, AR),
July 20, 2002
R. J., *b.* May 7, 2003, Johnson, AR
Calvin Edison Hogan, *b.* May 28, 2006, Johnson, AR
Mason Henry, *b.* June 7, 2011, Johnson, AR
Abigail Phydella Rose, *b.* December 27, 2013, Johnson, AR

FAYETTEVILLE CITY OFFICIALS:
MAYORS, POLICE & FIRE CHIEFS

IN FAYETTEVILLE'S LONG history—in 2028 the city will celebrate its bicentennial—it has had many and varied civic leaders. The following lists of mayors, police chiefs, and fire chiefs are intended to provide historians and interested citizens an entry point into the history of Fayetteville municipal leadership.

Over the years, the positions of mayor, police and fire chief have been directly impacted by the city's several incorporations. Fayetteville had at least six incorporations from its beginning until just after the turn of the twentieth century:

- 1828, October 17, as Washington Courthouse[123]
- 1836, November 3, as Fayetteville, by state legislature[124]
- 1841, January, by county court as "The Aldermen and Town Council of the Town of Fayetteville"[125]
- 1870, August 24, by county court[126]
- 1883, November 15, as a City of the Second Class—2500 inhabitants[127]
- 1905, June 20, as City of the First Class—5000 inhabitants[128]

Fayetteville Mayors

In its almost two-hundred year existence, Fayetteville has had many distinguished city leaders beginning with Alderman Pleasant Vincent Rhea on down to current Mayor Lioneld Jordan. Alderman Rhea, who according to the *Fayetteville Daily Democrat* "Ruled Fayetteville"[129] from 1841 to about 1851. Rhea was succeeded by James

P. Neal from 1852-1854.[130] It is uncertain who the mayor was from 1854-1858, but J. W. Walker served in 1859 as the first mayor under the city's new charter, which was granted by the state legislature. Walker was followed by Stephen Bedford whose term was cut short by the outbreak of the War Between the States.[131]

During the war, Fayetteville city government was suspended, replaced by military administration. After the war ended, civilian rule was resumed and the first mayor elected to office, in 1868, was Col. M. Larue Harrison who had commanded the First Arkansas Cavalry (Union) during the Battle of Fayetteville, April 16, 1863, and during its occupation of our town.[132]

The subsequent Reconstruction era in Fayetteville created, as it did elsewhere, some measure of local conflict with what was perceived as outside, and unwanted, federal and state intervention. Here in town, this conflict reached its peak with the municipal elections of 1871.

The weekly *Fayetteville Democrat,* owned and published by E. B. and W. B. Moore, crowed that the "Conservative" Democrat "Citizens" ticket had swept the elections. An unnamed acting governor in Little Rock did not agree, however, and replaced J. M. Pittman, the Democratic Party candidate who had apparently won the popular vote for mayor, with "Radical" Republican T. Murray Campbell. The Moores were so incensed by the installation of Campbell that they refused to recognize the new mayor or his city council, at least on the pages of the *Democrat.*[133]

When Reconstruction and the *Democrat* finally calmed down, Fayetteville had a long, settled period of regular elections (held each April), and a smooth transition from one mayor and council to the next ensued. With names like Van Hoose, Eason, Mulholland, Rollins, Philips, Taylor and Wilson, the list reads like a who's who of local public service in Fayetteville's civic past.

In the years of the Great Depression, Mayors T. S. Tribble and A. D. McAllister battled through an unusual period of local corruption. With the help of the Civil Service Commission—established to provide oversight to the police and fire departments—and the Good

Mayor Lioneld Jordan
City of Fayetteville

Government League, however, the more brazen lawbreakers, or "law-benders" at least, were swept from office and public prominence.[134]

George Vaughan succeeded Mayor McAllister just as World War II was starting and his administration was about a year into its second term when Vaughan announced in March 1944 that he could no longer serve as the city's top official because he had been inducted into the Armed Forces of the United States. George T. Sanders became Mayor Pro-Tem and when Vaughan did not return in time to reclaim his position, Sanders himself was elected mayor in 1945 and served two terms in office.[135]

In the years after World War II until the mid-1960s, men like Admiral M. Powell Rhea (the great-grandson of Pleasant Vincent Rhea),[136] long-time Fayetteville public servant Roy Scott, J. Austin Parish and Guy E. Brown held the post of mayor.[137]

From 1966 until 1992, Fayetteville adopted a City Manager/City Board form of government. Even though the city manager was responsible for the day to day operation of the municipal government, the elected seven-member board chose a mayor from among its own ranks.[138] Among the mayors during this era were Don Trumbo, Garland Melton, Jr., David Malone and Joe Fred Starr. In 1975, Marion Orton was chosen Fayetteville's first woman mayor (the second, Marilyn Johnson, would serve in the latter 1980s).[139]

Since 1992 when the Mayor/City Council form was re-adopted, Fred Hanna, Dan Coody, and Lioneld Jordan have served as the city's top official.[140]

Fayetteville Police Chiefs

The position of Fayetteville Police Chief was not created until 1906, after the city was incorporated as a first class city. Its equivalent, though, City Marshal, is traceable at least back to 1860 when M. D. Frazer held that position.[141]

Unlike the mayor-appointed position of police chief, the city marshals were elected by municipal vote. H. C. C. Botefuhr was city marshal in 1869[142] and Jefferson Gilliland was elected to that position in December of 1870.[143]

A city marshal with the unlikely name of A. K. Coward resigned his position in 1874 "in disgust"—most likely over lack of pay and the unruly behavior of denizens of "Smoky Row." Smoky Row was the name for a strip of liquor purveyors and saloons that used to be on East Center Street out in front of where the historic Washington County Courthouse now stands. Coward's replacement was Parson Elisha Robinson who was described in the local paper as a "South Methodist Minister."[144]

J. D. Henry, who was elected City Marshall in 1875, had a dangerous encounter with unfriendly Native Americans when on a visit to a friend over in the Indian Territory. According to the *Fayetteville Democrat,* a group of men from a local tribe armed with pistols were intent on doing harm to Henry's friend and attacked the man's house during the night. Henry, who was not the target of the attack, and his friend, who was, both escaped the assault unscathed.[145]

Just a few years later, on July 2, 1881, in a scene more reminiscent of Dodge City or Tombstone than sleepy Fayetteville, City Marshall W. D. Patton and Deputy Sheriff John I. Mount were shot down in cold blood near the Northeast corner of the Square by unknown assailants.[146]

It was suspected that Patton was murdered in retaliation for killing a man named George Reed, who was part of a gang operating out of West Fork during this time. The *Democrat* vowed that the murderers would be brought to justice, but no one was ever arrested or indicted for the killings.

Among other City Marshals during this era were George H. Pettigrew, W. A. "Toy" Gregg—who served for many years in various local law enforcement positions—and Lee Duggans. C. S. Tunstill was the last elected City Marshal, serving from 1904 until 1906.[147]

On June 20, 1905 Fayetteville was incorporated as a City of First Class, having 5,000 inhabitants. In early 1906, Capt. U. L. Smeltzer (or Smelser) was appointed police chief by Mayor C. A. Mulholland. Capt. Smeltzer resigned in 1908 to be replaced by Alexander C. Cruse.[148]

When W. H. Rollins became Mayor in 1909, he immediately appointed veteran law enforcement officer W. A. "Toy" Gregg as chief and Gregg served in this position, with one short break when he ran for county sheriff and lost, for the next ten years. 1909 was also the year that the city passed Ordinance #259, which delineated for the first time the powers and duties of the chief of police position.[149]

In 1930, Neal Cruse, the son of former police chief Alexander Cruse (who had served three terms just after the turn of the century), was appointed chief. A short four years later, after a virtual mountain of corruption charges had been leveled at him by the city and the

Fayetteville City Officials, 1928
(From Left—Top) Dennis A. "Slim" Burson, Unknown, Neal Cruse
(Bottom) Unknown (possibly Lem Guinn), Police Judge W. H. Rollins,
W. A. "Toy" Gregg, Earl Hand
Courtesy Fayetteville Police Department

Civil Service Commission, Neal Cruse was relieved of his position. Earl Hand took over as acting chief and held that position until 1939 when Ordinance #832 was passed abolishing the positions of Police and Fire Chief.[150]

Mayor A.D. McAllister served as *ex-officio* Chief of Police and Chief of the Fire Department until 1941, when new Mayor George Vaughan was elected and thus became the new *ex-officio* chief of the two departments.[151]

City Ordinance #852 was passed in May of 1941 again creating the "Seperate (sic) Office of Chief of Police of the City of Fayetteville." In September of that year Dan Allen was offered and accepted the position of police chief. Allen was chief until 1944 when he resigned to run for Sheriff of Washington County. Bob Day briefly acted as chief until May 1944 when Mayor Pro-Tem George T. Sanders became ex-officio chief.[152]

Finally, in March of 1945, City Ordinance #884 was passed describing the performance and duties of the chief of police. Sanders, by then officially elected mayor, appointed Pearl Watts as permanent chief of police, ending better than a decade of upheaval in the police department and laying the groundwork for the orderly and more stable position of chief that we know today.[153]

Chief Watts served from 1945 until 1962. Among his successors were Hollis Spencer, Glen Riggins, Richard Watson, and Gregg Tabor. The current chief of police is Mike Reynolds who began serving in 2019.[154]

Fayetteville Fire Chiefs

The beginning of Fayetteville's Fire Department is somewhat obscured by the smoky haze of distant history. W. S. Campbell, in his history *One Hundred Years of Fayetteville, 1828-1928,* says that George Albright was the first fire chief beginning just "after the Civil War."[155]

A few years after the war, in 1869, the weekly *Fayetteville Democrat* reported an early attempt to form a Fire Company and by 1872 the Washington Fire Company had been organized but it had no equipment. The next year local businessmen provided the company with ladders, buckets and such. In January 1874, however, the department—now called the Washington Hook and Ladder Company— disbanded.[156]

Finding the exact dates when the department reorganized and when Albright became its chief is problematical due to the paucity of source materials. But on January 22, 1876, a fire broke out at the Book Store on the East Side of the Square and the *Democrat* reported that Capt. George Albright was credited with putting out the flames before they could do major damage to the store. It appears Albright may have put out the fire all by himself.

In 1877 the *Democrat* reported a meeting of the apparently reconstituted Fire Company, and in 1880 there was a news story about the

"Fire Brigade" putting out a fire burning down on troublesome Smoky Row.[157] According to an article in the *Fayetteville Daily* for January 27, 1909, however, the fire department was officially established "in 1896." This date does seem to mark the beginning of the "modern era" because the department has been in verifiable, continuous existence since that time.

Uncertain as its beginnings may have been, we know that the following year, 1897, the fire department got its first horse-drawn wagon. Twenty years later, on October 1, 1917, the older technology was discarded when the first motorized fire truck was purchased and put into operation. This truck was replaced in 1918 by a "350-gallon pumper" and in 1925 the city bought a "750-gallon pumper" at the cost of $12,500.[158]

In the heart of the Great Depression, in 1934, the municipality of Fayetteville, like most of the rest of the nation, was struggling financially and otherwise. To help with local problems, a three-man Civil Service

Fire Engines on Block Street
Universtiy of Arkansas Libraries, Special Collections, Loc 1362

Commission was established with oversight powers for both the Fire and Police Departments. By the end of the 1930s, on August 17, 1939 to be exact, the city adopted the recommendations of the Civil Service Commission and passed City Ordinance #832 which eliminated the offices of Fire and Police Chief. Dropping these positions also enabled the city to save money at a time when meeting the budget was critical.[159]

From 1939 to 1941, Mayor A. D. McAllister served as ex-officio Fire Chief and Police Chief. In September of 1941, members of the Fire Department successfully petitioned the mayor and city council for the right to appoint their own acting chief and Henry George was selected for that position.[160]

From that time, George served as acting chief, except for a few months in 1946, until Burl Skelton was appointed temporary chief in November of 1948. Skelton was appointed permanently in 1949[161] and was the first man to serve as full-time paid fire chief. He served as chief until 1971.

After Skelton, some of the chiefs were Charles McWhorter, Paul Logue, Mickey Jackson and Tony Johnson. David C. Dayringer served as Fayetteville Fire Chief from 2010 until he retired on June 21, 2019. On July 8, 2019, Mayor Lioneld Jordan appointed Brad Hardin as the new chief of the Fayetteville Fire Department.[162]

FAYETTEVILLE MAYORS

P. V. Rhea—1841-1851 (approximate end date)
James P. Neal—1852-1854
Unknown—1855-1858
J. W. Walker—1859
Stephen Bedford—1860
Col. M. Larue Harrison—1868-1869
E. I. Stirman—1869-1871
T. Murray Campbell—1871-1872
J. R. Pettigrew—1872-1873
George A. Grace—1873-1874
Robert J. Wilson—1874-1876

Col. Alfred M. Wilson—1876-1877

A.S. Vandeventer—1877-1880

J. H. Van Hoose—1880-1881

W. C. Jackson—1881-1883

C. W. Walker—1883-1884

S. E. Marrs—1884-1885

W. C. Jackson—1885 (April to Dec.)

Robert J. Wilson—1886 (Jan. to April)

O. C. Gray—1886-1887 (April to Oct.)

E. B. Wall—1887-1888 (Oct. to April)

J. H. VanHoose—1888-1890

F. M. Goar—1890-1891

J. T. Lusk 1891-1895

W. S. Pollard—1895-1897

Jack Walker—1897-1901

Capt. J. T. Eason—1901-1905

C. A. Mulholland—1906-1909

W. H. Rollins—1909-1913

Guy Philips—1913-1914

Tom Taylor—1914-1917

Allen M. Wilson—1917-1919

J. M. Phillips—1919-1921

Allen M. Wilson –1921-1929

T. S. Tribble—1929-1935

A. D. McAllister—1935-1941

George Vaughan—1941-1944

George T. Sanders—1944-1949

Powell M. Rhea—1949-1953

Roy A. Scott—1954-1957

J. Austin Parish—1958-1959

Guy E. Brown—1960-1965

Don Trumbo—1966-1968

Garland Melton, Jr.—1969-1970

Joe Fred Starr—1971-1972

Russell Purdy—1973-1974
Marion Orton—1975-1976
Ernest Lancaster—1977-1978
David R. Malone—1978-1979
John Todd—1980-1981
Paul Noland—1982-1986
Marilyn Johnson—1986-1987
William V. Martin—1987-1990
Fred S. Vorsanger—1991-1992
Fred Hanna—1992-2000
Dan Coody—2001-2008
Lioneld Jordan—2008-present

FAYETTEVILLE CITY MARSHALS (ELECTED)

M. D. Frazer—1860
H. C. C. Botefuhr—1869 (as of January)
Jefferson "Bud" Gilliland—1870-1871
Wesley Barnes—1871-1872
Thomas Jennings—1872-1873
A. K. Coward—1873-1874
Parson Elisha Robinson—1874-1875
J. D. Henry—1875
W. F. Stirman—1877-1880
W. D. Patton—1881
Col. W. T. Barry—1881-1882
J. H. Cooper—1882-1883
A. B. Kell—1883
George H. Pettigrew—1883-1884
A. B. Kell—1884-1885
T. J. Taylor—1885-1886
H. S. Gray—1886-1887
J. T. Reynolds—1888-1890
H. F. "Dutch" Buie—1890-1892
W. A. "Toy" Gregg—1892-1894

W. P. "Pat" Moulden—1894-896
Lee Duggans—1896-1904
C. S. Tunstill—1904-1906

FAYETTEVILLE POLICE CHIEFS (APPOINTED)
Capt. U. L. Smeltzer (Smelser)—1906-1908
A. C. Cruse—1908-1909
W. A. "Toy" Gregg—1909-1913
A. C. Cruse—1913-1914 (Dec. to April)
W. A. "Toy" Greg—1914-1919
A. C. Cruse—1919-1921
R. F. Jackson—1921-1923
Harry Sanford—1923-1925
W. A. "Toy" Gregg—1925-1929
Samuel Guinn—1929-1930
Neal Cruse –1930-1935
Earl Hand—1935-1939 (Acting)
Mayor A.D. McAllister—1939-1941
Mayor George Vaughn—1941
Dan Allen—1941-1944
Bob Day—1944 (Acting)
Mayor Pro-Tem George T. Sanders—1944-1945
Pearl Watts—1945-1962
Hollis Spencer—1962-1975
Glen Riggins—1975-1979
Clint Hutchens—1979 (Acting)
Bob Jones—1979-1986
Richard Watson—1986-2002
Rick Hoyt—2002-2004
Frank Johnson—2004-2006
Gregg Tabor—2006-2019
Mike Reynolds—2019 to present

FAYETTEVILLE FIRE CHIEFS

George Albright—post-civil war-1897
Frank Mayes—1897-1906
Clay Duggans—1906-1917
C. W. Hansard—1917-1922
C. W. Winkleman—1922-1929
Clyde Walters—1929-1939
Mayor A. D. McAllister—1939-1941
Henry George—1941-1946 (Acting)
Carl Tune—1946 (Acting: May-November)
Henry George—1946-1947 (Acting: November-March)
Henry George—1947-1948
Burl Skelton—1949-1971
Charles McWhorter—1971-1977
Paul Logue—1977-1985
Mickey Jackson—1985-2001
Dennis Ledbetter—2001 (Interim)
Chris Bosch—2001-2005
Marion Doss—2005 (Interim)
Tony Johnson—2005-2009
David Dayringer—2010-2019
Brad Hardin—2019 to present

FAYETTEVILLE'S
OLD SCHOOLS

IN THE EARLY 1950s, Fayetteville's public school system was much smaller than it is today. There were only six public schools: five elementary schools—Washington, Jefferson, Leverett, Lincoln, and West Side (soon to be replaced by Bates), all of which taught grades one through eight—and the high school, which had grades nine through twelve.

Although Washington and Jefferson had been around in earlier incarnations since the late nineteenth century, the first public school in Fayetteville was actually Henderson School. Initially opening in 1866 and called "The Mission School for Negro Only," the school building was completed in 1868 near the corner of Lafayette and Olive. By 1892, this school for Fayetteville's black children was renamed[163] for "District Superintendent" Ebenezer E. Henderson who had come to Fayetteville in 1866 to organize the school district.[164]

The brick remains of Henderson School, which was later replaced by Lincoln School, can still be seen today as part of a private residence on Olive Street. In the old days of segregated education, black students wishing to continue their schooling past the eighth grade had to either be home schooled, privately taught, or attend a black high school in another town such as Fort Smith.

Washington School, the second oldest public school in town and also known long ago as the North or North Side School, stood about where it stands today in the block bounded by Lafayette and Maple on the south and north sides, respectively, and by Highland and Forest on the east and west sides, also respectively. The original Washington

School was built in 1885 by Albert M. Byrnes and the first classes were held there in 1886.[165]

By the late 1920s, however, city officials and the school board felt that the Washington School building needed more than just renovation. During 1930 and into early 1931, the "new" Washington was completed by E. V. Bird Construction. The school we know today, which faces Highland, was constructed slightly up the hill from the "old" school, which faced Lafayette. According to the *Fayetteville Daily Democrat,* first classes were held in the "modern" Washington School on Monday, February 16, 1931.[166] The school is still open today.

The original Jefferson, or South Side, School was built in 1890—again by Albert M. Byrnes—and was located on South Street just to the southeast from where Church Street intersects. The old Jefferson, like the one that replaced it, was made of red bricks. The west side of the old building was supported by three brick columns.

Work on the "new" Jefferson—also built by E. V. Bird Construc-

Jefferson School
J.B. Hogan

tion—was started in 1929 on the southeast corner of the intersection of South College and Sixth Streets. As described in the *Fayetteville Daily Democrat*, the first students to attend the new school did so on Thursday, February 19, 1931.[167] Although it ultimately closed as an elementary school after the 2005-2006 school year, the "new" Jefferson School building still stands today and is currently used as an adult education center.

In 1935, some of the bricks from the old Jefferson School (the one at South and Church) were used in the construction of a new school.[168] This school was located on the southeast corner of South Willow Avenue and East Center Street in the heart of Spout Spring Hollow, the historically and predominantly black section of town. The new school was named Lincoln and it replaced the older Henderson School. The first principal was Herman Caldwell and the library at the school was named after George Ballard, local poet.[169]

Lincoln provided Fayetteville's black children with public education until 1965 when the last of the city's elementary schools integrated. With integration, the need for a separate building for Fayetteville's African-American students ended. During the 1970s, its purpose completed, Lincoln School was demolished.[170]

On the northwest side of town, Leverett School, like the old Washington and Jefferson schools, has provided education for Fayetteville children since the late 1800s. The original Leverett School was built by Albert M. Byrnes in 1899 and was located at 1006 W. Maple on the northeast corner of Garland and Maple, where a University of Arkansas building stands today. Directly across the street from old Leverett School on the northwest corner of Garland and Maple was a large university burial site known as College Cemetery,[171] a fact now almost universally forgotten.

The "new" Leverett School, on the northwest corner of Cleveland (formerly York) Street and Garland Avenue, opened for classes on Monday, September 4, 1939.[173] Leverett School, built by E. V. Bird Construction, still stands at the same location today and is fully operational.

Leverett School
J.B. Hogan

Constructed in 1923 on Stone Street for $20,000, the West Side School provided education for the children of Fayetteville's southwest side. The West Side School was eventually replaced by Bates School but it still stands today as the Administration Building for the current Fayetteville High School.

Bates School was built specifically to replace the West Side School and classes were first held there on Monday, September 10, 1951.[174] Located at the intersection of Martin Luther King Boulevard, formerly known as Sixth Street, and Buchanan Avenue, Bates School educated children on the west side of town until 2000. For several years its buildings served as a Fayetteville High School Annex but they were razed in 2010 as part of an extensive renovation of Fayetteville High School.

The original Fayetteville High School was built by Albert M. Byrnes in 1908 on the west side of North School Street between West Center and West Meadow Streets. As the town grew and more space was needed for the expanding student body, annexes were added to

West Side School
J.B. Hogan

the existing building. The north annex was added in 1925 and the south annex in 1927.[175]

By 1952, Fayetteville had grown enough to require a new high school and the current high school was built up on the hill above Bates School facing Stone Street. In 1954, Fayetteville High School integrated without incident and with little fanfare. The old building was used then as the Fayetteville Junior High School.

The last of the pre-1960 elementary schools to be built in town was Root School, which opened in 1955. The school, located on Mission Boulevard (Highway 45) a short distance east of Old Wire Road, was designed by T. Ewing Shelton. The first day of classes was Monday, September 12, 1955. *The Northwest Arkansas Times* newspaper pointed out that of the 203 students attending the new Root School, a considerable number of them had transferred in from Washington School.[176] Root School is still active today.

By the late-1950s, Fayetteville Junior High School attendance had increased so much from the influx of students funneled into it from the several elementary schools that annex buildings were added on the east side of West Avenue just past Meadow Street below the school.

Responding to the rapid growth of students from the "Baby Boomer" generation, in the fall of 1959 Fayetteville added the new Woodland Junior High School on Poplar Street just off North College. Woodland, like Root School, was designed by T. Ewing Shelton. It opened for classes—even though construction was not quite complete —on Friday, September 18, 1959 with Benny Winborn as principal. It is still an active school today.[177]

At the same time Woodland Junior High was opened, Fayetteville Junior High School on School Street was renamed Hillcrest Junior High School. Hillcrest lasted until the spring of 1966 when it was closed.

That fall, Ramay Junior High School—named after long-time Fayetteville and Hillcrest Junior High principal M. O. Ramay—opened on the west side of town.[178]

Three years later, on June 13, 1969, the building that had once been Fayetteville High School, then Fayetteville, and finally Hillcrest Junior High School burned down. The building was soon razed[179] and eventually replaced by Hillcrest Towers, a high-rise public housing community.

With present day Fayetteville High School having undergone an almost total renovation in recent years, the city now has just four active schools left from the old days that are recognizable as they were first constructed. Root School and Woodland Junior High date from the mid-to-late 1950s, and the present Washington and Leverett schools go back to the 1930s. And while they may be older now, these schools are nonetheless a positive, enduring reminder of our long and significant educational past.

FROM THE LYRIC TO THE UARK
FAYETTEVILLE'S OLD MOVIE HOUSES

FOR A GOOD portion of the early to mid-twentieth century, Fayetteville had four walk-in movie houses: the Ozark, Royal, Palace, and UArk. To those who remember going to these old theatres in their heyday, the recollection may conjure up a sense of joy, nostalgia, and perhaps—because they are now part of our distant and receding past—a touch of melancholy as well.

With their multi-colored wall lights, stages still used for plays and live shows, and curtains that were drawn back with the first flicker from the projection room, the old picture shows may seem quaint today. In that older time, going to the movies was a far less common experience than it would later become. Attending a motion picture was something special, even an extraordinary event to many of those who were just able to rake up enough cash for the price of admission.

In the latter nineteenth and early twentieth centuries, however, before movies came along, a series of opera houses provided locals their theatrical entertainment. The first of these establishments, operating from 1879-1886, was on the third floor of the old Van Winkle Hotel down on Smoky Row at 26 East Center—directly across from the Mountain House/Hotel which would become the Oriental Hotel and then the Mountain Inn so familiar to older city residents.[180]

The second opera house, operating from 1886 to 1905 was on the Southwest corner of the Fayetteville Square at 17-19 West Mountain. This opera house was on the second story of what would become Budd's Department Store, then J. C. Penney's, and currently a brew pub.

Harvey M. Hudgins of Hot Springs was the owner of the opera house but John T. Woods managed it, until 1895 when Hudgins assumed those duties as well, and it was often referred to as Woods Opera House.[181] Woods himself had a separate opera house for a brief period during the 1890s. It was located on College Street, north of where the Ozark would be built a few years later.[182]

During 1904-1905, a new opera house was built on College just to the north of Center Street and was at first called the Knights of Pythias Hall and Opera House. On June 4, 1907, the *Fayetteville Daily*[183] reported that the new hall had become the Ozark Theatre, although the new name did not become official until June 15.

Ozark Theater
Courtesy of Professor James Chase

Of these old opera houses, the earliest one to show the "new" motion pictures was the Woods Opera House. On January 6, 1898 an advertisement in the weekly *Fayetteville Democrat* proclaimed that in addition to its regular theatrical shows, the opera house also had "Two moving picture machines."

Given the date of the advertisement, these machines were most likely Kinetoscopes. They were patented in 1891 by Thomas Edison, although his brilliant young British protégé William Kennedy Laurie Dickson headed the team that actually invented the device.[184] These machines were viewed individually by customers and were popular during the early days of motion pictures.

At the dawn of the twentieth century, motion picture shows in Fayetteville were predominantly of the "traveling" variety. In 1904, the Young Brothers Electric Theatre came to town and exhibited movies for eager local audiences. Where they set up in town and how much they charged for admission is not known but the show returned in 1906 featuring a "set of moving pictures" with the overall title *Fairyland*. The show, according to the *Fayetteville Daily* on May 4, 1906 "was considered very fine."

Another traveling show was that of Lyman Howe who presented movies at the Ozark Theatre each year from 1906 to 1909. In 1907 he brought movies of Victoria Falls and in 1908 there was a feature called *Lifeorama*. 1909 theatre-goers saw films of Egypt, Russia, and of a disaster in Sicily. Despite this being the era of the "Nickelodeon," with viewers watching programs individually, the *Daily* noted that for Mr. Howe's show the Ozark seated customers in its balcony for 25 cents and on the lower floor for 35 and 50 cents.

1907 was an important year for the movies in Fayetteville. Besides the traveling shows making their short stops in town and a brief run in March by a theatre calling itself the Dime Electric Show (owned by a C. McDonald, the *Daily* indicated), at least two different motion picture houses tried to establish more permanent businesses.

In April, the Scenic Theatre opened on East Center Street—possibly indoors in a building just to the west of the Van Winkle Hotel. The first show at the Scenic was 7:30 p.m. on Friday, April 5, 1907 and advertisements ran in the *Daily* through the first week of June. Admission prices were given as 10 cents for adults and 5 cents for children.

The movie house was open for "some weeks" in 1908, with ads running on June 1 and 2 under the name of Smith & Kerrens Scenic

Theatre, but on June 24, 1908 the Scenic closed for good. The reason for the failure was, the *Daily* said, "poor attendance." The owners took their show and left for "some point in Missouri" because, as the paper related, the owners "could not make the business pay here."

In the fall of 1907 another theatre tried to make a go of it in Fayetteville. This was the Marvel. From newspaper descriptions, it was located indoors in the Hight Building which was on North Block Avenue just below the Northwest corner of the Square and "adjoining Skaggs Drug Store." The Marvel opened on October 16, 1907 and, in addition to showing movies, it also had occasional vaudeville shows. Admission to the movies was a flat 5 cents, the standard Nickelodeon charge, but it was 10 cents for adults and 5 cents for children for vaudeville entertainment.

The Marvel did not last out the year, however, despite putting several ads in the *Daily* during October and November. On November 11, 1907, for example, the Marvel advertised a movie extravaganza entitled *The Life of Christ*. This feature had been filmed in four acts, with thirty-eight hand-painted color scenes, taking up four thousand feet of moving picture film.

One of the interesting aspects of the early movie houses was that the length of film reels, in thousands of feet, was often the most important item stressed in advertisements. The owners apparently wanted customers to get their money's worth, as measured by the amount of film shown and not necessarily by the quality of the movie on that film.

As for the Marvel's success, thousands of film feet or not, it was short-lived. Their last advertisement appeared in the *Daily* on November 22, 1907 and the Marvel was soon gone from the Square, forgotten by all but the most ardent of local historians.

Despite the June closing of the Scenic, 1908 was yet another big year for movie houses in Fayetteville. Lyman Howe's traveling show came to town again and there was a brief foray into the movie business —lasting only a few weeks—by a Mr. Hays.[185] Shows also were displayed in the windows of Baum's Store on the East Side of the Square. The *Daily* told of a show at Baum's on May 30, 1908 that resulted in

two boys from Madison County slightly hurting themselves while ex-
citedly running across the Square to see the movie. In all that year, Fayetteville gained four more theatres, with each striving for permanence.

All of these new theatres started out as "air domes." Air domes,
or airdomes, might be viewed as sit-down precursors to later drive-
in movie theatres, such as the 71 Drive-In, which opened on North
College in October, 1949. These theatres were warm weather establishments where films and other forms of entertainment were shown
to crowds packed into roofless structures. They normally consisted of
four walls, a ticket window at the front, and an elevated stage at the
back where the movies were projected onto a rudimentary screen.[186]

In late June or early July 1908, the Pastime Electric Theatre opened
on Center Street. It was most likely located in an airdome theatre that,
at that time, stood on the south side of the street just to the west of
the Oriental Hotel.[187] This new "open air" theatre, as stated in a June
24 advertisement in the *Daily*, was "nearing completion." An ad on
August 13 listed admission to the Pastime Electric as 5 and 10 cents.

Unfortunately, the Pastime came to a sudden, surprising end. On
September 9, 1908, a troupe from Kansas had been booked to perform
illustrated songs which were a staple of the early movie theatres. One
of their singers happened to be a black man and a local woman, unnamed, refused to play piano for him.

The resultant hubbub immediately forced the Pastime out of business, as described by its owners in a letter to the *Daily* the next day,
September 10. Pastime ads continued to appear in the paper through
September 26, 1908, but there's no evidence any other films were
shown there after the "racial" incident.

Just about when the Pastime was going out of business, another
movie house sprung up to replace it. This was the Vaudette Theatre.
In the September 10, 1908 *Daily*, this venue was called a "New Air-
Dome" and was said to be located on the "Van Winkle" lot, the old
hotel having recently been razed.

The Vaudette, according to the *Daily*, gave "its first public moving
picture exhibition" on Saturday, September 26, 1908. On opening

night, and on many nights to follow, local bandleader Frank Barr and his orchestra provided music for the theatre. Barr was a well-known musician in town and this connection to local movie houses would not be his last. First night admission to the Vaudette was standard for the time: 5 cents for children and 10 cents for adults.

By November 2, 1908, with the weather cooling down, the Vaudette had apparently found indoor quarters for it was said in the *Daily* that their "room," with a capacity of 250, was "comfortably heated." One week later, on November 9, the theatre advertised "Talking Pictures at Vaudette." This was twenty years before real talkies came along, of course, but the ad was referring to an early attempt to get around this technological roadblock called "TA-MO-PIC." This system, the *Daily* explained, employed actors hidden behind the movie screen where they recited the lines of the silent films.

In January 1909, the Vaudette did what many movie theatres of the time did when ticket sales were slow—they brought in Vaudeville shows, but kept admission prices at the low rate of 10 cents. On April 13, the Vaudette advertised in the *Daily* that they were located at the Opera House—at the time this almost certainly referred to the Ozark —and that they were showing "2000 feet of the very latest motion pictures." On May 11, they claimed an attendance of 1,000 and on May 15, having begun using the airdome again, it was reported that bad weather had forced them back into "their building."

No further advertisements for the Vaudette appeared in the paper until May 16, 1910. Six weeks later, on July 1, there was an ad for a boxing show, and on July 27 one for "Vaudeville every night," but the Vaudette's days were numbered. On September 27, 1910, a last ad appears in the *Daily.* Like the several theatres before it, the Vaudette quietly closed, to fade silently into Fayetteville's nearly forgotten past.

The next movie house to open in Fayetteville would completely buck the trend of fly-by-night, come-and-go businesses. This was the Lyric Theatre, first managed by two men named Whitten and Rigs (or Riggs). The "New Lyric," as it was referred to in early *Daily* ads, was an airdome located near the train depot at the corner of West and Dickson Streets. It opened on or about September 15, 1908 and advertised movies through October, including some that were "hand-colored." Admission was given as 5, 10, and 15 cents.

Whether the Lyric had shows during that first winter is not known, but by the following spring the *Daily* related that Frank Barr, the well-known local musician and orchestra leader, had taken over the theatre. He began showing movies there on April 17, 1909. Some six weeks later, Barr moved his airdome from Dickson Street to 17 North Block just off the Square.[188] Admission at both locations was a flat 10 cents.

For nearly five years, the Lyric remained in the same location, only using the Hudgins Building next door at 15 N. Block to show indoor movies during the winter and on rainy summer nights. Then, on December 17, 1913, Barr unveiled a new, permanent Lyric building at 101 North Block, at the corner with Meadow Street—where the Ozark Cleaners building still stands today. The *Daily* described the year-round structure as being "45x75 feet" with "trap windows all over the house." It was "equipped with nice chairs" and there would not be "a post in the building."

The paper crowed that this movie house would be "one of the best equipped moving picture houses in the state and Mr. Barr is to be congratulated upon his progressiveness in this town." As for Barr, he was so happy with the new digs that he took out an advertisement to say: "We have heard so many complimentary remarks about our new building, we are a little swelled up and can't help it."

Through economic upturns and downturns, admission price increases—boosted by a required war tax during and after World War I—Barr kept the Lyric open continuously for many years. Early in 1910, he was the first to openly invite "negro patrons" to his theatre, and at that time, according to an article run in the *Daily*, he employed as many as nineteen people in his local operation.

Over the next years, the Lyric continued to be a fixture on the local movie house scene, providing motion pictures, live entertainment, and benefits for local causes such as the creation of a new park at College and Meadow Streets in May of 1914. By February of 1917, however, the Lyric was experiencing financial problems. On February 22, an advertisement highlighted the difficulty of "keeping the theatre open at low prices." Barr himself wrote in the May 10 daily *Fayetteville Democrat* complaining about "how hard it is to get good movies with the stars people want to see" and continue to "charge low prices."

Still, the Lyric stayed open. Admission went up to 15 cents for adults and 6 cents for children (both including war tax) and Barr kept the movies coming until the fall of 1918. This was the time of the great Influenza Epidemic that swept the United States killing thousands of people. Fayetteville was also hit by the malady and in the *Democrat* for October 9, 1918 the city issued a quarantine on all public gatherings, naturally including the movies. Once the city quarantine was lifted on November 2, 1918, Barr reopened the Lyric.

Despite continuing economic difficulties at the theatre, Barr managed to keep it afloat for a while longer. Finally, as chronicled in the *Democrat* of September 6, 1919, he finally got out of the local movie business altogether by selling the Lyric to E. C. Robertson of El Dorado.

Robertson himself was primarily interested in opening a new theatre in the remodeled building that had once housed the Baum Brothers Store on the East Side of the Square. Robertson declared in the *Democrat* his intention of keeping the Lyric open, but only for special shows. His interest would be in promoting a new movie house called the Victory.

Occasional movies were shown on the weekend and other entertainments such as vaudeville shows and boxing matches were held at the Lyric during the rest of 1919 and into 1920. There was another brief, two-week long city influenza quarantine in February of 1920 and by that fall and winter the theatre was seldom used. Finally, with little fanfare, the Lyric passed into history early in 1921. Over two decades later, in June of 1945, it was razed to make room for a new building that would house the Ozark Cleaners.

Back in the fall of 1908, shortly after the Lyric had first opened for business, yet another theatre tried to make a go of it in Fayetteville. This movie house was another airdome and it called itself the "New"

Princess from the beginning. The Princess was situated on the north side of East Center Street, most likely near the lot where the Van Winkle Hotel had stood, but its precise location is not known.

The first advertisement for the "New" Princess Theatre, in the October 5, 1908 *Fayetteville Daily*, described the movie house as having "comfortable chairs—well elevated" and listed admission prices as 5 and 10 cents. Although there was only one more ad in the paper during the rest of the year (November 4), the Princess managed to survive into 1909.

On January 24, 1909, for example, it was advertised that they would have "8000 feet of Motion Pictures every night this week." Ads continued to appear in the *Daily* throughout March and on April 19, responding to contemporary concerns about the morality of the "new" motion pictures, the Princess made it known to their clientele that "every reel" of film shipped to them was "inspected by (the) Chicago Police Department." If the movie was deemed "clean" it was then sent to local distributors thereby guaranteeing that only "first class pictures" would be shown.

Despite its attempts to show only "clean" pictures, the Princess apparently was unable to develop a steady customer base. On May 26, 1909, a month after their last ad appeared in the *Daily*, the Princess was gone—yet another casualty in the competitive, volatile movie theatre scene that existed in Fayetteville during the first decade of the twentieth century.

At the beginning of 1909, the Lyric, Vaudette, and Princess theatres were all showing motion pictures in town. At year's end, however, only the Lyric and Vaudette would still be operating but during this time a theatre briefly popped up on Dickson Street with one of the most intriguing names of any of the old movie houses. Located at 416 West Dickson Street, in the heart of the current club and restaurant area, this new venue was the Bijou Dream Theatre—Pittsburg, Pennsylvania, and Chicago, Illinois also had theatres with this name.

Despite its evocative name, the Bijou Dream Theatre lasted only a short time. Its first and only advertisement was in the February 9,

1909 edition of the *Daily*. Admission was the typical 5 and 10 cents, but what movies it showed, as well as the reasons it failed so quickly are, again, lost in the mists of distant time.

Some two years later another movie venue opened that would become something of a local staple. This new theatre was an airdome and was appropriately named the Ozark Airdome because it was located near the corner of College Avenue and East Center, across the street from the courthouse and the Ozark Theatre. It opened on May 29, 1911 with a full schedule of "vaudeville and picture shows."[189]

Admission, which didn't change during the Airdome's first incarnation, was 5 cents for children and 10 cents for adults. When winter came, they leased the Ozark Theatre and held their movies inside, out of the inclement weather. The Ozark Airdome kept its name until the fall of 1914 when advertisements for the theatre disappeared from the *Daily*.

On April 22, 1915 a new set of owners stated in the daily *Fayetteville Democrat* that they had leased the Ozark Airdome and would soon re-open the venue under the name "Skydome." The new theatre, according to the paper, was "entirely separate and apart from the Ozark management" although they would be using the same location as the "old Ozark Airdome."

Admission at the Skydome would remain 5 and 10 cents, but they charged 10 and 20 cents for some special showings. An ad in the Wednesday, April 28, 1915 edition of the *Democrat* announced that the Skydome would open "Friday Night" (April 30, 1915). A first night highlight was that "one lady" would be "admitted free" with each 10 cent ticket purchase.

During the Skydome's run, one of its more interesting programs was a film about Fayetteville itself, which played on September 29, 1915. This film, entitled *The Magic of the Hills*, was the winning entry in a contest that had been announced in the *Democrat* on August 17. *"Fayetteville To Be Seen In Movie Film,"* the *Democrat* front page headline proclaimed.

A professional movie production crew, the newspaper explained, one that had made a similar movie in Ft. Smith, was to arrive in town on September 1 to begin filming. The Skydome offered a $10 prize to the person writing the winning scenario. Local actors were to be used in the movie.

"Fayetteville Movie Makes Decided Hit," the *Democrat* page one headline read on September 30. The lead actors were Scott Hamilton and Lillian Lawson. Miss Lawson, it was disclosed, had been made "an attractive offer…to engage in professional motion picture acting" by a producer who purportedly witnessed the film's debut. There's no evidence the young lady ever appeared in another film.

As prior noted, the Skydome, like the Ozark Airdome before it, used the Ozark Theatre for its winter headquarters. Shows were held inside the Ozark during the winters of 1915-1916 and 1916-1917. Early in 1917, however, the Skydome was close to the end of its nearly three-year run. The last Skydome show in the Ozark was held on February 9, 1917 and the next day the *Democrat* confirmed that the theatre had closed its indoor run at the Ozark and was looking for new quarters.

All was silent on the Skydome front until April 26, 1917 when C. W. Winkleman told the *Democrat* that he had taken over the theatre and would be opening it again early in May. On May 4, 1917, an advertisement in the paper confirmed that the theatre would begin operations on May 7, but that the outdoor venue would once again be called the Ozark Airdome rather than the Skydome. On that opening night admission was 5 and 15 cents, with a lady or child free with each paid ticket.

Throughout the rest of spring, summer, and into the early fall, the Ozark Airdome faithfully presented its shows—never changing the basic admission price. Despite ownership's best efforts, however, this would be its last year. The final ad for the theatre appeared in the *Democrat* on September 26, 1917, about the time the show was usually moved indoors. This year, though, there were no winter shows. The Ozark Airdome had closed for good.

Back in the summer and fall of 1911, with the Ozark Airdome established and the Lyric Theatre completing its third year of operation, two more movie houses tried to make a go of it in Fayetteville. The first of these was more a rumor than a reality because it doesn't seem to have actually opened despite an August 25 story in the *Fayetteville Daily*.

On that day, the paper indicated that a new, unnamed theatre was to open down in "Quicktown" in the "southwest part of town." Quicktown was the area in the vicinity of the corner of what is now Martin Luther King Boulevard—formerly Sixth Street—and Government Avenue in south Fayetteville. No more was ever heard of this proposed motion picture house.

Slightly more successful was another try at putting a theatre down on Dickson Street. This was the Orpheum Theatre located at 424 West Dickson and its owner was O. L. Champion. The first advertisement for the Orpheum appeared in the *Daily* on November 9, 1911 and other ads appeared through the middle of December.

Advertisements picked up again on February 21, 1912 and ran until March 20. A March 15 ad repeated the theatre's address and gave its admission at 10 cents. The Orpheum lasted through the spring and into the summer but finally on August 27, 1912 its last ad appeared in the *Daily* and, like so many theatres before it, the Orpheum was heard of no more.

For several years after the closing of the Orpheum, no new theatres appeared in Fayetteville. The Air Dome and Skydome, along with the Lyric—and to a lesser extent the Ozark—provided movie entertainment for local audiences. Finally, in October 1919, only a month after he had come to Fayetteville and bought the Lyric Theatre from its longtime owner Frank Barr, E. C. Robertson of El Dorado opened the Victory Theatre in the old Baum Building on the East Side of the Square. Simultaneously, the Lyric was allowed to simply fade out of the movie business.

A story in the daily *Fayetteville Democrat* for October 20, 1919 declared: *"Victory Theatre to Open Oct. 27."* In fact, the new theatre didn't open until Friday, October 31. Calling itself "Arkansas' Classiest Movie House," the Victory's first show, starting that evening at 6:30 p.m., was *Bonnie Bonnie Lassie* starring Mary McLaren. Admission was 11 cents for children under fourteen and 22 cents for adults—war tax included.

Victory Theater
Courtesy of Professor James Chase

The Victory had a nice run in town, lasting until it would be replaced by the Palace Theatre in the fall of 1926. In its seven year run the Victory survived another influenza quarantine in February of 1920, was active when the *Fayetteville Democrat* officially became the *Fayetteville Daily Democrat* on November 29, 1920, and showed perhaps its most memorable film, *Robin Hood,* on March 17, 1923. This Douglas Fairbanks hit cost locals the extraordinary matinee price of 25 and 55 cents, and then 75 cents and one dollar for the evening show. All admissions included the war tax.

In early May 1925, the first indication of the eventual closing of the Victory was signaled by a story in the *Daily Democrat* stating that an option had been taken out on the Baum Building by an unnamed, but non-resident party. On May 30, the identity of this person was revealed. W. F. Sonneman, a motion picture entrepreneur from Waco, Texas had purchased the Baum Building.

The effect this would have on the Victory was not fully known for better than a year. On September 14, 1926, an advertisement in the *Daily Democrat* reported that there was "Not much left of the Victory

—Except—Very Fine Pictures." The imminent closure of E. C. Robertson's flagship theatre was undeniably clear.

On September 29, 1926, amid indications in the *Daily Democrat* of Sonneman's hurried remodeling of the Baum Building, an advertisement in the paper referred to the Victory as the "little show." With construction crews working three shifts in a rush to complete the new Palace Theatre, the Victory's last ad ran on Friday, October 15, 1926 and its "Last show in this house" (the Tom Mix horse opera *No Man's Gold)* was held the next night, Saturday, October 16, 1926. Like so many movie houses before it, the Victory was gone, relegated to the status of forgotten Fayetteville history.

The same year that the Victory had begun operations, 1919, another theatre opened in Fayetteville but its existence was brief and unsuccessful. This movie house was called the Monarch and it seems to have lasted less than a month. The first advertisement for the Monarch appeared in the daily *Fayetteville Democrat* on November 4, 1919 and gave its location as the Rogers Building on School Street. More ads appeared in the *Democrat* that month including pleas to "Don't Forget the Monarch," but they were to no avail. The last ad appeared in the paper on November 14, 1919 and the Monarch theatre came to an unceremonious end.

After the brief tenure of the Monarch, the next theatre to open in Fayetteville was the Royal. Owned and managed by department store moguls E. A. and A. L. Budd, it would be a fixture on the South Side of the Square for decades to come. Contrary to dates published in the primary histories of Fayetteville, the Royal does not date from 1921 but actually opened its doors, as shown in the *Daily Democrat,* on Friday, December 10, 1920, with the feature film *Trumpet Island.* Admission on opening night was 10 cents for children and 20 cents for adults.

By late spring 1921, the Royal was popular enough to inform patrons that it would be expanding its facilities. On May 13, 1921 both a front page story and an advertisement on the inside of the *Daily Democrat* trumpeted the enlargement of the Royal. The remodeled theatre

Royal Theater

University of Arkansas Libraries, Special Collections, Picture Collection, oversize 5-147

would seat 1,200 patrons, readers were told, and when it reopened—the scheduled date was July 1, 1921—there would not only be movies but regular vaudeville shows as well. The July 1 date turned out to be a bit optimistic, as did the size of the expansion.

During the month of July and well into mid-August, 1921, no ads appeared for the Royal. Then on August 16 the theatre reappeared with an advertisement, followed by more ads on August 17 and 18 as well, advising customers that it would open on Friday, August 19. Right on the altered schedule, the "New" Royal Theatre reopened as promised with the feature film *Reputation* starring Priscilla Dean. Admission prices were 10 cents for the balcony and 20 and 30 cents for the lower floor. According to the paper, some 960 customers attended the reopening, sixty more than the remodeled theatre supposedly could hold.

From mid-1921 until 1925, the Royal and Victory theatres provided nearly all of the movies in Fayetteville. The Ozark, which had displayed movies along with its traditional theatrical fare from 1910 to 1914, almost exclusively presented stage shows from 1915 until early in 1925. In February of 1925, as disclosed in the *Daily Democrat,* E. C. Robertson, owner of the Victory Theatre, leased the Ozark. Robertson would shortly turn the Ozark into primarily a movie house. There was still a theatrical season, but it was greatly reduced in scope and size.

As noted previously, 1925 had also seen another important development on the Fayetteville movie theatre scene. On May 6 an option was taken out on the Baum Building (home of the Victory Theatre) on the East Side of the Square. The buyer was the aforementioned W. F. Sonneman and one of the reasons he came to town from Texas was to get into the local movie business.[190] He did so with considerable energy and success, eventually owning and managing every theatre in town.

For much of the next year, while the Royal and Victory competed against each other and the Ozark went through a couple of remodeling and repair phases and began another limited theatrical season, not much was heard about Sonneman and his plans for the Baum Building. Those plans, of course, would directly impact the Victory. In mid and late September 1926, then, Victory ads began appearing in the *Daily Democrat* referring to the "little" movie house's diminished facilities, which were the result of the Baum Building being under heavy reconstruction. The Victory was slowly being squeezed down and out.

On September 15, 1926, the paper told of men working hard to install the outside electric sign for the Palace Theatre and indicated that the remodeling was almost done. It was hoped that the new movie house, representing an estimated investment of $150,000 by Sonneman±an enormous amount for those days—would open in early October. Meanwhile, the Victory continued its inevitable contraction and decline.

On Thursday, October 14, 1926 the first advertisement appeared for the Palace Theatre and the next day the Victory ran its last. On Saturday, as the Victory closed down, a Palace ad in the *Daily Democrat* heralded the first movie at the new showcase theatre: *Son of Shiek.* It starred the recently deceased Rudolph Valentino in his "last big production."

Palace Theater
Fayetteville Public Library, Digital Collection

The Palace Theatre opened officially on Thursday, October 21, 1926 at 7 p.m. with the advertised *Son of Shiek*. Admission was 15 cents for children and 35 cents for adults. In the next day's *Daily Democrat,* it was reported that 1,600 people had attended the premier event and the paper even ran a congratulatory editorial piece in addition to the front page news story. With the opening of the Palace, Fayetteville's stable of movie houses would be unchanged for some fifteen years, but it was hardly a stagnant time.

On October 6, 1927, one year after the Palace completed the Fayetteville theatre trinity, Hollywood released a motion picture that changed the industry and the movie-going experience almost as much as the creation of motion pictures had itself. This movie was *The Jazz Singer,* starring Al Jolson. It was the first "talking picture." Practically overnight, "talkies" were all the rage and movie houses around the country competed to be first with the new technology.

In Fayetteville, the first sign that the talkies were headed this way actually came in the form of advertisements from the Joie Theatre out of Ft. Smith. The Joie ran ads in the *Daily Democrat* on July 30 and

September 7, 1928 letting Fayetteville movie-goers know that it had the real thing —talking motion pictures.

"Hear Them! See Them!" the July 30 Joie ad read, referring to the Warner Brothers Vitaphone talking picture *The Lion and the Mouse* starring Lionel Barrymore. The September 7 ad was even more enthusiastic, describing the film *Lights of New York* as the "First 100% All Talking Picture" and "The Greatest of All."

On February 4, 1929, the Royal made a play to be the first theatre in Fayetteville to show a talkie. Unfortunately, their management—led by J. W. Hunter, once manager of the Ozark, who had taken over the Royal late in the summer of 1927 when W. F. Sonneman became manager of both the Palace and the Ozark—chose the wrong "new" technology. The Royal, now advertising an admission price of always 10 cents for "Any Seat, Any Time," went with a process called Synchrotone.

As detailed in the *Daily Democrat,* The Synchrotone technique used a record with the actor's voices synchronized to the action on screen. This was a kind of higher tech version of the old TA-MO-PIC method where actors stood behind the screen and recited the lines of the film such as was used by the Vaudette Theatre back in 1908. The Royal ran their Synchrotone movies for three days and nights and got a write-up in the *Daily Democrat* which included the not particularly strong endorsement that the "banjo player also was reported to be very good."

On February 5, 1929, at the exact time the Royal was trying its experiment, the Ozark stole all the local movie thunder by announcing in the *Daily Democrat* that the "Highest Type Talking Pictures" were coming there soon, even setting a tentative date of either February 20 or 21. On February 7, the paper related that the *"First Talking Screen of Kind in Country Received at Ozark."*

Because Robert Levy, a New York City engineer contracted to install the new equipment at the Ozark, was delayed in coming to town, the opening of the talking film was put off, as well. On March 5, 1929 a new hoped-for date of March 15 was set for "Talking Films Opening at Ozark." The Ozark just missed this date but on Saturday, March 16,

1929 a large, bold-font headline on page one of the *Daily Democrat* declared that *"Photophone Marks New Era In Fayetteville."*

So the first talking picture in town using this new Photophone system was a two o'clock matinee at the Ozark on Monday, March 18, 1929 with three follow on shows later in the day. The first feature talkie was *Mother Knows Best* starring Madge Bellamy. This historical program, which the paper said "Places City On Map As One Of Most Progressive In State," had a temporary admission price of 50 cents.

Once the Ozark was established as the talking pictures leader in the city, the Palace and Royal theatres hurried to follow suit. Despite several *Daily Democrat* ads declaring it would soon have talkies, the Royal was aced out for second place in the sound picture sweepstakes by the Palace. On Monday, June 3, 1929 the Palace introduced its Vitaphone system with the feature *On Trial* starring Pauline Frederick. Admission was 10 cents for children and 35 cents for adults.

The Royal kept trying to get their own talkies and, after several delays and postponements, at 7:15 p.m. on Monday, June 17, 1929 the "little theatre that could" finally began its own true sound era with the movie *Times Square* starring Arthur Lubin and Alice Day. An article in the *Daily Democrat* stated that the Royal system was called a "Photo Talker" and had been installed by a company out of Dallas, Texas. Admission for the first talking picture at the Royal was 10 cents for children and 25 cents for adults.

Following the introduction of sound films in Fayetteville, the Royal, Palace, and Ozark remained the city's only movie theatre options for more than ten years. During this stretch of time, the Royal took up several of the non-movie headlines.

On July 21, 1932, an article in the *Daily Democrat* disclosed that an acting stock company, the Orpheum Players of Springfield, Missouri, had leased the Royal for a two week stay. The group put on stage shows between screenings of movies and took up residence in local apartments. The manager brought in for the duration of the lease was a man named W. S. Sutherland, who was expected to remain in town to run the Royal when the group moved on.

After the Orpheum Players moved on, however, nothing more was heard of the Royal until November 2, 1932 when an advertisement appeared in the *Daily Democrat* announcing a "New Sound" and "New Manager" at the theatre beginning that day. The first movie under the unidentified new management was *Makers of Men* starring Jack Holt.

On April 7, 1933, Royal management changed again when W. F. Sonneman leased the theatre from E. A. Budd. This made Sonneman the controlling party of all three movie theatres in town. The latest incarnation of the "New" Royal would, the *Daily Democrat* reported, "feature first run Western pictures each weekend and second run pictures of other kinds during the remainder of the week." Admission prices at the Royal would continue to be "at a smaller price" than "either the Ozark or the Palace."

For the next few years, the local movie business scene settled in under Sonneman's solitary guidance, but then part of that empire went up in flames. On Monday, January 15, 1940, the Royal burned to the ground in a fire that also claimed the adjacent Budd's Mercantile and the Royal Barbershop and Café, as well. As described in the *Northwest Arkansas Times,* the theatre was a total loss, but the Budd brothers, who owned the property, and Sonneman, who had a long term lease on the Royal with the Budds, immediately went to work restoring their burned out businesses.

The next day, January 16, E. A. Budd outlined plans to rebuild the mercantile and the Royal. Sonneman told the paper that he was not only going to help rebuild the Royal, but also planned to construct a new theater on Dickson Street, too, although the exact location and name was not yet known.

Never one to procrastinate, Sonneman was back in business with the rebuilt Royal on Thursday, May 23, 1940, with the feature film *Frontier Town.* The admission listed in the *Times* was 15 cents for all comers on opening night, but by the weekend the regular prices of 10 cents for kids and 20 cents for adults was in effect.

With the Royal, Palace, and Ozark already his, Sonneman went to work on making his dream of building a theatre on Dickson Street

that would cater primarily to the university crowd become reality. It
didn't take long for that goal to be reached. Before the end of 1940, a
series of modern, yellow brick buildings—including a movie house—
went up on Dickson Street near the University of Arkansas.

On Wednesday, January 16, 1941, the last of the old-time indoor
movie theatres opened at 645 West Dickson Street with the expressed
intent of showing pictures that would be "especially selected to appeal
to the University crowd." With a blitz of advertisements, self-promot-
ing news stories, and congratulatory greetings from other businesses in
town scattered throughout that day's *Times,* the UArk Theatre presented *Haunted Honeymoo*n starring Robert Montgomery on its gala first
night. Admission for the evening was a flat 30 cents—including a 3
cents defense tax and a 1 cent sales tax.

Along with its sister establishments, the opening of the UArk gave
Fayetteville its four theatre complement so familiar to those living here
in the 1940s and 1950s. During these years, local movie-goers came to
consider the Royal, Palace, Ozark, and new UArk as fixtures in town—
as unchanging as the historic Washington County courthouse or Old
Main on the University of Arkansas campus.

In the summer of 1948, local film fans learned that after years of
owning and managing all of Fayetteville's theatres, W. F. Sonneman
had made the decision to divest himself of his movie empire. On July
1, he put an advertisement in the *Times* for an all children's show that
"Old Man Sonneman" was presenting as a way of "saying Good Bye."

It was related in the paper of July 3, 1948 that the Malco Theatre
Group, with Loris Stanton as the new local manager, had taken over all
four movie houses in town and that the Ozark Theatre would be closed
some months for "extensive remodeling." That same day, several local
businesses ran advertisements thanking Sonneman for his contributions
and also welcoming the new Malco management. In the days and weeks
ahead, while the Ozark was being redone, the Malco Group ran consis-
tently large, eye-catching ads for the Palace, UArk, and Royal.

Then, on Friday, October 22, 1948, the *Times* declared: *"New
Ozark Theater To Open Monday."* The article described the "new"

Ozark as having seven hundred and thirty "leather and velour covered" seats, five hundred and eighty-eight yards of carpeting, a new "Super Simplex" projector, fine new tile bathrooms, and with a large concession stand built in the rear of the theatre. On Monday, October 25, 1948, the refurbished Ozark re-opened for business with the feature film *The Saxon Charm* starring Robert Montgomery and Susan Hayward.

During the next decade, the four theatres evolved into the establishments that most people of the era remember. The Royal was the cheap theatre, the kids matinee theatre, the fading, decaying home of the B-Western movies. The Palace, after closing in late 1953 for an extensive remodeling after a small fire, came back strongly in early 1954. For a number of years more it held forth on the East Side of the Square with slightly higher admission prices, an improved décor, and movies a bit older or less successful than those playing down at the Ozark.

The UArk continued to be the university theatre, often showing racier, more adult-oriented films, while the Ozark maintained its refrigerated coolness as the finest theatre in town, with the newest pictures and finest ambiance.

Nothing, of course, lasts forever, and that cliché is especially true in the movie theatre business. Time, the growth of television, the arrival in town of the first multiplex theatre (as recorded in the *Times*, the Malco Twin Cinemas opened August 26, 1970) and the decline of the Square as the business hub in town began to drive the old movie houses out of business.

One by one these theatres, no longer in the hands of local, individual entrepreneurs like W. F. Sonneman, dropped by the wayside. The Royal, usually hanging on by a thread, anyway, was the first to go. Its last show, as advertised in the *Times*, was a double-feature on Sunday, February 5, 1956. The twin-bill starred John Wayne in *Old California* and Johnny Weismuller in *Tarzan and the Ape Man*.

The Palace lasted more than a decade longer than the Royal, but by the spring of 1969 it was no longer showing movies. From then until the spring of 1974 it mostly put on live country music shows like the Ozark Opry,[191] usually on Friday evenings in the summer.

On May 16, 1974, with the destruction of the East Side of the Square imminent as a result of Fayetteville's version of urban renewal, a final advertisement in the *Times* noted the "last" Arkansas Country Opry music show on Friday, May 17. The Palace, like so many movie houses in town before it, was gone.

The Ozark, on the other hand, continuously operated as a movie house right up until the day its doors were closed forever. Although it remained a part of the Malco theatre chain, the Ozark suffered from the growth of the dual screen venues then taking hold in Fayetteville. By the mid-1970s, film patronage was shifting northward, out Highway 71 (the Malco Twin Theatres) and up to the new Northwest Arkansas Mall (the Malco Mall Twin Theatres).

In the spring of 1977, Malco announced in the *Times* that they would be opening the Razorback Twin theatres on North College. With the arrival of the Razorback, the Ozark was odd theatre out. On Tuesday, April 19, 1977, the Ozark showed its last feature *Raggedy Ann and Andy,* a musical. With that final program, over seventy years of theatrical shows, vaudeville, and movies came to an end.

Although no longer a part of the Malco chain, the UArk remained a continuously operating movie house—even splitting into the UArk 1 and 2 with the former showing "art" films—through the spring of 1974. Then, after being off local radar for over eighteen months, it re-emerged in late December 1975, still as twin theatres and still showing mostly art and retro films. By the spring of 1976 it was a single theatre again and remained so through March of 1977 when its ads dropped out of the *Times.*

After another eighteen month hiatus, the UArk reappeared in the middle of October 1979 calling itself the UArk Arts Center. Movies, again mostly art and retro films, were shown on the weekends into 1980. In July of 1980, its name changed again, this time to "Alternative Films/UArk" but its movies were still of the art and retro variety. Finally, in late 1980, the UArk closed its doors for good.

On Saturday night, December 13, 1980 the UArk ran an advertisement in the *Times* for its final movie, *Foul Play* starring Goldie
Hawn and Chevy Chase. The last of Fayetteville's old indoor movie
houses was gone.

Today, there is not a single trace left of either the Palace or the
Royal. Urban renewal and the destruction of the Square saw to that.
The UArk marquee can yet be seen on West Dickson Street, however,
and the Ozark building was saved and renovated in the mid- to late-
1990s. The Ozark was rescued from the wrecking ball through the
efforts of Jonathan Story, a junior high student at the time, and local
businessmen like banker John Lewis. The upgraded Ozark building still stands on College Avenue next to the historic Washington
County Courthouse.

Although these faint memories are perhaps not enough to fully
remind Fayetteville of its movie theatre past, at least something remains of those bygone days. The UArk façade, lately renovated, and
the restored Ozark building now stand as partial symbols of a distant
era, as echoes of a time long gone, an age nearly lost. And until the
last person who attended one of these movie houses is gone, the old
theatres that once graced Fayetteville will remain in our collective
local memory and will not have been completely lost or forgotten
in time.

The following list summarizes, in mostly chronological order, the
old time movie theatres and venues in Fayetteville from 1898 to the
closing of the UArk in 1980.

FAYETTEVILLE OPERA HOUSES/STAGE THEATRES

Opera House
Van Winkle Hotel, 26 E. Center Street, third story
Years: 1879-1886

Woods Opera House
17-19 W. Mountain (Southwest corner of the Square), second floor
Years: 1886-1905
later Budd's Dept. store, later Penney's, currently a brew pub.
John T. Woods, Manager, 1886-1895;
H. M. Hudgins, Hot Springs, Owner/Manager, 1886-1905

Woods Opera House
North of where the Ozark Theatre would be located, on the same
side of College Street
Years: 1892-1896 (ca.)
John T. Woods, Owner/Manager

Knights of Pythias Hall and Opera House
Next to old Washington County courthouse on College, built in
1904-1905; renamed the Ozark Theatre (1907)
Years: 1904-1907

*Tent shows: general entertainment performances appearing in town at such
locations as the corner of Meadow and College, the Stone lot on East Center Street, and often during the 1910s and 1920s on the Boles Lot (just
north of Dickson Street and west of St. Charles Avenue).*

FAYETTEVILLE THEATRES (MOTION PICTURES)

Opera House (Indoors)
17-19 W. Mountain Street (SW corner of the Square)
Years: 1898
Admission: Unknown

Young Bros. Electric Theatre (Temporary traveling show)
Unknown Location
Years: 1904, 1906
Admission: Unknown

Lyman Howe's "moving picture show" (Indoors)
(Temporary traveling show)
Ozark Theatre (Knights of Pythias Hall and Opera House)
Years: 1906-1909
Admission: 25, 35, and 50 cents (1907 and 1909)

Dime Electric Show
Unknown Location
Years: 1907
Admission: Unknown
Opened: 3/25/1907; C. McDonald, owner

Scenic Theatre (Indoors)
East Center Street
Years: 1907-1908
Admission: 5 cents children, 10 cents adults (1907-1908)

The Marvel (Indoors)
Hight Building, N. Block Avenue, below NW corner of the Square
Years: 1907
Admission: 5 cents, movies;
5 cents children, 10 cents adults, vaudeville shows (1907)

Baum Brother's Store (Indoors)
East Side of the Square (where Victory and Palace were located later)
Years: 1908
Admission: Unknown

Mr. Hays (Temporary)
Unknown Location
Years: 1908
Admission: Unknown

Pastime Electric Theatre (Airdome)
Unknown Location
Years: 1908
Admission: 5 cents and 10 cents (1908)

Vaudette Theatre (Airdome)
also used indoor facility
Van Winkle lot, on north side of East Center Street
Years: 1908-1910
Admission: 5 and 10 cents (1909-1910)

Princess Theatre (Airdome)
East Center Street, north side
Years: 1908-1909
Admission: 5 and 10 cents (1909)

Lyric Theatre (Airdome) *then indoors*
At (near) the depot (West Avenue and Dickson Street), 1908; 15-17
N. Block Avenue (until 1913); thereafter, 101 N. Block Avenue
Years: 1908-1921
Admission: 5, 10, and 15 cents (1908);
adults 15 cents and children 6 cents, including war tax (1917)

Bijou Dream Theatre
416 W. Dickson Street
Years: 1909
Admission: 5 and 10 cents (1909)

Ozark Airdome (Air Dome)
inside Ozark Theatre in winter, 1910-1914
23 E. Center Street
Years: 1910-1914, 1917
Admission: 5 and 10 cents (1911-1914); 5 and 15 cents (1917)

Skydome (Air Dome)
inside Ozark Theatre in winter
23 E. Center Street
Years: 1915-1917
Admission: 5 and 10 cents;
10 and 20 cents for special movies

Orpheum Theatre
424 West Dickson Street; O. L. Champion, owner
Years: 1911-1912
Admission: 10 cents (1912)

Victory Theatre (Indoors)
10-12 S. East Avenue (East Side of Square in Baum Bldg.); E. C.
Robertson, owner—El Dorado, AR
Years: 1919-1926
Admission: 11 cents under 14, 22 cents adults (1919)

Ozark Theatre (Indoors)
4 North College Avenue
Years: 1905-1977
(theatrical and vaudeville shows, boxing matches, movies)
Admission: 5 and 10 cents, movies;
10 cents balcony and 15 cents floor, vaudeville (1910-1911)
Opened (as opera house): 1905 (built by Knights of Pythias, 1904-
1905); changed to Ozark Theatre, June 15, 1907; Owner/Manager:
W. D. McNair (early 1910s); W. F. Sonneman (1927-1948);
Malco Theatre Group (1948-1977)

Monarch Theatre (Possibly indoors)
Rogers Building on School Street
Years: 1919
Admission: 5 cents, children under 12; 10 cents, adults
war tax included (1919)

Royal Theatre (Indoors)
13 W. Mountain Street (South Side of Square)
Years: 1920-1956
Admission: 10 and 20 cents (1920)
Opened: December 10, 1920; E. A. Budd and A. L. Budd, owners/
managers; W. F. Sonneman, owner (1933-1948); Malco Theatre
Group (1948-1956)

Palace Theatre (Indoors)
13 S. East Avenue (East Side of Square);
took over Victory Theatre space (Baum Building)
Years: 1926-1974
Admission: 15 and 35 cents (1926)
Opened: October 21, 1926; W. F. Sonneman, owner;
Malco Theatre Group (1948-1974)

UArk Theatre (Indoors)
645 W. Dickson Street
Years: 1941-1980
Admission: 30 cents (1941)
Opened: January 16, 1941; W. F. Sonneman, owner;
Malco Theatre Group (1948-1970s)

HISTORY OF FAYETTEVILLE'S
WILSON (CITY) PARK

FOR OVER ONE hundred years, Fayetteville's City Park, officially named Wilson Park, has provided citizens with a pleasant recreational area where they and their families could picnic, play, and swim. Although the park is no doubt familiar to most locals, its history may not be quite as well known.

Fortunately, the history of City Park falls into three distinct phases that can be identified through its ownership and management. As early as 1906, the park was privately owned, maintained, and operated by A. L. Trent, a benevolent and civic-minded man.

In the mid-1920s, a group of local businessmen—led by Dr. Noah Drake of Drake Field fame—purchased the park from Trent. Dr. Drake and his fellow investors formed the City Park Company and that organization ran the park—building the first permanent swimming pool and several stone cottages, remains of which still stand today—until the 1940s.

The city of Fayetteville purchased City Park from Dr. Drake—who had bought out the other investors—in late 1944 and has owned it ever since. Under municipal ownership, the park was expanded greatly and the tennis courts and ball field,[192] among other improvements, were added over the years.

What we have today, though, is owed to a large degree to the original owner of the city park area: A. L. Trent. According to W. S. Campbell, in his book *One Hundred Years of Fayetteville, 1828-1928*, Trent had been a cashier at the old Washington County Bank before

A.L. Trent
100 Years of Fayetteville by W. S. Campbell

becoming an insurance man.[193] He was also a practicing Methodist
and a member of the Chamber of Commerce.[194]

In the early years of the twentieth century, Trent purchased the
land in and around what would become City Park.[195] Through his
own good will he provided Fayetteville with a place for individuals and
families to gather in "a place of beauty"[196] and in good weather swim
and boat in what was then called Trent's Pond.[197]

In 1908, an anonymous writer going by the name "City Park Poet"
penned a tribute to the natural beauty of this new addition to Fay-

etteville. In the poem *Athens of Arkansas,* the author tells the audience that "By being more friendly with Nature and Art," we "have added to town a beautiful park" and:

> *To sum it all up—to come to the test,*
> *There's but one addition that we can call best,*
> *The one by Mt. Nord through Englewood shade,*
> *The place of all places that Nature has made,*
> *The place she has made and sealed with her mark*
> *The beautiful place we call CITY PARK.*[198]

Besides anonymous poetic renderings of the park's fine qualities, Trent himself (there is no evidence that he was the City Park Poet) liked to write occasional letters to the newspaper touting his park and its facilities.

On October 21, 1916, over a month after the park had closed for the season, he wrote a letter printed in the *Fayetteville Daily.* He thanked the public for their "patronage" and said he "hoped to make the Park a still more inviting place." To do so, however, he noted that it was "entirely beyond" his "means or ability to do so."

Lobbying for the city to take ownership of the park ("of course the city should own the park," he said), Trent reminded readers that three years before he had offered the park and the springs, two one-half acre deeds, to the city, if they would agree to improve the property. With no response to his offer, he continued maintaining the park by himself.

He stressed in the letter that the park, if maintained at a high level and advertised throughout the region, could bring in visitors from Texas, Missouri and steal some of the thunder of other "Summer Resort" destinations like Winslow and Eureka Springs.

The following summer, he wrote another letter to the paper that provides a glimpse into the life of our city nearly a century ago. His purpose was to announce an increase in the price of swimming at City Park to 25 cents whether swimmers provided their own suit or not.

It was the same price, Trent noted, as charged in area towns he had visited like Muskogee, Oklahoma and Ft. Smith.[199]

Trent reminded his customers that previously he had offered a 5 cent reduction in the price if they brought their own swim suit. Morning short swims "before breakfast" would remain 10 cents, but patrons were requested to be out of the water by "7 o'clock" so that "the boy who waits on them can go to breakfast, too."[200]

By the early to mid-1920s, City Park was beginning to enter what might be called a transitional phase. Trent was still its owner and manager, but other voices with other plans for the park were being heard. In April 1923, for example, it was suggested that the city of Fayetteville buy the park. An unidentified "prominent citizen" said that because the town was "growing rapidly" it could not expect "private individuals" (meaning Trent) to maintain this "valuable ground as a public playground free of charge."[201]

A $40,000 bond investment, it was suggested, would provide "20 acres of land," which included almost 17 acres to the west of the park known as Wilson's Pasture, for use as a tourist camp. This would give Fayetteville a park "worthy of its name" and one "where the tourist public may be made comfortable and happy."[202]

The same "prominent citizen" mentioned above advocated municipal intervention because this "beautiful hill-side which has been compared favorably by travelers in Athens to the most beautiful natural amphitheatre in the world must be cut up into building lots unless Fayetteville does something to save it."[203]

Early the following year, 1924, the Fayetteville Chamber of Commerce met to further discuss plans for a tourist park. They proposed that Wilson's Pasture, which it was believed could be purchased for $10,000, "be utilized for an auto park." By the end of March 1924, the Chamber had begun a Tourist Camp fund that with a goal of raising $1500 would finance an auto park to "lure tourists from all sections of the country."[204] By April 2, the paper reported that the camp had had its first guests and they "Like it."[205]

Even though the auto park was already in use, by mid-April

City Park with Old Main in background
Fayeteville Public Library, Digital Collection

the Tourist Camp fund drive was still in process and had taken in $1,067. Yet another $500 was still needed to reach the earlier-announced goal.[206]

Near the end of the month, the paper reported that internationally renowned author, historian, and philosopher Will Durant, on a visit to Fayetteville "several years" before, had said that the natural amphitheatre in City Park "rivaled that at Athens." Durant's comment mirrors frequent comparisons between Fayetteville and Athens so often repeated by well-meaning local boosters of this and earlier optimistic eras.[207]

On May 1, 1924, the Chamber of Commerce suggested what they believed should be the next big improvement to City Park. *"Swimming Pool Urged for City By C. of C. Boosters"* a page one story in the *Fayetteville Daily Democrat* reported. "A concrete swimming pool," W. F. D. Batjer, Secretary of the Chamber said, could be built for an estimated $3000 and would be "a great drawing card for tourists and ... vacationers."

Despite Batjer's hopeful projections, plans for a "concrete" swimming pool in City Park did not begin to firm up until March of 1926. A. L. Trent, still owner and manager of the park, offered to build a pool and continue to maintain the park without charge if the city would provide free water. In a letter to the *Democrat,* Trent responded to the "considerable agitation" the city had gone through in regard to "buying a site for park grounds, tourist camp, etc." These efforts by the city, he noted, had seemingly "failed."[208]

Later in the month, however, a solution was found. With Dr. Noah F. Drake as its head, a private company was formed by local stockholders, including Drake and Trent among more than forty others, with the goal of purchasing City Park and building a swimming pool there.[209] City Park Company was the name of the new ownership group and by the end of March 1926 some $14,706 in stocks had been purchased by investors.[210]

On April 3, 1926 it was announced in the *Democrat* that City Park had been purchased from Trent for $8,500. The official date of the sale would be August 6, 1926.[211] Work on the proposed new pool and a playground for children would begin in ten days.

The pool was to be located south of Trent's Pond, which it was said would be preserved (it was not).[212] There were also plans to build a band shell by the pool where musical shows could be performed for patrons who sat in chairs or on blankets and watched the entertainment from above on the rolling hillside south of the pool.

Once the announcement of a new swimming pool had been made, a contest was held to find a name for the park itself. On April 14, the Democrat reported that "City Park" was the name selected for City Park. Two ladies, Miss Vera Drake and Mrs. Fred Armstrong split the $10 contest prize for their shared suggestion. Not quite two weeks later, April 27, the paper noted that ground had been broken on the new swimming pool.

Just over a year later, on May 1, 1927, the pool was opened to the public. The *Democrat* reported that nearly 1,000 people attended the opening of City Park with close to 200 of them availing themselves "of swimming privileges." The pool was described as being 60 by 160 feet in size and that it and other improvements to the park had cost almost $40,000.

Wilson Park, Remaining Stone Cottages
J.B. Hogan

The tourist camp had also been expanded and now consisted of six small houses and three stone cottages.[213] Tourist camp capacity was estimated as "150 cars or 450 people." A. L. Trent's son-in-law and daughter, Mr. and Mrs. Keith Carson, would reside in the park and be in charge of "grounds, tourist camp and concessions." Frank Barr, well-known local bandleader and former movie house entrepreneur, was the "general park director."[214]

In the summer of 1928, the tourist camp did landmark business. From June 15 until the first week of September some 4500 tourists and 937 cars were listed in the record books of the park.[215]

For the next fifteen years, City Park remained under the aegis of the privately owned City Park Company but there was a continual, low level discussion concerning the appropriateness of municipal ownership of the park. In October 1933, Dr. Drake offered to sell City Park to the city of Fayetteville for $20,000 but in those cash-strapped days of the Great Depression the offer went unanswered.[216] Finally, during the difficult days of World War II, city ownership moved closer to reality.

In May of 1942, the City Park Company was dissolved with Dr.

Drake taking sole ownership of City Park.[217] About two and a half
years later, in December of 1944, the city finally agreed to buy City
Park from Dr. Drake for $16,000.[218] City Park was then officially
owned by the government of Fayetteville and it remains so today.

At times over the years, the large tract of land west of City Park
proper, known as Wilson's Pasture after the prominent local family
that owned it, had been rented for tourist camp parking and other
recreational uses. In mid-1945, with Victory in Europe assured and
hopes of a Pacific victory in the offing, an influx of college-bound
veterans began arriving in town to attend the University of Arkansas
on the GI Bill.

Fayetteville Mayor George T. Sanders and the city council initiated
a program that allowed returning vets to park trailers throughout the
grounds of City Park for an affordable fee while going to school or read-
justing to civilian life. Although opposed by some, the trailer program
brought in needed income to less than overflowing municipal coffers.

In the summer of 1945 Charles Morrow Wilson, third generation
scion of the highly regarded Wilson clan and an internationally known
and respected author, offered to sell Wilson's Pasture to the city on the
condition that the park be named in memory of his mother Mattie
Morrow Wilson.[219] Wilson envisioned the new, expanded park as a
"beautiful and valuable"[220] place for local residents to enjoy an undeveloped natural site in the heart of Fayetteville.

On August 5, 1946, the *Northwest Arkansas Times* reported that
the city would purchase the 16 7/8 acre tract from Wilson. The price
of the land to the city was $15,500. The actual sale price was $22,500,
minus the author's donation of $7,000.[221] Twelve days later, on August
17, it was announced that the contract for the land was signed. City
Park now encompassed 22 acres in all.[222]

Wilson presumed that the verbal agreement between himself and
the city of Fayetteville would keep the newly purchased area "an ornamental city park." On August 20, however, Mayor Sanders announced
in the *Times* that veteran's trailers could now be parked not just in the
old City Park area but in the new section, as well.[223]

A few months later, in the fall of 1946, Mrs. Roberta Fulbright, owner of the *Northwest Arkansas Times*, wrote in her "As I See It" column that the city should honor A. L. Trent, the man who had founded City Park. Mrs. Fulbright proposed that a day in October be set aside as A. L. Trent day.[224] Mrs. Fulbright's suggestion did not come to fruition, but her idea seems like a valid one even now.

From December 1947 through the spring of 1949, a controversial proposal to build a Boy's Club in City Park caused a fair amount of rancor between proponents and opponents of the plan. On December 15, 1947, the *Times* reported: *"City Park Site Accepted For New Boys Club Building."*

Almost from the beginning, the proposal had its detractors, but by late March 1948, plans had been made to start work on the new Boy's Club.[225] W. W. Higgins, director of the Boy's Club board, estimated that a building would cost around $35,000 and would be built "just north of the present swimming pool."[226] The recommended location was shortly changed to the west end of the park, the area formerly known as Wilson's Pasture and recently purchased from Charles Morrow Wilson.

By the end of the year, opposition to the plan had grown to such proportions that Wilson himself, who was also upset by trailers being allowed in the area he had sold to the city, wrote a letter of protest to the *Times*. The new Boy's Club building, he said, would grossly violate the "gentleman's agreement" he had made with the city to ensure that City Park (especially the western part that he had sold to them) would "be used as an ornamental public park for the benefit and good of the general public of Fayetteville."[227]

In the January 5, 1949 *Times*, proponents of the Boy's Club plan began to retreat from their position. Protesters sensitive to Wilson's point of view suggested that the Boy's Club building be built in the northeast section of the park as had initially been planned, and not on the west side.

That same day, Mrs. Fulbright devoted her "As I See It" column to the controversy and suggested finding another place for the Boy's Club outside of City Park altogether. Wilson was so annoyed by the whole affair that the next day he offered to buy back "the land in question (the old Wilson's Pasture) in its entirety at the amount of money received by me from the city."[228]

Fortunately, the election of Admiral M. Powell Rhea as mayor of Fayetteville in 1949 helped bring the Boy's Club controversy to an end. Rhea, while serving on the Boy's Club executive board, had opposed building the new club in Wilson Park and shortly after he assumed office it was also reported that the trailers in City Park would not be replaced.[229] A little over a year later, in July 1950, the Fayetteville city council voted to remove the trailers by June 1951.[230] With the trailers on the way out and the Boy's Club plan no longer viable, both controversies simply faded away.

By January 1951, some four and a half years after his sale of Wilson's Pasture, Charles Morrow Wilson's desire to have City Park renamed for his mother had still not been fulfilled. Alderman Hugh Kincaid addressed the council on January 29 and requested City Park be renamed Wilson Park. The council voted to leave the name as City Park but approved a plan to erect a plaque to the people who expanded it and then "await the reaction of the public."[231] Neither the plaque nor a public reaction to it seems to have been forthcoming.

For several years there had been plans to build tennis courts in City Park and in 1951, the courts—"long under construction"—were finally opened on August 18.[232] Just a few days later, the old tourist cabins (seven in all), which had slowly fallen into decline over the years, were sold to local entrepreneur H. O. Bailey for a total of $852. Bailey bought the cabins to use in opening his own tourist camp on Highway 71 south of town.[233]

As for the Boy's Club, in the fall of 1951 the *Times* reported that the club would move temporarily to the White Chapel Assembly of God Church building on south College.[234] The church was located just south of the Rock Street intersection with Archibald Yell Boulevard (it is currently a vacant lot). By the mid-1950s, the Boy's Club used the facilities of the National Guard Armory before a new building was erected at Harmon Field in the late 1950s.

Wilson Park Ballfield Today
J.B. Hogan

In 1954, the area once known as Trent's Pond was leveled and put into shape for youth baseball. The Sherman Lollar Little League began play on the new City Park ballfield in the summer of 1955 and operated exclusively until Walker Park was opened in the south part of town in 1961.[235] Today, the field at Wilson Park is used for softball leagues.

With regard to the long-delayed renaming of City Park to Wilson Park, the next attempt to do so was registered in a *Times* editorial of August 22, 1960. With the recent addition of Walker Park in south Fayetteville, the writer observed, it was now "a good time to name the park in the north section of the city, now called City Park. And the name it should have is Wilson Park." The editorialist went on to give details of the 1946 sale of Wilson's Pasture and concluded that the renaming "would be a gesture of recognition to Charles Morrow Wilson and the family which has so long lived in this area."

Despite the several attempts and exhortations to rename City Park, no official change was made. The split or simultaneous usage of the two names is apparent in city maps of the era. The 1962 Fayetteville city map lists City Park but four years later the 1966 version uses Wilson Park. In keeping with the dual names, the 1966 phone book uses City Park.

In the latter 1960s, Fayetteville took an important step with regard to its growing park system. The city council proposed and adopted Ordinance #1526 which created the Department of Parks and Recreation. Some sixty years after A. L. Trent had privately provided the city a public park, municipal management of all parks in town was complete.[236]

On June 16, 1969, over twenty years after Charles Morrow Wilson's sale and gift of Wilson's Pasture to the city of Fayetteville, City Park was finally, and officially, renamed Wilson Park in honor of the writer's mother Mattie Morrow Wilson. Mayor Garland Melton, Jr. suggested at a city council meeting that City Manager Wesley Howe "be given the latitude to have the proper inscription placed on a plaque formally naming Wilson Park."[237]

The *Times* for June 30, 1969 ran a laudatory editorial on the dedication and renaming of the city's flagship park. And while the name change was and is official, even today perhaps as many people still refer to our main in-town recreation area as City Park as those who call it Wilson Park. Traditions—even when they are just names—can be extremely slow to change or die out.

GROWING UP IN EARLY TWENTIETH-CENTURY NORTHWEST ARKANSAS

Excerpts from a letter by Clarence St. Clair "Buck" Gilbert[238]

CLARENCE ST. CLAIR "Buck" Gilbert was born November 21, 1908 in Whitener, a tiny Madison County community west of Hindsville, Arkansas. On August 25, 1978, Gilbert began a long letter that told of his childhood in Northwest Arkansas during the early 1900s. The letter eventually reached nearly seventy-five handwritten pages[239] and Gilbert finished it, after a two-year break, on June 14, 1980. He died June 21, 1983 in Tishomingo, Oklahoma.

The following excerpts have been chosen for their value in describing the life not only of a young boy, but also that of his family and the communities in which he and they lived at the dawn of the twentieth century. Gilbert's memories are funny, poignant, and reflect the personality of an adventurous, high-spirited boy who became a man of equally high-spirits and one with a highly defined sense of humor and a personality that still shines forth from his words and memories.

Spelling, grammar, and punctuation have not been corrected in order to retain the flavor and character of "Buck" Gilbert.[240]

When I came into this world I couldn't speak a word of english. Of course I was very young at the time, but being a very smart little boy, it wasn't long until I was cussin' and gripin' just like everyone else

I was born at Whitener Ark. Nov. 21-1908 or 1909 I'm
not sure which for some of my records say one thing and some
say another. My Dad[241] was a blacksmith, my mother[242] read
the bible a lot and my Dad cussed a lot, so two of the first
words I learned to say were, God and Damn, and I took off
from there Some of the stories I intend to tell in this writing
may be rated pg. or X, so you may want to censor it before
you let the kids read it

I had blond curly hair until I was about 3 years old, when
I got a desease called Exema kinda like the itch, only much
worse. I had sores all over my body and in my hair they had to
keep my head shaved for 2 or 3 months, Dad got some medicine from old Dr. Moore at Hindsville, it was used in my bath
water, and just set me on fire That's when I learned some more
words like the first two, and a few I invented myself. One day
mother saw an advertisement in the *Household*[243] magazine, under patent medicines Dr. Hobson's Exzema Cure,[244] in no time
at all I was well again, but I didn't have curly hair any more

About that time I had my first taste of Tabaco, Dad had
an old pipe that had gotten too strong for him so he gave it
to me. I sucked on it for some time, until mother got mad
and threw it in the stove, but I have been smoking pipes and
ciggaretts ever since

Ike Vaughn owned and operated the general store at
Whitener, Mr. Vaughn had two kids one boy about my age
and a girl about 3 years older. The girl's name was Elsie and
we called the boy Buster, when Buster and I were about 5 or 6
years old we played together a lot.

Mr Proctor the mail carrier and his wife lived right next
door to the store, one day Buster and I snuk into Mrs Proctors chicken house and stole some eggs, we took them in the
store and traded them for choclate candy. I know Mr Vaughn
knew where we got the eggs, but he didn't like the Proctors,
so didn't ask any questions but just let us have the choclates

and laughed, after that Mrs Proctor didn't get as many eggs as before, but Buster and I had plenty of choclates....

We moved from Whitener to Sonora,[245] where I started to School when I was Seven, we didn't live there very long for I dont remember but one old man who lived across the pasture from us and we called him Uncle Newt One morning mamma baked some mince pies and sent my sister Thelma[246] and I to take him one, and to ask him if it would make him mad if she didn't send him another one for supper

Well that old man sat down and ate the whole pie, and got so sick he almost died

One other thing I remember at Sonora at School we had a water cooler on a stand in the back of the room, we all had folding metal drinking cups that we carried in our pockets, one big boy went to the cooler and filled his cup with water came back to his seat and started lapping it like a dog, the teacher told him to stay after school and he would give him a whipping, at recess some of the kids were teasing the boy about it and the teacher said he was going to give them a whipping to, I was scared for I knew if I got a whipping at School Dad would give me another one when I got home. so I went to the teacher and told him I was sick, and he let me go home I don't know what happened and I didn't inquire about it either, (at least I didnt get a whipping)....

Oops! it was bound to happen, I forgot one move we didn't move from Whitener to Sonora we moved in with Grandma Gilbert[247] and Uncle Dick[248] somewhere in the mayfield community, I never knew my Grandpa Gilbert,[249] if I had to write about him it would be a blank page, all I know about him is what my Dad told me, my Dad told me Grandpa made a liar and thief out of him.

He used tobbaco but forbid his boys to use it, so they stole his tobbaco and then lied to him about it. he also kept his axe very sharp and wouldnt let the boys use it, he would sharpen his axe on the grindstone and would use water on the stone to keep the metal cool, which would leave a gray film on the axe,

when grandpa was not around Dad would sneak his axe out and use it, then he would put the axe on the grindstone again and leave the film on, so his Dad wouldn't know he had used it, until one day he was chopping some wood with it and missed the wood and split his big toe, Grandpa came home while Grandma was bandaging Dad's toe, but he never said a word about Dad using his axe,

I don't even know, when or where my Grandpa died or where he is buried....[250]

Dad and Uncle Dick were digging a water well in the front yard, had it down about 30 ft and were just about ready to give up, they had hit some hard rock and had to use dynamite and it was dangerous and expensive, one day Uncle Dick was lowering Dad down on a rope with the winlass, when Dad noticed a wet spot on the wall about 10 ft from the bottom, they put a ladder down in the hole and Dad climbed back up to the wet spot and dug out some of the dirt then said I can hear water running he took a crowbar and drove it back into the wall of the well about 3 ft and water started comming out around the crow bar. he pulled the bar out and water came gushing out through the hole. they had a good water well, it filled the hole about half full and it staied that way as long as uncle Dick lived there....

I gotta get back to Sonora or I'll miss the moving wagon to Hewitt Springs

Hewitt Springs[251] is a watering place about 3 or 4 miles South & east of Springdale

We lived on one hill, Mr. Rass Jones a retired railroad man livied on the next hill and the spring was in the holler (in case you dont know what a holler is it's a small canyon) between the two hills....

As I said before I don't know why we moved here so I

Gilbert Siblings
(From Left) Helen, Buck, Phydella
Martha Hogan Estes

guess we didnt need a reason to move away and we did just that after about 3 months—moved into an old shack just south of Healing Springs[252] several miles west and a little north of Springdale....

Just below our house in the hollow (holler) was a railroad track, around 4 O'clock every afternoon a little old train would go up the holler...Several times a bunch of big boys would come out and bring buckets of water, and several bars of P. and G. soap,[253] and just before the train came by they would soap the track, the wheels on the little ole Engine would slip and he couldn't make it up the hill, the boys would be hiding in the bushes beside the track laughing like crazy. HO! BOY!

Hold onto your hat and climb in the wagon we're movin again, (and we hadn't been here long enough to find our way to the out house in the dark) (well, what the Heck, it wasn't a very fancy out house anyway)

This time we went 4 or 5 miles north to a little place called Osage Mills,[254] the blacksmith there either died or wanted to quit any way his tools were for sale, and Dad borrowed $45.00 from Hewdie Crank and bought the tools, his name was really Hugh but everyone called him Hewdie....

Our house was at the east end of the Street where the road forked, one went north to Bentonville the other went Southeast to Cave Springs

Dads' shop was at the other end of the Street where the road forked again one went south past the School house to Healing Springs the other went northwest across the creek to nowhere in particular....

There were 4 houses and a Church on the north side of the street between our house and the shop. Mrs. Terhune the School teacher, Mr. Vassar the Infadel Mr. and Mrs. Rutherford and a boy my age and Mr. and Mrs. Cliff Bright and their little boy Dickie, we called him the little bright boy, his Dad was a fur trapper and big buyer,

On the street going south there was Mr. and Mrs. Morris a retired couple, Mr. Wall and his wife and 2 girls, Herb Gamble who owned the general store, and Mr. and Mrs. Sikes, who had 4 children 3 girls and one boy Sammy....

On down the road about a half mile was Uncle Eddie Piercie's place, almost everyday one of us kids had to go to Uncle Edies and get a gallon syrup bucket full of seperated milk in those days, it had been put thru a cream Separator, so we called it separated milk....

My brother Carl[255] could do about anything he put his mind or hands to, he built us a real neat sled with steel runners, it snowed about a foot deep one day, and after it thawed for a couple of days, the weather turned real cold and there was about 2 or 3 inches of ice on the ground, there was a hill behind our house, and an old road coming down off to one side of our house, we pulled that sled up to the top of the hill through the bushes (we couldn't go up the road it was too slick) when we got to the top we eased that ole sled out on the road and jumped on it. there was just one thing wrong, we had forgotten there was an old wood gate at the bottom of the hill, Carl who was sitting in front saw what was going to happen and he bailed out I didnt have time to think or do anything so I just closed my eyes and lowered my head and went right through that gate about 40 miles an hour, I was skinned up a little and didn't have any broken bones, but that old gate went to peices like a bomb had hit, if it had been a good gate it would have killed me, HO! BOY!

….Not long after we moved to Osage my Grandma Gilbert died [November 10, 1913] and Uncle Dick moved in with us and bought a small farm about 2 miles west of Osage up on the post oak flats.

He had two roan horses, one named Baldy the other one walked kinda funny so we called him Old Sprad, we didnt have a lawn mower so we would put the horses in the yard and they would mow the grass, it saved a lot of work and the horses got fat on the grass I liked to sit up on Ole Sprad and ride around the yard while he mowed the grass one day a bee stung him or a horsefly bit him, and he took off around the house ran under the cloths line and dragged me off, didn't hurt me much, but sure knocked the wind out of me, for a while after that, I didn't care too much for horse back ridin'….

This next story is just to show how folks in the olden days made do with what they had at hand.

I went to spend the night with my friend Curt Downing, it was his birthday and we were going to have ice cream and cake,

Mr. Downing put the milk and sugar and vanilla in a 1 gallon syrup bucket with a tight fitting lid, put it down in a big bucket, crushed the ice in a burlap bag with the flat side of an axe, and filled around the little bucket with ice then rotated the little bucket round and round holding onto the bail or handle every few minutes he would take the lid off the little bucket and with a long spoon scrape the frozen cream from the sides of the bucket, after repeating this procedure several times, we had ice cream as good or better than we can buy now at the "Dairy Queen"

In 1917 the Germans were trying to overrun Belgium, France and England, it was an election year in the United States *[1916 was actually the election year]* and we were already shipping ammunition and supplies overseas to the French and English,

Woodrow Wilson who was campaigning for president, was telling the people, if they wanted to keep their husbands, sons and sweethearts out of war, to vote for him,

Not long after he took office the Germans supposedly sunk one of our ships and the President and Congress declared war on Germany[256]

My brother *[Carl]* was only about 15 years old at the time, he was so mad at them Germans he wanted to join the Army, he thought he could take Dad's ole single barrel shotgun and kill all those Germans in just a little while

The war didn't affect me much one way or another as I was too young to realize what was happening. the one thing I do remember was rumors going around that we were going to have to eat cornbread, for they couldn't ship cornmeal overseas as it would spoil before it got there

It wasn't patriotic to eat biscuits during the war. for it might deprive our soldier boys of having bread to eat....

One day we got word that two Okla outlaws had robbed the Bank at Cave Springs, and were coming our way, riding on one horse, one facing forward and the other facing backward, brother Carl grabbed Dad's ole shotgun and went down the road a little way and hid in the bushes he waited about 3 hours and the bank robbers never came by, (probably a good thing they didn't, or he might have got shot.

(In northwest Ark. everyone thought all outlaws and bank robbers came from Okla.)

Remember Mr. Vassar the Infidel? I think he was a communist but we hadn't heard that word yet. Although he read the Bible all the time, and almost had it memorized, he didn't believe one word that was written in it, he also believed that man decended from monkey....

When the Armistice was signed ending the war[257] everyone was so happy they had to celebrate in some way. some got drunk, some had fireworks, Dad and some of his friends shot Anvils

This requires a bit of explaining of just how it was done, so here goes.

A good blacksmiths anvil weighs some where between 150 and 200 lbs. in the bottom of the anvil is a square hole about 1 1/2 in. across and 4 or 5 in. deep. place one anvil upside down on a big block of wood sawed from a tree, fill the square hole with black gun powder let a little string of powder extend to the edge of the anvil, place another anvil upside down on top of the other one with the powder in it. heat the one end of a 10 ft piece of rod iron in the forge, touch the red hot end to the powder on the edge of the bottom anvil it will blow the top anvil off onto the ground, and make a big boom that can be heard for miles....

Some times I had to help Dad in the shop. when he was shrinking wagon tires it was my job to turn the blower that kept the fire going in the forge, then help him carry the hot tire over and slip it on the wheel with two pair of long handle tongs, then I had to dip water out of a barrel close by and pour on the hot tire to cool it, and also keep it from catching the wood wheel on fire.

Another job I had to do sometimes was hold the horse's halter while my Dad nailed shoes on them, it wasn't bad at all if the horse was gentle, but sometimes we got hold of a wild one, when this happened we had a long pair of tongs called a twitch. Dad would place the horse's upper lip in one end of the tongs, squeeze the handles to-gether, and it was my job to hang onto the tongs, if I hung in there I could control the meanest horse, if I didn't hang on the horse could hurt my Dad, who had one of the horse's legs clamped between his knees, I also knew if the horse hurt my Dad, my Dad was goin to hurt me, so needles to say I hung on....

When Mr. Gambol sold the house we lived in at Osage Dad went to Cave Springs and rented a house, and came home with Wesley Stroud in a model "T" truck, we loaded up the furniture, and away we went....

Cave Springs was a big town to me, there was a Resturant, 2 grocery stores a Hardware store, a railroad, Depot and a 3 room School house there were about 40 kids in my room with one teacher 3rd 4th and 5th grades

I dont remember much about this place except there were

Gilberts at a Family Reunion, ca. 1970s
(From Left) Leslie, Helen, Buck, Phydella
Martha Hogan Estes

two families at the edge of town who were having a feud kin-da' like the Martins and the Coys. Each family had two boys in school and almost every day after school on the way home these four boys would get into a fight, and they used any thing they could get their hands on to fight with, ball bats, sticks, rocks fists and feet, sometimes it would get pretty bloody, and it almost scared me out of my britches

I dont think we lived in Cave Springs more than three months until Dad decided he would try farming for awhile Uncle Tom Johnson at Spring Valley[258] was looking for a sharecropper, so we loaded up Wes' Strouds model "T" truck and moved to Spring Valley….

By this time moving from place to place had became a way of life for us, and we thought nothing about it, when Dad took off one day and came back a few days later, and said he had leased 160 acres close to War Eagle Mills[259] in Benton County Ark. $60.00 cash for 1 year when we got ready to move Dad built a couple chicken coops, we had no chicken house so our chickens roosted in some trees in back of the house, with the help of our dog and all us kids we caught them chickens and put them in the coops.

The next day Uncle Houston Scott[260] (mothers brother) and Jim Vanwinkle came over real early with two wagons we loaded up and took off for War Eagle Mills….

we didn't have a horse, cow or pig, some man over at Mayfield[261] told Dad he had a blind grey mare we could use if we would take good care of her, Dad and I walked to Mayfield on Saturday, staid all night with Grandma Scott,[262] picked up the old mare the next morning and I road her home….

There was about 6 acres of fairly smooth land just outside our yard fence, we put posts around it and stretched one smooth wire about 4 ft off the ground and stapled it to the posts, we then lead the mare around it several times, we would lead her up to the wire real slow until it touched her chest, after that when we wasn't working her to the plow or sled which we hauled wood or anything that needed to be moved from one place to another, we would turn her loose in that little pasture and she never hurt herself or got into any trouble.

when the grass got tall in our yard we would bring her inside and use her as a lawn mower, sometimes even now I wish I had a nice gentle old mare to mow my lawn for me

She was so nice and fat and slick sometimes I would sit upon her back and ride around while she mowed the lawn, one day when I was sittin on her and her head was down chompin the grass, I thought it would be fun to slide down her neck, I made it down to her ears, but it scared her I guess for she tossed her head up high, and I went end over end in the air and hit the ground on my back, it didn't hurt me much, but it sure knocked the wind out of me, believe it or not, I didn't do that any more

When she was in her little pasture I could go to the front gate and whistle real loud and she would start toward me, if she stopped all I had to do was whistle again and she would come right up to me, and I would pet her and talk to her, I would try to have something different for her to eat, even if it was just some pea vines out of the garden

Although me and that old mare had a lot of trouble when we started cultivating the small corn and beans, I loved her and I think she loved me,

Imagine if you can, a small boy, 10 or 11 years old, trying to cultivate small corn with a blind horse and a double shovel plow, but we did, and I'm still here 60 years later and I know if there is a horse heaven that old mare is there, eating oats and alfalfa hay....

War Eagle Mills was just a small place with two General Stores a Blacksmith shop and a water powered mill where they made flour and corn meal, and seven or eight homes close by. there was a small strawberry patch on the place where we lived, we picked the berries and sold them to everyone that would buy them and used the money to buy flour, sugar salt coffee baking powder and soda. these were just about the only things we needed that we couldn't grow on the farm....

Before the first of January we heard from Mr. Bettus the man who owned the land he spent a year in California and didn't like it, so he was coming back to Ark. and wanted his place back.

Dad took off again, he was back in a few days, had rented an old log house south of Spring valley. Made a deal with Uncle Houston and Jim Van Winkle to move us again, this place was close to a small creek called Vaughn Branch,[263]

Uncle Melvin Gilbert[264] owned about 200 acres of timber about 1/2 mile south of our house That winter Dad I cut and split about 10,000 fence posts for him, he paid us 3¢ each for splitting them and I think he sold them to Welch Grape vinyards at Springdale for 10¢ each....

The Sanders Brothers who owned the general store at Spring Valley, also farmed and bought and fed a lot of hogs, early in the fall they were moving a bunch of pigs one got away and got lost in the woods, and they couldn't find him,

Late in the winter Uncle Houston and Dad were out in the woods huntin' squirels and found this old pig, which had grown big and wild, they scared him out of a brush pile, he took after Uncle Houston who dropped his rifle, and climed a tree, he then started after my Dad, who was carrying a shotgun when he got close to Dad, he shot him right in the face with both barrels, uncle Houston went home and got the team and wagon—they loaded him in the wagon brought him home and we had fresh meat to eat.

My pal Kermit had a Jenny to ride (a Jenny is a female burro) I think) anyway one Sunday we decided to ride her over to uncle Melvins, to see my cousins Willie and Roy. when we came to the creek she wouldn't go across, Kermit thought he could take her back up the road a little way, kick her into a gallop, maybe she would cross the creek before she had time to think about getting her feet wet but when she came to the creek she just stopped suddenly and Kermit went flyin' over her head and landed in the creek he tried it two or three times and the same thing happened every time, by that time we decided, we didn't want to go to uncle Melvins anyway....

The old log house we lived in was damp and cold, there was fog along the creek almost every morning, and we had bad colds all winter, so Dad decided it wasn't a healthy place to live, he went to mayfield mountain, it was owned by mrs Ballew a widow, she reserved two rooms in the house and we moved into the rest of it.

Dad started me to plowing a small field and cultivating the apple orchard with the double shovel, and took off for Haberton[265] to open a blacksmith shop, that some other blacksmith had walked off and left.

He only came home on weekends, and after a coupla, months, mrs. Ballew told him if he wasn't going to farm the land we would have to move out so she could get someone who would farm it for her (I don't think Dad intended to farm it in the first place, he just wanted a place for us to live for a while)

Harve Ferguson owned the General store the blacksmith shop and a house between the store and the shop, so, we moved into the house, we hadn't lived there more than two or three months until mr. Ferguson sold the house and store to a man from Texas and we had to move again. this time, just down the road about a quarter of a mile, into an old two story house called the Harp place

The School was a little way down the road east of the store on the north side of the road, when we started School in the fall the weather was still rather warm, and in the afternoon we would open all the windows to let in what breeze there was, there were two long benches up front, which were called recitation benches kinda like church pews without any backrest on them, when we had, fourth fifth or whatever arithmetic class we were all called up front with our slates, sat on the bench and the teacher gave us problems to work, when we finished a problem we would give it to the teacher to check we didn't have any erasers for our slates, so when the teacher gave them back to us after checking them, we just spit on the slate and wiped it off with the palm of our hand (not too sanitary but it got the job done)....

[Gilbert tells how student harassment forced the school's male teacher to quit three weeks into the school year. The replacement teacher is more than the rowdy students had in mind, however.]

....word got around on Sunday afternoon there would be school on monday, we all went back on monday, and when the bell rang we all trooped in, standing up front was a tall skinny lady and in the back sat three board members, one member introduced her as mrs. Lottie Couch and if she couldnt handle us by herself they would help her.

we hadnt been there more than ten minutes until she had whomped two or three kids on the head with a geography book, and believe you "me," when she whomped you, you staid whomped. Rumors filtered down to us, that she was so mean no other school in the county would hire her, I think her motto was "Readin' writin' and Rithmetic taught to the tune of a hickory stick" I dont know about the other kids, but I know she taught me more Readin' writin and Rithmatic than any other teacher I ever had. If we didn't get our lessons done during study period she kept us after School until we did, and sometimes she would walk us home and explain to our parents why we were late

On the playground she was one of us, we played, Stink-base, Blackman, Crack the whip and Scrub up Baseball,[266] and she took her place in the lineup just like the rest of us.

A "School Bully" didn't have a chance, if a big kid picked on a little one, she clobbered him good, in a little while we didn't have any "School Bullys"....

Buck Gilbert and Martha Hogan Estes
Martha Hogan Estes

At home I slept upstairs, there was holes in the roof and
one morning when I awoke there was snow on top of my cov-
ers, about this time we had to move again....

We moved into an old rambling two story house (called
the Nelson place,) about a mile east of Zion[267] in the Zion
School district but we walked back to Haberton and finished
the School term there....

[Two year gap in letter, resumed on July 14, 1980]

....I have to go back a little way, for between Cave Springs
and Spring valley there was a short stop at Hewitt Springs
with some real important stuff....

The State was building a new hiway between Springdale
and Spring valley,[268] and needed a blacksmith, so Dad went
to work for them....dirt and rocks were plowed up with four
horses and a rooter plow so the slips and fresnoes[269] (also
pulled by horses) could move it from the high spots to the
low places, plow rooters and grade blades didn't stay sharp

very long in the rocky ground, and had to be sharpened quiet often, that's where the Blacksmith came in.

as this road had to go thru the timber sometimes, the trees had to be removed, a crew of men with seven foot crosscut saws and axes would cut the trees down then the teamsters would latch onto them with log chains and as many horses as it took to drag them off to oneside

But hold everything, we still have them big Red Oak and post oak stumps (some of them as much as thirty inches in diameter) in the way, they couldn't get enough horses around one of these stumps to pull it out of the ground, so thats where the powder monkey came in, in case you don't know, a powder monkey is a man that fools around with black powder and Dynomite, this powder monkey was something to write about. he would put as many as 40 sticks of dynamite under one stump, he blew some of them so high, parts of them never did come down, pieces of them lodged in the tree tops off to the side, and some of them were still up there several years later, when I traveled the road accasionally.

One day the road building contracter was in Dad's shop and told Dad this powder monkey was just costing him too much money for dynomite

Dad said, I've had some experiance with explosives and I dont believe it is nessesary to blow them stumps so high, if he could just put enough dynomite under them to split them up a little and loosen them in the ground, a good team of horses could pull the pieces out of the ground and drag them off to one side,

The man said, Joe I'll fire that powder monkey and hire you a helper in the shop, if you will take the job, and I think you can blow them stumps in the evening after the men quit work for the day, and if you can do it I'll double your wages. Dad took the job and blew the stumps with five sticks of dynomite where the other man had been using forty sticks, he saved the man more than enough money to pay his wages and the stumps didn't go so high any more, which wasn't nessesary in the first place.

Remember Uncle Newt the old fellow to whom we gave the mince pie? Well this same road went along the south side of his land, made a sharp turn and went north along the east side, the hiway people wanted to round off this corner so cars could go around without slowing down so much but when the men went out to move his fence back, Uncle Newt was sittin' on a stump with a double barreld shotgun Uncle Newt sez. The first man that pulls a staple out of that fence, gets a load of buckshot in the seat of his pants

after two or three trips and a promise of a hundred dollars for the little dab of land, (which established a new high for the price of land in Arkansas) Uncle Newt climbed down off the stump and went home, and they didn't have any more trouble with him

....my folks moved from the old Nelson place to the Anderson place about a quarter mile east of Zion store....

After attending ten different schools, (Sonora, Healing Springs, Osage Mills, Fishback,[270] Springvalley, War Eagle mills, Springvaley again, Mayfield, Habberton and Zion, I finally finished eighth grade and that was the end of my School days

I started working for Lee Dutchman full time at fifteen dollars a month with bed and board, (I would have said room and board but I had to share a room and bed with a little four year old boy.

Lee Dutchman was a fruit and vegatable farmer also milked eight cows and his wife Effie churned and sold home made butter in Springdale. All the work was done by man and mule power, Lee Dutchman had three mules, Joe, Jerry and Molly, and one combination saddle and buggy mare, old Bess.

All the things we had to do on that farm would have made cold chills run up and down Abe Lincolns back.

In the spring and summer we were up at five o'clock in the morning, first we fed the horses, then milked the cows, separated the milk, fed the calves, sloped and fed the hogs, fed and watered the chickens, when we were thru with all that Effie would have breakfast ready. Ham and eggs fried taters and gravy, hot biscuits, and some sorghum molasses and strawberry jam on the side by this time we didn't need any coaxing to eat a good breakfast....

Lee Dutchmans farm equipment consisted of a six foot orchard disc, two twelve inch soil turning plows and two double shovels.

On an average day I could plow two acres with a twelve inch turning plow...at noon I unhook the mules, climb on ole Jerry and head for the barn, pump water from the well with a hand pump into a log hollowed out to form a watering trough for the mules, feed them some corn and I'm ready for lunch, after lunch while the mules are getting' a little extra rest, I pump some more water and give the pigs and chickens a fresh drink, bridle the mules jump on ole Jerrys back and head for the field to plow another acre

[Gilbert's letter concludes with a life lesson]

My Dad always said, a poor boy had three choices, he could, work, steal or starve, I didn't want to go to jail for stealing, I had missed a few meals and I didn't like to do that, so I worked for fifteen dollars a month.

EARLY HISTORY OF FAYETTEVILLE
MUNICIPAL AIRPORT[271]

Dedicated to Glenn D. Estes, First Flight Service Station Chief at Drake Field

Kitty Hawk

On December 17, 1903, over the sands of Kitty Hawk, North Carolina, Wilbur and Orville Wright made two centuries of theory and experimentation a verifiable reality. With their first flight, lasting all of twelve seconds, the Wrights proved that man could fly in a heavier-than-air machine.

In the following years, flying fever quickly spread across the United States and Europe as technological advances produced better and more powerful airships. An exciting expression of the new airplanes and their swashbuckling pilots were racing competitions which began to proliferate around the world and nation.

In January 1910, the first international air competition was held in Los Angeles, California. By this time, Glenn H. Curtiss was making his own airplanes and in Santa Ana, California, Glenn Luther Martin, a successful auto dealer, was teaching himself to fly and had gained a reputation as one of the most famous "pioneer birdmen."[272] To increase interest in and sales of his product, Curtiss scheduled an exhibition tour to communities in the Midwest in 1911. He contracted Martin to be the aviator.

First Flight in Fayetteville

The Washington County Fair Association, presided over by Fayetteville's Jay Fulbright,[273] saw an opportunity to enhance attractions at their sixth annual event by adding the appearance of one of these newfangled airships. In late August 1911, the Association had acquired the services of Roy Burgess,[274] an aeronaut from Michigan, but negotiations evidently fell through as Burgess did not appear at the fair.

Still, on opening day of the fair, Tuesday, October 3, 1911, in addition to a parade of automobiles and "a greater number of fine horses" from the Square to the Fairgrounds—then located at Razorback Road between Mitchell and Nettleship Streets, local crowds were promised "an attraction that is something out of the ordinary." The out of the ordinary attraction was an airship[275] "for which," the *Fayetteville Daily* reported on Wednesday, October 4, "many came miles to see."

The aircraft the crowd watched that day was a biplane, powered by a Curtiss "O" series V-8 engine. The paper said the plane had a wingspan of 40 feet-3 inches, was 35 feet-2 inches in length, and weighed 1150 pounds. It was piloted by Glenn Martin.

The *Fayetteville Daily* reported that on the October 3 flight Martin took off at four p.m. "from the north side of the inner part of the fair grounds," headed south "and rose gracefully as a bird getting higher, and higher all the time, until he reached a height of 1,800 feet. A mile or two south of the fair grounds he circled to the west and came back around over the grand stand and went northeast over the south part of town, reaching Cantor (sic—Cantor is probably a typographic error for Center) Street."

"Again circling to the west," the newspaper story continued, "he passed over the grand stand once more and then flew south for a half a mile where he circled to the east and came back down where he started, alighting easily and without a jar. The wind was blowing at the rate of 33 miles an hour which made it exceedingly hard sailing when squarely facing it, as he was when going south." The October 6, 1911 *Springdale News* reported that Martin had, wind-aided or not, reached a speed of 65 miles an hour.

The flight attraction at the Fair was such a success, the *Fayetteville Daily* noted, that some people were heard to say that for "straight flying those who had seen exhibitions in St. Louis and Kansas City declared they had never before seen anything equal to Martin's performance." It was said that the "exhibition was simply fine—far beyond the expectations of the most sanguine." Those who witnessed the event numbered about 10,000. During the entire flight, Martin had been airborne approximately fifteen minutes.

Searching the Heavens

In response to local interest in the new flying machines and their daring pilots, flights began to be regularly scheduled at the Washington County Fair. The 11th annual Fair, as described in the September 15, 1916 *Springdale News,* would include the following feature for September 26-29: "The Airship—One of the greatest aviators [unnamed] in the country will make two flights daily in one of the latest model airship(s) doing all kinds of stunts way up in the clouds."

By the time the United States entered World War I—war was declared against Germany August 6, 1917—aircraft had become the latest offensive weapon. Deadly, yet romantic tales of aerial combat captured the interest of the world. The reality of a new method of destruction also instilled a note of fear into citizens who had been convinced that distance from the battlefront was an assurance of security.

The war also contributed to LeRoy Williams of Fayetteville becoming one of our earliest native aviators. He had been drafted into local Company B, Arkansas National Guard, which was mobilized August 5, 1917. Company B later became Battery B of the 142nd Field Artillery and during this restructuring Williams was assigned to other duties that allowed him to become a pilot—one of the first in the area.[276]

The vulnerability to aerial attack remained such a concern to the military that as late as 1923, five years after the war ended, defense safeguards were still being implemented. On December 4 of that year, the 206th Coast Artillery, Anti-Aircraft, First Battalion, Battery A, Arkansas National Guard was organized in Fayetteville under the command of Capt. E. K. Hooper. Three powerful searchlights were installed, the last throwing a beam that could be seen some forty miles away. At the time, Battery A was the only Searchlight Unit in the state. [277]

Mr. Zerbe Comes to Town

Pioneer aircraft manufacturers had soared into prominence with their contributions to a new era of military strategy during World War I. The biplane became the industry standard but experimentation continued at a feverish pace. A triplane design enjoyed some success but the advantages of an extra wing were marginal. There were some innovative souls, however, who thought that if two wings were good, more had to be better.

In the spring of 1920, one of these innovative men, Jerome S. Zerbe, arrived in Fayetteville to produce a fully enclosed passenger aircraft for a group of Missouri businessmen. A former instructor at Polytechnic High School in the Los Angeles area, Zerbe had previously constructed a quintaplane (five wings) attached to a motorcycle for entry in the Dominguez Hills Air Meet in Los Angeles in January 1910.

That venture met with disaster when upon racing down the field for takeoff a front wheel fell into a hole causing the craft to pitch forward on its nose. No further attempt was made by Zerbe to pursue the experiment and he disappeared from the area.

Having apparently recovered from his earlier humiliation, the daily *Fayetteville Democrat* for October 23, 1920 relates how Zerbe had reemerged and set up shop in a livery stable on East Mountain Street in Fayetteville, just off the Square, to build his "Air Sedan." According to the newspaper story, the plane was near "Completion" and would launch a test flight "From Local Field Within Three Weeks."

The Air Sedan consisted of four short-span, double-cambered, forward-staggered wings mounted to a plywood-clad cabin designed to hold four passengers.[279] Zerbe also incorporated the concept of warping the wings to control air flow in a manner similar to that used and later rejected in the Wright Brothers *Flyer I* machine.

Tom Flannery agreed to test-fly the plane, but although the 90hp Le Rhone rotary engine was powerful enough to lift the craft, one account of the flight says it sprayed the windshield with castor oil, rendering visibility almost impossible.[280] According to a later retelling of the story in the *Northwest Arkansas Times* of June 15, 1986, Zerbe's experiment failed to get any higher than forty or fifty feet in the air, but managed to land without incident.

That same issue of the paper, in addition to contradicting the time frame of the flight (the 1986 *Times* story says the flight occurred in March of 1919 as opposed to the fall of 1920 as reported at the time), also says there was "some evidence to indicate" that at least one additional attempt was made, but the plane crashed.

Pilot Flannery was said to have walked away unhurt. The failed test flight seems to have brought Zerbe's inventiveness to a close. He left Fayetteville shortly thereafter and all but vanished into history.

America Takes Wing

The period after Armistice Day (November 11, 1918) saw increased aviation activity around the nation, and local pilots, discharged from service, acquired their own personal craft to continue the adventure they had enjoyed in the air. They also were able to earn income by providing sight-seeing excursions, pilot training, crop-dusting, mail delivery service, aircraft racing and by staging exhibitions for a fee.

At these popular exhibitions, pilots demonstrated such show-stoppers as "loops," "barrel-rolls," "stalls," "falling leaf" descent patterns, and other stunts to take the breath of their mesmerized audience. Assistants standing on the fuselage behind the pilot would "wing-walk," that is, riding through the skies while performing tricks that would literally take "daring" to new heights.

Perhaps the single most significant event in the budding world of aviation, one that eclipsed the barnstorming exhibitions and captured the entire world's heart as well, was the solo transatlantic flight of Charles A. Lindbergh on May 20-21, 1927. Practically every man, woman and child knew of "The Lone Eagle" crossing the sea in his *Spirit of St. Louis*. The romance of the early airways had reached its zenith.

Looking for a Place to Land

During the 1920's, local aviators were faced with the same problems that the rest of the nation was experiencing. Open fields and pastures were the only places in which they could take off and land with reasonable safety.

Such sites were limited in mountainous communities like Fayetteville. The fairgrounds, University of Arkansas Experimental Farm, and the old Sportsman's Club Golf Course were all used.[281] These areas were available to pilots on a permission-only basis, however, so at times any accessible field in the county might not be available for use as a landing strip.

Talking It Up

Locally, aviators began using the Country Club golf course on Winslow Road, now the location of the Entree Division of Tyson Foods, Inc. on South School Avenue, as a landing field. A parachute jump exhibition was scheduled there for Sunday, May 15, 1927. The *Daily Democrat* reported on Saturday, May 14 that the passenger-carrying aircraft used for the jumps would "be here for a week or 10 days."

The exhibition was under the management of Charles W. Hardin, pilot R. Newton and a mechanic. "An airport could easily be constructed here," Hardin told the *Daily Democrat* on May 19, "and Fayetteville, on a direct line between St. Louis and Tulsa and other places in that region that already have regular fields, should be equipped with such a station. Commercial planes would, of course, be brought in if there were a field here, and there are also air mail possibilities."

That was all the Fayetteville City Council Chamber of Commerce aviation committee, chaired by P. G. Walker, needed to hear. A special meeting was scheduled for May 24, according to the *Daily Democrat,* and Major J. Carroll Cone, of the Arkansas National Guard in Little Rock and state auditor, accepted an invitation to speak on "The Future of Aviation in Arkansas." Not surprisingly, the committee was composed of former combat aviators including Walker, Hugh Rogers, and Roy Brumfield.

The Chamber of Commerce itself urged local citizens to attend the meeting as a show of support for a landing field. The request was apparently honored because Major Cone delivered his speech at a meeting in the Palace Theater where he spoke on the future of aviation in Arkansas and America. He also addressed the specific future of a Fayetteville airfield.

If a landing field were to be located here, the May 25 *Daily Democrat* quoted Cone as saying, then "state financial aid can be secured." Also, the city would be listed on government maps and others as a landing place for commercial and private aircraft. There were two air mail routes in the state at this time, he noted. Fayetteville would add to that number and "stand a good chance to be listed" as a landing place for a planned route from Atlanta to Dallas.

In the same article, Cone was said to stress that a permanent field "accessible to the city and purchasable at a reasonable price" should be acquired. "There is no place in the state where an air port is more needed than in Fayetteville," he said, "if not for business reasons then for patriotic ones."

C. M. Lawson, president of the Ely-Walker Dry Goods Company of St. Louis and of the Campbell-Bell Dry Goods Company and Price Clothing Company of Fayetteville, paid a visit to his local family on the first weekend of June 1927. He took the opportunity to share his views on the airport issue with the newspaper.

In the June 4 *Daily Democrat,* Lawson opined that an airport would be "one of the best means possible of giving Fayetteville nation-wide attention and facilitating means of passenger and mail transportation." He had with him "a report from a Washington commercial news bureau advising cities and towns interested in obtaining an airport to communicate immediately with Wm. P. MacCracken, Jr., Assistant Secretary of Commerce, Washington, who will offer free help including complete specifications for acquisition of an airport."

Besides help with the acquisition, Lawson continued, the government may "in many cases" assign an engineer to "work with your authorities during all stages." The benefits of the federal assistance to the city were spelled out in the report. "I don't know how much land would be needed," Lawson added, "but I believe a few thousand dollars spent here for a landing field, not in a half-hearted temporary way but with the idea of being permanent, would in the end be worth a great deal to the city."

Touching Down

Acting on Lawson's report, P. G. Walker and the aviation committee engaged in communications with the Department of Commerce for assistance in establishing an airport. On November 28, 1927, Scott D. Hamilton, secretary of the Chamber of Commerce, stated in the *Daily Democrat* that the South Mountain Development Company, owner of the Country Club, in conjunction with the Chamber would provide the property required for an airport on the present golf course that "will be included in the government's future memos, logs, and bulletins."

The association authorized Walker's committee, the newspaper article continued, to "proceed at once with placing airport markers on certain designated sections of the present golf course, which will be made into a temporary port according to instructions from the Aeronautics Branch of the Department of Commerce." Those instructions were detailed in a letter from Major General Mason M. Patrick, Chief of the U. S. Air Corps.

In addition to the letter from Maj. Gen. Patrick to the committee, the chief of the Air Information Division of the Dept. Of Commerce, Ernest Jones, also wrote, the paper said, "asking for complete information concerning the proposed local field and assuring that Fayetteville will be included in the airport maps and the Airway Bulletins sent to all airports automatically issued by the Army and Navy to all service pilots."

The Chamber of Commerce aviation committee was augmented in its efforts to steer airport establishment and to secure the appropriate equipment to carry out their mission by G. A. M. Johnson, H. O. Davis, and G. W. Chamblin of the Lions Club and Joe Bates, J. H. McIlroy, and Morgan McMichael of the Rotary Club.

Scott Hamilton had been pulled from the joint committee to assist the Development Association in transforming a portion of the old golf course for use as an airfield. He was assisted by Johnson, Chamblin, Bates and Hugh Rogers.

"The airways will not affect the fairways," the association promised local golfers through the *Daily Democrat*. A new location for the Fayetteville Country Club on South Mountain had been negotiated and golfers were assured they could proceed on the current links until the new ones were ready. "By spring," Hamilton said, "both the new airport and the new golf course will be in such condition that we expect both to attract summer visitors."

P. G. Walker also stated in the article that the new "port" would be 2,200 feet in length. It was defined as "a locality adapted for landing or taking off of aircraft which provides facilities for shelter, supplies and repair of aircraft; or a place used regularly for receiving or discharging of passengers and cargo by air."

Surveying the Field

One month after the announcement assuring an airport for Fayetteville, the airfield was suitable enough for an unexpected drop-in. According to the December 29, 1927 *Daily Democrat,* a W. W. Walker, "accompanied by his wife...and the plane's mascot, a German police dog," was en route from Huron, South Dakota to Hot Springs flying an Alexander Eagle Rock.[282] Walker had attempted to find a landing place at several communities, but the only suitable field was the one at Fayetteville.

Walker described the neophyte airport as the most desirable landing field in this part of the state. He told members of the Chamber of Commerce aviation committee that "the site was excellent provided that the field was maintained properly." After refueling, the Walkers continued their flight.

On February 28, 1928, the *Daily Democrat* reported that Lieutenant Taylor Robertson, newly commissioned in the 154th Observation Squadron out of Little Rock, had arrived at the airport in his new Waco 10[283] three-passenger plane on February 24. With Robertson were two passengers, including his father.

"As far as location goes," Lt. Robertson told the paper, "the proposed airport at the Country Club golf course south of town is ab-
solutely the best near Fayetteville." He had been using the field since
his arrival, offering rides advertised in the *Daily Democrat* on February 28 at $3.00 per passenger and would be available at the field
until March 4th.

"Within two miles from town," he continued, "and on the main
road, the field would offer almost immediate service to the town." The
"main road" was known as Greenland Road—previously Winslow
Road—at that time. It is present-day U. S. 71B.

"With a little work," Robertson suggested, "it can be made into
a good field. Grading on the south end, the cutting down of rough
spots and the filling up of ditches would enable a big ship to land and
take off easily. Power and telephone lines would have to be put un-
derground near the field and some trees would have to be cut away."
He further stated that with his small plane, he had only used a small
portion of the field.

A Change in the Wind

Exactly three months after the announcement that an airport
would be established on the old Country Club golf course, the dream
began unraveling. Despite some glowing reports about the proposed
airfield, there were valid complaints from local aviators.

One of the issues regarded the proximity of McCullom Mountain
to the landing strip. Not only might this mountain be a surprise to
an approaching aviator, but as a natural hazard it also required some
advanced maneuvering to negotiate the short distance between the
mountain and the field.[284]

At a city council meeting in the evening of the same day that Lt.
Robertson had made his observations of the temporary airport known
publicly, February 28, 1928, discussion ensued about the viability of
that particular site for a permanent airfield. The *Daily Democrat* noted
that Mayor Allen M. Wilson had appointed an airport committee to
study the issue and be prepared to make a report to the council at the

following week's meeting. Dr. Noah Fields Drake was named chairman of the committee.

The city council meeting revealed the existence of two schools of thought on the airport issue. There were those who wished to retain the old golf course site because it was essentially in hand. An opposite camp desired a study to determine the best site from a number of optional proposals and then the activation of a funding mechanism to answer the needs of a Class A facility.

After city council discussion, Mayor Wilson stated in the March 6, 1928 *Daily Democrat:* "It is the consensus of opinion of the council that a special election should be held to decide upon a bond issue for the purchase of an airport. In doing this, the city will protect itself by securing beforehand options on all desirable landing fields. Land suitable for a Fayetteville airport can be purchased at from $100 to $200 an acre, the committee named by the council at its last week's meeting reported."

"The election," Mayor Wilson went on, "will be held within the next 60 days and in order to give all civic groups ample time to discuss the matter and to offer suggestions, we have asked every recognized civic group to name one representative and to have that representative present at a meeting of the council set for March 17, at which time the council will receive suggestions as to what the civic groups desire to have included in the bond issue to be submitted."

The mayor also presented some of the other items that would be worthy of including in the special election: a city hall, fire apparatus, park, National Guard armory, auditorium, more street paving and street equipment, all to be considered as soon as the city would be able to afford them. The airport and a new city hall were headline items.

At its March 22, 1928 meeting, the city council voted to secure options on sites for both a landing field and a new city hall and to make a careful study of the bond question. As noted in the *Daily Democrat,* Lions Club representative T. L. Hart stated that a $100,000 bond issue bearing 5 percent interest could be retired in 20 years. Of that amount, he added, about "$30,000 or $40,000 would be required for a landing field."

U. S. aviator Lieutenant L. S. Hewitt was a guest of the airport
committee, chaired by Dr. Drake, at the May 3 city council meeting to
offer his input on site selection for a new airfield. The *Daily Democrat*
for May 5, 1928 indicated that sites for which an option had been
obtained by the city were: the old golf course, available for $10,000;
the Allen Davis 50 acre property on the Springdale highway north of
town, $13,000; 43 acres of Jake Drake's property north of Leverett,
about $11,000; 55 acres of Hunt property, North College, $10,000;
the Parker property north of the Drake property; and the Dowell
property on the Siloam Springs highway. The last two parcels were not
seriously considered "because of high cost of putting in shape."

After the sites had been inspected, Lt. Hewitt stated in the paper
that he regarded the golf course site, where he had landed on his arrival, as the most favorable location for a landing field. His second
choice was the Davis property. Chairman Drake made his report to the
council for their further consideration.

The Chamber of Commerce aviation committee was understand-
ably pleased by Lt. Hewitt's site selection. "We like to have our judgment backed by the army fliers and the council," a committee member
told the *Daily Democrat* on May 8, 1928. "At the time the Chamber
of Commerce was working to create interest in securing an airport the
council was not interested." But now, the Chamber spokesman added,
we "are gratified to have had the city take the matter up and we hope
it will be able to put the deal through to a successful conclusion, either
through bond issue or other legitimate means."

Chamber president J. T. Berson told the paper that the aviation
committee "was responsible for Fayetteville being placed on the aviation map of the U. S. Department of Commerce and has fostered the
need of a field for several years. The above committee made a thorough
study of all available local fields and recommended last year that the
present golf course be secured as a temporary landing field. Naturally
we are pleased that the U. S. Army representative who was here last
week to make a survey for the council approved the selection we announced by the aviation committee of the Chamber of Commerce."

The Long Stall

Meanwhile, the city council was having trouble getting a handle on the cost of their ambitious city improvement project. It was their intention to lump several desired projects into one bond issue to put before the public vote and to provide for the consideration of each item separately.

At a special meeting of the city council on May 16, 1928, described in the *Daily Democrat* the next day, a committee was appointed to work with the Chamber of Commerce for the express purpose of determining a realistic estimate for each of the items, including an auditorium, a new city hall, an outdoor amphitheater, a hospital, and an airport. Aldermen N. F. Drake, J. F. Stanford, and V. L. Jones were named to the committee. The city now believed that all the items under consideration could be secured for $200,000.

When the special committee met with the Chamber's Citizens Committee, composed of Tom L. Hart, Scott D. Hamilton, and Roy Wood, after the council meeting a week later, the figure of $200,000 was upheld. Estimates for the individual items proposed were determined. The airport estimate, as reported in the *Daily Democrat* of May 22, was cut in half from the earlier figure of T. L. Hart to $17,500.

Despite the grinding deliberations of the city council, aviation enthusiasts in the community were treated to a series of stirring aerial events. On May 24, 1928, an advertisement in the *Daily Democrat* announced that the Lone Star Flying Circus would be performing May 27 on the "Flying Field" located at the "New Country Golf Course on South Mtn." The event was sponsored by Batteries 'A' and 'E', 206 Coast Artillery (Anti-Aircraft).

The "Champion Wing-Walker of the World," E. E. "Shorty" Radack, was the featured performer. Shorty would, the *Daily Democrat* promised, "jump from a speeding airplane to the ground in front of the audience without the aid of a parachute or any other apparatus of any kind." And to "see 'Shorty' get off the airplane," the paper added, it would be necessary for you "to be directly on the Flying Field."

As the council toiled on in meetings, the landing field at the old golf course grew stagnant. Months went by and nothing happened. The repercussions from the lack of attention that the field was getting were soundly felt in September 1928 when Fayetteville was excluded from a state air tour, sponsored by the Little Rock Chamber of Commerce, because of, the *Daily Democrat* disclosed on September 5, "poor landing conditions and no equipment."

The Lions Club had donated $100 in the vain attempt to bring the four plane tour to Fayetteville, according to Charles M. Taylor, chairman of the proposed event, at a meeting at the Mountain Inn Hotel. Taylor told the *Daily Democrat* that he hoped the incident would arouse sufficient interest in the city that it would lead to improvements at the local field.

He gave the paper four reasons why the air tour had bypassed Fayetteville: the "present condition of the field on which, due to ditches, and the like, it is impossible to land with safety except under certain wind conditions, and with a light load; the amount of work that would be required to put the field in condition so that planes could land under any conditions; the routing of the fliers 120 miles off their course; and the general lack of emergency landing fields in this section due to its mountainous character."

Purchasing a Landing Field

Fayetteville was going to have to make a commitment one way or the other. The city did not own the land containing the present "airport" and it would be imprudent to make any improvements on the property because of that fact. In addition, setting up a landing field was going to incur liability and nothing could be done to address that issue without ownership.

Purchasing the land seemed a necessity beyond the umbrella of a bond issue, which seemed to be staggering under its own weight. The cost of putting the old golf course into shape as a landing field would be an additional expense to a city that really didn't have a particularly healthy budget. However, if the city was serious about acquiring a municipal airport, they were going to have to demonstrate it. The fact that Fayetteville had been excluded from the state air tour did arouse the city leaders as Charles M. Taylor had hoped.

Dr. Drake and the airport committee concluded that, for better or worse, the old golf course was the best site available for an airport. At a meeting of the city council on March 18, 1929, Alderman Drake presented a proposition "to purchase by the city... 78 acres of land being the old golf course, for an airport... for the sum of $5,000."[285]

On March 27, a meeting of the city council was called to enact the purchase of the airport from the South Mountain Development Company. Under the provisions of Ordinance #701, five warrants, payable over five years to South Mountain, passed and were approved. There would now be a Fayetteville Municipal Airport.[286]

Dr. Drake Lends a Hand

The city's shallow pockets were then revealed. One year before, the old golf course had been available for $10,000 but a price half that figure was negotiated. Mayor Wilson had speculated that land for an airport could be acquired for $100 to $200 an acre but the city was now able to purchase that land for approximately $64 per acre. Payments over five years on the bargain purchase price should not have been too big a problem, but even with the better purchasing price, there wasn't enough extra money in the city till.[287]

At a meeting of the city council on June 10, Dr. Drake proposed to give the city $3,500 toward the purchase of the 78-acre tract west of Highway 71—the old golf course—for use as an airport if the city would provide the remaining $1,500.[288] On June 11, 1929, Dr. Drake stated in the *Daily Democrat* that the project was an important one for Fayetteville.

"Although there seems at the present time no immediate need for an airport," he said, "the time is close when the need will be an urgent one and if Fayetteville doesn't purchase the site at the present time, the land when the need arises may not be available."

He also pointed out that money would still be needed for furnishings and repair of the field to make the airport one of the best available

Noah Drake
University of Arkansas Libraries, Special Collections, MS D789

and acceptable for government purposes. Aviation experts had attested that the ground was suitable and that all the work necessary to complete the field would be the drainage of low marshes and the creation of hangars. And, as Charles Taylor had already pointed out, there were still discrepancies at the field that had to be dealt with.

"Expressions of appreciation for the generosity of Mr. Drake were made by the mayor (now T. S. Tribble) and members of the council." Alderman Clem Pearson moved to accept the proposition and Alderman C. T. Harding seconded it. After a vote of six ayes and two absences, the motion passed and the purchase of the property was declared effective immediately.[289]

The price of $5,000 for the property on the west side of Highway 71 had been established back in March when ten persons in Fayetteville had bought seven acres east of the highway for the sum of $2,500. The June 11, 1929 issue of the *Daily Democrat* listed the persons buying each of 10 shares at $250. Among them were: W. P. McNair, N. F. Drake, George Appleby, W. N. Gladson, C. M. Lawson, Charles W. Appleby, and Floyd Hight.

On June 17, Alderman Clem Pearson introduced an ordinance for the purchase of an Aviation Field, appropriating $1,500 to be paid to the South Mountain Development Company. Ordinance #706 was passed and approved.[290] On July 8, Alderman Drake received council approval to direct the city engineer, E. M. Ratliff, "to investigate and report as to construction of runways at the Aviation Field."[291]

From Fairways to Airways

At last, there was activity at the aviation field that would attract entrepreneurs. On October 7, 1929 Finley Anderson went before the city council and proposed "instituting a flying school" at the airport. Clem Pearson moved that a committee comprising Mayor Tribble, the city clerk, the city attorney, the city engineer and Alderman Drake be "authorized to contract with the Ozark Flying Corporation for the establishment of a flying school and the use of the city airport for that purpose." The motion, seconded by Alderman C. T. Harding, passed unanimously.[292]

On October 24th (Black Thursday) and 28th (Black Monday), 1929, the stock market, which had been fluctuating wildly since summer, experienced record-setting declines and went into freefall until hitting bottom on November 23rd and stabilizing. During that period, economic activity was virtually suspended across the nation until some sign of normalcy was assured. President Herbert Hoover and Secretary of the Treasury Andrew W. Mellon issued proclamations of optimism, but the market said otherwise.[293]

The optimistic tone from Washington was good enough for the authorities of the Ozark Flying School because their contract with the City was approved by the first week of December. At a meeting with the council on December 9, Mr. Anderson urged the standing airport committee to make improvements to the existing field. The committee was "empowered to take the necessary steps" for those improvements.

This charge would include providing tile for drainage and contracting with Mr. C. E. Pierce for ditching and filling. The committee was also asked to secure from the authorities of the Flying School payment of the moneys due under the terms of the contract with the City.[294]

At a council meeting the following week, Dr. Drake proposed that the Street Department be authorized to use street working equipment to grade a fence row on the farm of W. F. Drake[295] for use of the Ozark Flying School, "said School to pay expenses thus occasioned." The proposal passed unanimously.[296]

It was reported at the city council meeting of December 23, that the grading and drainage at the airport would cost "approximately $1,000." The council approved a motion to open work for bids and "to accept the bid which they judged the best."[297]

Shift in Approach

In early February 1930, the *Daily Democrat* reported that Dr. Drake and Art T. Lewis had been named to the Chamber of Commerce aviation committee and for the next few months the emphasis remained on keeping the airport where it was. The committee, with the approval of the city council, worked hard to put together a $20,000 bond issue to improve the existing golf course airport field and the issue passed on May 20.

But by mid-summer there was a shift in approach. The city's desire for an A-1 airport that would attract larger passenger and cargo planes, and with them better local business opportunities, led the aviation committee to take out an option on 160 acres of land four miles west of town on Highway 16 as a possible site for a new airfield. The property, according to the July 23 *Daily Democrat,* had been "highly recommended by Martin C. Hoffin, airport specialist from the United States Department of Commerce."

On August 2, 1930, however, the *Daily Democrat* reported that rather than pursue the Highway 16 property, the aviation committee instead had taken a contract for "approximately 150 acres of land four miles south on highway 71." Members of the committee were listed as: Morgan McMichael, chairman; Mayor T. S. Tribble, E. M. Ratliff, Dr. N. F. Drake, Don Fuller, W. P. McNair, and W. S. Campbell.

Averaging $80 an acre, the *Democrat* article detailed, the new location would cost about $12,000. Hoffin, the federal airport specialist, had unofficially suggested this property "as the best possible site for an airport, near Fayetteville." The land would be paid for by the earlier approved $20,000 bond. It was expected that the city would also recoup money from the sale of the existing airfield at a later date.

A New Location

City Engineer Ratliff received the Department of Commerce requirements for an A-1 airport on August 12, according to the paper, and work on the field, including clearing and leveling of the land, was already underway. The land for the new airport had been purchased from H. E. Hefflefinger, G. Selle, Robert Campbell, G. F. Dickson, and J. Frank Moore.

In the general aviation excitement of the time, the paper reported on August 18 that "E. V. Bird Buys First Airplane." Bird, a successful local builder, bought the aircraft, "a government inspected and licensed ship," from his brother-in-law Clinton Thompson of the Spartan Aircraft Company of Tulsa whose "headquarters will be here." Bird would have the "first locally owned" airplane in town.

"Airport Site Now Complete" the *Daily Democrat* for August 27 announced, and the story went on to relate how Mayor Tribble had received word from Durango, Mexico that H. O. Ward had agreed to sell a 20-acre strip that would fill in the 160 to 170 acre site needed for the field. Work on the new site was expected to "begin in the immediate future."

During the fall of 1930, while title and deed work was being finished, plans for "preliminary construction" of the new airfield were
put in place. Finally, toward the end of the year, the *Democrat* reported
that "field work on the topographical survey of the airport" had been
completed. The survey was required as a preliminary step "in determining work needed to make an A-1 landing field on the site."

On January 3, 1931 plans for work on the new airport were approved and in March, City Engineer Ratliff reported that progress was
being made on the airfield. By summer, the runways were being graded. "Three runways have been graded, 300 feet wide" a *Daily Democrat*
story on June 23 said, with a fourth being graded that same day. Lieutenant W. D. Hopson of Little Rock, the story continued, had "landed
the first plane on the new field" just the day before (June 22).

Work continued through the summer and up into early fall, when,
according to a *Democrat* article of October 1, 1931, tentative plans
were made to have an airport dedication on October 15—if an army
blimp could be brought in for the special event. The dedication day
came and went but nothing was reported in the paper.

The aviation committee considered a new date for the airport dedication early in 1932. On March 9, the *Democrat* reported that plans
were being made for an air show in July and that the *"Local Port Dedication Is Set for Late Summer."*

It would "not be advisable," the committee suggested, to hold
these events before Bermuda grass was sewn on the runways and other
improvements were made to the field. On May 10, there was another
reference to dedicating the airport in conjunction with an air show but
the plan seems never to have been completed.

Stalled Out Again

During 1933 and 1934, air shows did come to Fayetteville, including that of Reg Robbins on August 15, 1932, a big American Legion
show on August 13, 1933, and a 23-airship air tour that hit town on
October 27, 1934. There was still an effort, albeit bit by bit, to improve
the airfield. E. M. Ratliff attempted to tile the runways and improve

drainage in July of 1934, but the harsh economic realities of the Great Depression seem to have stymied local desire to enhance the airport.

In 1934, the Aeronautics Branch of the Department of Commerce was renamed the Bureau of Air Commerce.[298] In July of that year, C. V. Holderbaum, airport inspector for the Emergency Relief Administration (ERA), checked on the progress of Fayetteville's airport.

After inspection, Holderbaum declared it was "in condition to provide airplane landing facilities for any type of planes." He cautioned, however, that "the field cannot be considered an all-weather field until more adequate drainage facilities have been installed." He concluded his report by stating that the field was practically complete.[299]

This overly optimistic report did not necessarily reflect reality. In fact, things became so bad that in the spring of 1935, on May 20, the *Democrat* ran an editorial based on information given by pilots landing at the airport that referred to the field as a "menace." In "its present condition," the paper said, its "runways are a bog. Its signs are wrong… Its tile-draining is wrong, a joke. The field yet will cause death of pilot and passengers unless its shortcomings are corrected soon."

Fixing a Menace

The editorial triggered an immediate response. The next day, May 21, City Engineer Ratliff asked to be relieved of his responsibilities relating to the airport. The *Democrat* related that Ratliff had told the city council that the city had refused to spend any money on the airport after the ERA had changed prior Department of Commerce plans for the field.

ERA inspector Holderbaum fired off a letter, printed in the May 27 *Democrat* reiterating the airports problems and leaving city leaders with a challenge: "In spite of unfavorable criticism of and apparent dissatisfaction with present conditions at the field," he wrote, "it still is believed by many that Fayetteville should have an airport. Whether it does or does not have one, is a matter which rests solely with the community."

Holderbaum's words seemed to fire up local leaders. The next day,

May 28, the city council considered a proposal to lease the airport to a flying school in exchange for improving the landing field. By the fall, the Ozark Eagles Flying School had reached an agreement with the city and promised, as reported in the October 12 *Daily Democrat,* to build "a hangar on the airport." The hangar was finished, according to the paper, by October 25 and there was a 24 hour filling station service at the airport as well.

On November 6, the *Democrat* ran a story describing an $11,000 airport improvement project that was being submitted by city and state officials to the WPA. If approved, this project called for the building "of a 60 by 80 (foot) hangar," the installation of "a tile drainage system," and "placing metal boundary markers and providing turf sod on the landing areas."

On December 14, the paper reported that the WPA would provide over $34,000 for the airport project, but on January 7, 1936 the much more modest figure of $11,000 was approved by the Bureau of Air Commerce. Nonetheless, a corner had been turned and Fayetteville was on its way to having the top notch airport it had wanted for so long.

Throughout the rest of the 1930s, the airport got better and better. In the fall of 1936, a huge tri-motor airplane landed in town and stayed for several days giving rides to awestruck locals. In May of 1937, 74 U. S. Army planes from Kelly Field, Texas visited the Fayetteville airport and in July of 1938 plans were made for a new hangar and, as detailed in the paper, "$23,000 in other airway improvements."

Big Changes—For the Better
In 1940, with another great war on the horizon, two things happened to enhance the Fayetteville airport yet again. In late June, the United States War Department requested that the city make its airfield available as part of the national defense system. The city was eager to meet that request. The second important occurrence relating to the growth and modernization of the airport was the arrival of Raymond J. Ellis.

Ray Ellis
Fayetteville Public Library

Ellis, who had gotten his flying training in Muskogee, Oklahoma, came to Fayetteville in September 1940 to help improve the struggling Civilian Pilot Training Program (CPTP) which had started at the Fayetteville airport in November 1939. Ellis also began operating the Fayetteville Flying Service, "the city's first permanent flight service."[300]

With pilots training for what would become World War II and with a professional aviator in Ellis on hand, progress at the airport moved quickly. In July 1942, Mayor George Vaughan, the city council, and the Chamber of Commerce—with input from City Engineer

Edgar Brown, Chamber of Commerce Secretary W. S. Campbell, and Ellis—called for a special election to provide a $100,000 bond issue for airport expansion. In the July 14 issue of the *Northwest Arkansas Times,* Campbell said that "the city has an obligation…to hold up this part of the state. A modern airport would do that and more."

The bond issue vote was scheduled for August 25, 1942. As detailed in the *Times,* citizens were asked to fund the purchase of land to nearly double the current airport size of 160 acres as well as the construction of "three runways from 4,000 to 4,800 feet in length." Improvements would also include the addition of another hangar and a small administration building. The bond issue passed by a margin of 406 to 308.

Ray Ellis Takes Charge

In early 1943, the city rewarded Ray Ellis for his success with the pilot training program (the CPTP) and his professional handling of the airfield and its facilities by approving his request to lease the airport. The Fayetteville city council approved the lease on January 11, 1943. Ellis signed the lease on January 18 and his tenure as manager of the airport, which lasted some three decades, became effective February 1, 1943.[301]

White Hangar[302]

During 1943 and 1944, an all-wood hangar was constructed at the Fayetteville airport. Ground was broken on May 1, 1943 and the hangar was designed and constructed by assistant City Engineer Henry George. With supplies scarce because of the war, timber from the nearby Boston Mountains was used and metal for doors and such were taken from old "barns, cars, buildings, and junk yards" to construct the building. George and seven other men built the 136' x 150' hangar for $15,000. When completed it was able to house close to forty aircraft.[303]

Dedication at Last

With the airport moving forward into modernization and with a full-time professional aviator in charge of the field, the long delayed dedication of the Fayetteville Municipal Airport could finally take place.

White Hangar
Fayetteville Public Library, Digital Collection

The *Times* celebrated the event with a special "Dedication Edition" on June 27, 1944. The edition featured pictures of city councilmen and Ray Ellis on its front page, and inside were features on the history of the airport and a laudatory editorial declaring that the airport was something of which "not only Fayetteville, but the whole Northwest Arkansas section can be proud." The next day, June 28, 1944—thirteen years after the first attempt to do so—the airport and the new White Hangar were formally dedicated.

Drake Field: an A-1 Airport

Three years later—in the upbeat aftermath of World War II—on April 14, 1947, in appreciation of Dr. Noah F. Drake's earlier generosity in helping purchase land for the airstrip and for his dedication in bringing a first-class aviation facility to Fayetteville, the new airport was renamed Drake Field. Fayetteville, at long last, had its A-1 airport.

HISTORY OF
COLLIER DRUG STORE

FOR NEARLY SEVENTY years, Collier Drug Store on the corner of Dickson Street and St. Charles Avenue has been a Fayetteville fixture. Opened on April 25, 1950, the family-run business has served generations of local residents.

Always high-tech inside and out, Collier Drug is a link between old Fayetteville and its newer self. Four generations of Colliers have operated drug stores in town and their history actually predates the current location by another three decades.

On April 1, 1917,[304] Melvin M. Collier, the patriarch of the family and it's longtime drug store business, became manager "with an interest in" the Red Cross Drug Store[305] located on the North Side of the Fayetteville Square.

Collier came to Fayetteville by way of Prairie Grove, where he was said to have "had considerable experience in drug stores" and was "a member of the lower house of the legislature."[306] Even back then, from its beginning, the Collier run business was ahead of its time, offering customers such "cutting edge services" as "delivery and charge accounts."[307]

Over the next decade, the Red Cross Drug Store became an abiding presence on the Square. Then, in 1930, after graduating from Fayetteville High School where he starred on the first Bulldog football team to play at Harmon Field, Morris G. Collier—Melvin's son—completed pharmacy school in St. Louis and began working full-time in the family business.

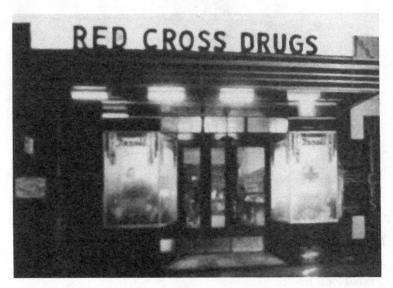

Red Cross Drug Store
Courtesy of Mel Collier

The next major event that befell the now second-generation drug store occurred on April 27, 1932. On that long ago day, a terrible fire spread across the Square and became a major blaze that nearly consumed the Red Cross store. The bold newspaper headline reported: *"$40,000 Fire At Red Cross Drug Co. Today."*[310] As devastating as that fire was, especially coming just as the Great Depression was deepening throughout the country, the Colliers regrouped, rebuilt, and reopened the Red Cross store in the fall of 1932.

After the great fire, the Red Cross Drug Store went through a period of stability that lasted through the rest of the Depression and World War II. As post-war technological advances swept the nation, however, the Colliers—Morris had become partners with his father in 1943[311]—believed they and Fayetteville were ready for a drug store upgrade.

In 1948, with his father now retired, Morris Collier purchased a lot on the northwest corner of Dickson and St. Charles streets.[312] What he had in mind, he said at the time, was a new drug store off the Square that would "be as much self-service as possible, in the modern trend of service."[313]

Morris Collier
Courtesy of Mel Collier

Matching the service would be the new building itself, described as "modernistic" in the *Northwest Arkansas Times*.[314] This new building was to be "of pink brick" with "an all-glass 106-foot front" and topped by "a 28-foot stucco tower with the name 'Collier' in metal."

It would feature air conditioning,[315] "tarazza floors," and as any kid from the era can tell you, "automatic electric glass doors"—an absolute marvel for the time and the first in Northwest Arkansas. The store also had another kid- and family-friendly feature: a full-service soda fountain.

Before the new store was built, however, the man who had started the family business that has endured for decades in Fayetteville,
Melvin M. Collier, passed away on July 24, 1949. The "widely known
druggist"[316] was eulogized as a "valued citizen," one always willing to
do his part for "civic betterment."[317] Fayetteville and the many groups
in which he took an active part, the *Northwest Arkansas Times* stated,
would "feel the loss his death has brought about."[318]

The following spring of 1950 brought happier news: the opening of
the new Collier Drug Store. On April 24, a large advertisement appeared
in the *Northwest Arkansas Times* announcing the new store. The next
day, April 25, 1950, Collier Drug Store, owned and managed by Morris
Collier, opened for business in its "modern Art Deco building."[319]

The store, which was built upon the site of a former skating rink and
the old Citizens Laundry,[320] was hailed as "Northwest Arkansas' Most
Modern Super Drug Store." In addition to the soda fountain[321] and the
"magic eye" that automatically opened the glass front doors, Collier's
offered Rexall prescription drugs, cameras and supplies, and "quality"
service. As Morris Collier said in the opening day ad: "We dedicate this
store to build a business ... that will advance continually ... to create a
personality that will be known for its strength and friendliness."[322]

For a few years after opening the new Collier Drug Store, the Collier family still operated the Red Cross Drug Store on the Square. In
January of 1953, the Red Cross Store was burglarized with the crooks
taking between $600 and $1,200 from a basement vault.[323]

About two and one-half years later, the *Northwest Arkansas Times*
reported that in the early morning hours of September 2, 1955, a far
worse fate befell the Red Cross store: it was ravaged by fire. The store
suffered widespread losses that ran into the "thousands of dollars."

Because of the heavy damage to the Red Cross store, on September 12, 1955 the Collier family chose to have a liquidation sale of its
remaining assets. Following the sale, the operation was moved to the
newer Collier Drug on Dickson Street[324] and, after nearly forty years of
continuous service on the Square in Fayetteville, the Red Cross Drug
Store closed its doors for the last time.

Collier Drug Store, with Presbyterian Church in Background
Courtesy of Mel Collier

In 1960, the next generation of Colliers joined the family business when Morris H. graduated from pharmacy school. Just four years later, Carl Collier also completed pharmacy training and began working for the family, as well. According to the store website, during this time, the family company was incorporated making each of the working members an owner.

In the mid-1960s, the Dickson Street store needed a bit more room and "Collier expanded into the vacated Dyke Lumber Company building to the north."[326] Then at the end of the decade, in June 1969, Collier had their first branch expansion: adding the new Collier Rexall East Drug Store and Western Shop at East Gate Shoppers City.[327] Four years later, in 1973, Colliers became the first pharmacy in Arkansas and the fourth in the United States "to use computers for prescription tracking and for keeping pharmacy records."[328]

Over the following decades, Colliers continued to expand, adding a branch in north Fayetteville in 1986 and the North Hills Fayetteville store in 1994. The following year, 1995, they added their first out-of-town store in Pea Ridge.

Also in 1995, the family suffered the loss of Morris Collier, who passed away January 18. He was eulogized in the *Northwest Arkansas Times* by long-time employee John Page as a "customer-oriented" man of great energy who "thrived on people," still working occasionally even after retirement "just to chat" with customers and friends. Louis Bryant, Jr., another employee with years of service with Colliers, said: "You can't find a better person than Mr. Collier."[329]

Carl Collier, Morris' son, had taken over the reins from his father upon the elder man's retirement and along with his children Mel and Meredith (who has since moved on to real estate work)[330] shaped Collier's future during the 1990s and into the current century.

One of the hallmarks of recent years has been more expansion. In 2005, the north Fayetteville store was closed and moved to Farmington, and that same year a branch was opened in Johnson, giving Colliers five stores in Northwest Arkansas.

In 2017, Collier Drug Stores celebrated an important anniversary: one hundred years of business and service to the local community. "Fayetteville's last family-owned drugstore,"[331] beginning in 1917 with the Red Cross Drug Store on the Square and continuing into the new millennium with five branches in town and the surrounding area, had survived—flourished—for a full century. Colliers marked the milestone by producing a 2017 calendar featuring historical photos of their stores, family members and employees.

No history of Colliers would be complete without mention of at least two of their longest-serving employees—John Page and Louis Bryant, Jr.

Page, a pharmacist, began working at Collier's in 1961 and had 37 years of perfect attendance. He has been past president of both the Arkansas State Board of Health and the State Board of Pharmacy. The importance of his work and contribution to the local area was recognized by the City of Fayetteville which honored him with a John Page Day and presented him a key to the city.[332]

Bryant worked as a deliveryman at Collier's for "nearly 60 years,"[333] becoming a virtual fixture there. Bryant, who passed away in 2007, was thought of so highly by the Collier family that they had a "one-day store closing to celebrate and honor his life."[334]

Today, Collier Drug Store remains a Fayetteville institution. Now in business for one hundred years, the Collier family has begun a second century of service to Fayetteville and the surrounding area.

Under the direction of young Mel Collier, the family's fourth generation in the business, Collier Drug is certain to continue as one of Fayetteville and Washington County's oldest and most respected family businesses far into the foreseeable future.

GEORGE BALLARD:
FORGOTTEN FAYETTEVILLE POET

THE HISTORY OF Fayetteville's African American community, for the most part, has been under-reported or ignored. Information about the people and life here is often hard to come by but worth the effort to dig out. In the decades after the Civil War, many families moved into the area roughly bounded by Washington and Walnut Avenues on the west and east and by Spring and Rock Streets on the north and south, respectively.

While most of the families ended up in this part of town, variously known as Vaughan's Valley, Tin Cup, Spout Spring, or simply the Hollow, some lived outside of the area in places like Red Hill, which is up North Highway 71B (College Avenue) near the present day Veteran's Administration Hospital. By the 1950s, other families had made their way into South Fayetteville, the traditionally poor white part of town, including those of horseman Otis Parker and musician Ralph "Buddy" Hayes. Wherever they have lived, though, our city's black population typically has had to fend for itself.

Yet—and despite the geographic, economic and social limits imposed on them by decades of segregation—many members of the community still gained recognition for their contributions to the culture and life of Fayetteville.

Counted among these would be Patrolman Lem McPherson, killed in the line of duty in 1928; James Hoover, indispensable long-time employee of City Hospital; and Louis Bryant, who worked many years for Collier's Drug.

In addition to these men, many other families from the Hollow have contributed to our history. Names like Carr, Young, Buchanan, Deffebaugh, Pettigrew, Manuel, Blackburn, Morgan, just to select a few, will be recognizable to long-time residents of the city. Regrettably, and despite their role in making Fayetteville what it is today, many of these people are now almost forgotten.

Of those lost to time—or nearly so—one who most assuredly should not be is the poet George Ballard. At his peak during the 1920s and 30s, Ballard was not as well-known as some of the other local authors during this active literary period, such as Charles J. Finger, Charles Morrow Wilson, Murray Sheehan and Rosa Marinoni. Nonetheless, Ballard is a writer of import and worthy of continued evaluation and interest.

Born January 4, 1882 in the rural community of Cincinnati in western Washington County, George Pool Ballard grew up on a farm. By early 1902, however, he had moved to Fayetteville and married Rosetta Dart.[335] The young couple lived in a small house on East Mountain Street just behind the historic Washington County Jail, which was new then, having been built just five years before in 1897.

Like most African American men of his time, Ballard worked at whatever jobs he could find to make a living for himself and his family. He shined shoes in a barber shop, worked as a mechanic, and was the jail janitor in February 1928 when six prisoners escaped, knocking Ballard down in the process as they fled custody.[336]

By the time he was run over in the jail break, he had already achieved some level of notoriety as a poet. This was true primarily because of a poem he wrote in tribute to Woodrow Wilson upon the president's death February 3, 1924. The poem was published in the *Fayetteville Daily Democrat* on February 6, 1924 and within ten days had garnered Ballard "wide recognition" not only here in Fayetteville but in other parts of the nation, as well.

Simply titled "Woodrow Wilson—A Tribute," the poem was praised, besides here in Arkansas, by readers in Iowa, Arizona and Florida. A letter from the Reverend Frank W. Court, Methodist Episcopal minister from Davenport, Iowa, commended Ballard for his "excellent production" and wished him "every success."[337]

"*Each human heart is touched with grief,*" the poem begins, "*The nation bows its head/For over the wire the news is flashed/'Woodrow Wilson is dead.'*" The final verse reads:

> *He has no need of "worldly peace"*
> *He leaves the league behind*
> *He has signed his name where angels sing*
> *"Blest be the tie that binds."* [338]

The poem, in the manner of the age, is signed: *George Ballard (colored), Fayetteville.*

Some three weeks after the Woodrow Wilson tribute poem was printed in the *Daily Democrat,* Ballard had yet another poem published in the paper. This one was entitled "A Toiler Speaks" and was written in response to author John J. Montague's poem "Contentment." Montague's work described a "white-collared" hero, a "soft-handed, dressed-up" man "content to live idle and clean-collared" while the work of the world was done by those "not afraid to soil their hands or garments."[339]

Ballard's response printed in the newspaper was rapid, sharp and to the point, although it's fair to say the version of "A Toiler Speaks" published in the 1928 collection *Ozark Ballards* was improved by editing. A portion of the poem from the book is quoted here:

> *I always feel proud of the work that I do,*
> *It's a kind that the public demands.*
> *I can not spoil my complexion like you*
> *For I am a dark-collar man*

> *Although my face may be black as a crow,*
> *And my hands be covered with dirt*
> *It gives me great satisfaction to know*
> *That I'm not a mere collar and shirt.*

So give me the overalls, jumper and cap,
Although they may tend to degrade.
I have no use for the white-collared man
Who does nothing but sit in the shade.[340]

This time the poem was simply signed: *George Ballard.*

The year 1928 was special in Fayetteville. It was the city's centennial and all stops were pulled out to make sure it was celebrated properly. Events were held throughout town during the week of July 4. Speeches were made, plaques dedicated and pageants held all to commemorate the one hundredth anniversary of Fayetteville.

For the centennial event, Ballard composed a poem entitled "Parable," which makes light-hearted use of the Golden Goose story to salute his adopted city. He also wrote a more direct poem for the one-hundred year anniversary of Fayetteville which he titled "Centennial" (100 Years of Fayetteville) July 4, 1928."

In part, the poem reads:

If you want, in looking back,
To see how time has flown,
Just look around in Fayetteville
And see how she has grown.

Our streets are paved with concrete,
Our electric lights, aglow—
Our homes were lit with candle light
One hundred years ago.

A dozen generations,
Like the flower and the weed
Have passed into the great beyond
That others might succeed.

We have the same old babbling brooks,
The same old rivers flow;
But Fayetteville was not the same
One hundred years ago.

In addition to his poems, Ballard suggested a float for the centennial parade that celebrated "Negroes of the Old South." Featured on the float would be old-timers and former enslaved men "Uncle" Sam Young and Charles Richardson, among others. Modern Priscilla, an African American women's group, was in charge of the float.[342]

1928 also saw the culmination of Ballard's poetic work with the publication of his book of verse, the cleverly titled *Ozark Ballards.* The collection includes forty-one poems, including those already mentioned here and was edited by Lessie Stringfellow Read, then editor of the *Fayetteville Daily Democrat.* The newspaper's parent company, Democrat Publishing and Printing, put out the book.

Ballard dedicates his book to "Members of the Colored Race Who Thus May Be Encouraged To Seek Self-Expression Even In A Crude Way" and to all the "White Friends Who Have Lent Help And Encouragement."[343] He also includes a short poetic "Appreciation" for Mrs. Lessie Read who he calls "a kind and gentle friend" who "helped me to succeed."[344]

Read's introduction to *Ozark Ballards,* while certainly positive, sometimes seems almost apologetic about the "colored" poet's work. Read tells us that while friends "have encouraged" Ballard, "not even these expect him to become another Paul Lawrence (sic) Dunbar."[345]

"Judged as true poetry," Read adds, "it is not possible to rank the 'ballards' very high." She does allow that some "University students and newspaper editors have been kind" to Ballard and see "a real if latent talent" in his poetry. Ballard," Read tells us, "knows nothing of the technique of writing." "My verse," she then quotes the poet, 'just comes to me and I write it down."[346]

Despite this rather lukewarm, patronizing support, which seems to imply that Ballard's literary output is as much that of a savant as a

Lessie Stringfellow Read
University of Arkansas Libraries, Special Collections, MS L541

poet, this nearly forgotten writer's work can stand on its own. George
Ballard was a poet—plain and simple. Any decision as to the quality of
his work can and should be left up to his readers.

   Ozark Ballards is divided into seven sections, the third of which,
"Summer," contains only the single poem "Memorial" a tribute to
American servicemen. The first section, "Lines to Notables" includes
the previously-mentioned poem on the death of Woodrow Wilson
and another for John Coolidge, Sr. (father of then-President Calvin
Coolidge).

OZARK
"BALLARDS"

By GEORGE BALLARD

Ozark Ballards
Fayetteville Public Library

"Just Before the Fight" is a pre-match, poetic analysis of the 1927 Dempsey-Sharkey heavyweight championship bout:

> *The sporting world would like to know*
> *If Dempsey is so very slow*
> *That Sharkey with his mighty clout*
> *Can knock the former champion out.*
>
> *And so they pay a million smacks*
> *To bring together these two Jacks,*
> *To watch them battle, round by round,*
> *'Till one shall knock the other down.*
>
> *But then (however that may be) —*
> *We all will see what we shall see—*
> *At eight o'clock they let them go*
> *And soon we'll say "I told you so."*[347]

Among the poems included in "Spring" are "Spring Fever," the earlier-discussed "A Toiler Speaks," "Ode to a Car," and "Wearing O' the Green:"

> *There is not a snake in Ireland*
> *Or so the people say,*
> *For good St. Pat prayed a prayer*
> *And drove them all away.*
> *And ever since that mighty prayer*
> *There's not a snake been seen.*
> *And so the Irish celebrate*
> *By wearing of the Green.*[348]

Writing in the age of Prohibition, Ballard calls his next section "Interlude and Drinking Songs" but the poems, among them "The Little Brown Jug," "Bootlegger," and "Pessimism" are mostly against the use of alcohol. "Drinking Song," however, reveals a more ambivalent attitude towards the issue:

> *Don't you feel like cussin'*
> *Your dear old Uncle Sam*
> *When you're blue and bilious*
> *And want a little dram?*
>
> *You would give a dollar*
> *Just for a little nip*
> *Just a little wee bit—*
> *If it only wet your lip.*
>
> *When you think of prohibition*
> *It gives your heart a pain!*
> *Ah, yes, it is heart breaking*
> *But we have it just the same.*[349]

Poems in the section "Miscellaneous" include the nostalgic "Lament for Dobbin," the modern (at the time) "Buick" and "The Thrill of My Life," which chronicles the discomfort felt during an airplane ride—a still unusual experience in 1928. "The Man Hunt" may have been inspired by the prison breakout that Ballard experienced up close and personal. The last poem is "Wonder:"

> *If we should chance some future day*
> *To sail the ocean wide*
> *I wonder what our eyes would see*
> *Upon the other side?*
>
> *I wonder if the grass is green*
> *Upon the mountain high,*
> *I wonder if the flowers bloom*
> *And do they ever die?*

> *I wonder if the housetops there*
> *Are covered o'er with snow*
> *Or if we'd find the weather fair*
> *If we should chance to go?* [350]

"Fall" is the next section in *Ozark Ballards* and it contains "True Fame," the aforementioned "Parable," and "At the County Fair"—the only poem in the collection in which Ballard uses dialect. The poem "Exempt" is an interesting take on serving in the military:

> *The boys on the farm*
> *Are all right we are told*
> *And it is seldom*
> *They die with T B.*
> *So when Uncle Sam*
> *Got himself in a jam*
> *No farmers were sent over the sea.*
>
> *For Hoover had said*
> *That the boys on the farm*
> *Should stay there*
> *To reap and to sow.*
> *And if the poets were mad*
> *The farmers were glad*
> *For there was none of us*
> *Rearin' to go.* [351]

The last section of the book, "Winter," naturally includes poems on the passage of time, as well as the coming of Christmas and New Year. The penultimate poem in both this section and the book is "Old Year:"

Farewell Old Year, your time is short,
We hate to see you go,
Your kindly deeds you've measured out
Alike to friend and foe.

For twelve short months you've been with us
And watched our rise and fall
You've measured out your blessings rare
Alike to one and all.

And when the Court House clock tonight
Rings out your funeral dell
If I am in my bed asleep,
Farewell, Old Year, Farewell! [352]

In the years after the publication of *Ozark Ballards,* George Ballard seems to have mostly dropped out of the public eye. On April 15, 1929, the paper reported that he had opened a "shine parlor" at 103 N. Block[354] and the following year he and three other men were hurt, though none seriously, in an automobile accident in Fayetteville.

Not much can be found about him during the next few years, but when he does reappear it's for a positive reason. During 1935-1936, Henderson School, built just after the Civil War for the African-American children in town, was replaced by a new school which was at first also called Henderson but later renamed Lincoln School.[355]

Dedication for the new school was held at 8 p.m. on the evening of May 21, 1936. Guests that night included Dr. Nolen Irby of the Arkansas Department of Education, who gave the "principal" address; F. S. Root, long-time Superintendent of Fayetteville Schools; James W. Dinwiddie, architect for the new school; Reverend J. W. Webb, pastor of the St. James Baptist Church; and State Senator Robert J. Wilson, scion of one of the oldest and most respected families in town.

Another guest was Fayetteville Mayor A. D. McAllister who was on hand to present one of the evening's biggest honors. The new

George Ballard
Fayetteville Public Library

school, which was meant to be one of the finest schools for our African-American children in this age of segregation, would proudly have the George Ballard Library.[357] It was a fitting display of respect for the popular local poet.

One of the few references to Ballard after this date indicates that during World War II he went down to Camp Chaffee to shine shoes for the soldiers. Besides some trips to Los Angeles to visit a sister, we know little of his last years.

On December 3, 1951, George Pool Ballard, poet, died at his

home. He lies today in an unmarked grave somewhere in Oaks Cemetery, last resting place for many—if not most—of our African American citizens from that time, on the south side of town just below the National Cemetery.

In July 1978, during Fayetteville's Sesquicentennial celebration, the entertaining poem "Parable," written for the 1928 Centennial, was reprised. The poem's final verses are an upbeat tribute to Fayetteville by George Pool Ballard, forgotten poet of the Hollow:

> *So if you live in Fayetteville*
> *Don't treat her with abuse,*
> *Don't kill her to get all the eggs*
> *Like the farmer did the goose.*
>
> *Just try to be contented,*
> *And help your town to thrive;*
> *Do everything within your power*
> *To keep the goose alive.*[359]

DEATH OF PATROLMAN
LEM McPHERSON

A Shocking Killing

On an otherwise mostly quiet Saturday night, April 28, 1928, one of the most shocking killings in Fayetteville history took place. Just before eight o'clock that evening, two shots rang out from the Hollow, east of the historic Washington County Courthouse.

Then came a third shot.

When the air was still again, Fayetteville Police Patrolman Lem McPherson, 48, lay dead on the ground. The killer: Everett "Eb" Williams, 26, a local bootlegger recently released after a nine-month term in the Washington County jail.

Williams, who would elude final capture for the better part of a week, eventually was caught, arrested, tried and convicted of second degree murder and sentenced to twenty-one years in prison. But what caused the shooting between the two African American men— one outside the law, the other sworn to uphold it?

Trouble Brewing

Only six days before the shooting, Williams had completed a sen-

NEGRO PATROLMAN SLAIN SATURDAY DURING MAN HUNT

Lem McPherson Killing
Fayetteville Public Library

tence for the illegal transportation of alcohol, a common enough crime in those days of Prohibition, and had been set free. Post-incarceration life for him, however, was as unhappy as it was brief. He believed that while he was in jail his wife Henrietta had received the attentions of a number of other men, including Patrolman McPherson.

By the day of the shooting, Williams had become highly agitated over the matter and spent Saturday afternoon, according to witnesses, drinking and "gunning" for McPherson. Williams' wife, Henrietta, had drunk so much alcohol herself that day that she was arrested and spent the rest of the weekend in jail.

A Brief Encounter

Left by himself, Williams ended up walking north on Willow Avenue where he encountered and was joined in his stroll by a woman named Nellie Newton. While the two walked up the street, Williams and Patrolman McPherson had their first encounter of the day.

"I just hope he says something to me," Williams was reported to have told Newton as the lawman approached them.

Despite the soon-to-be killer's bravado, there was no real confrontation between the two antagonists at this time, perhaps because Patrolman McPherson was carrying his police revolver at his side. The two men may have made their hostility to one another clear, but they went their separate ways—for the time being.

On the Prowl

As afternoon turned into evening, Williams—now an object of interest to Fayetteville Police, who had begun actively looking for him—went in search of a weapon. He found what he was looking for in the home of another local resident, Major Blackburn. Without Blackburn's knowledge, Williams took the steady workingman's .12 gauge shotgun and headed towards Webb's, a popular restaurant on North Willow.

"I ain't lookin' for y'all," Williams told brothers Sam and Embrus Young as he passed Webb's restaurant prior to the shooting.

The Youngs knew who the armed man was looking for, as they had spoken to Patrolman McPherson some time earlier. At that time the officer said he knew Williams was looking for him and that he would "take care of him."

Inevitable Confrontation

With the Fayetteville Police in general and Officer McPherson specifically looking for Williams and with him looking to "come to a settlement" with McPherson, it was just a matter of time before a confrontation between the two men would take place. Finally, as it neared eight p.m., they faced each other for the last time.

A short distance from Webb's restaurant, near a ravine and a field with a small house in it (just west up Spring Street from the intersection with Willow), the bootlegger and the patrolman faced off. The Youngs were nearby but when they saw the two men displaying guns, they hustled out of harm's way. Suddenly, two shots were heard almost simultaneously, with Embrus Young stating emphatically in court that Williams had fired first. Only seconds later, a third shot rang out.

"I've got you now," Williams said before running off into the darkening night.

In the Aftermath

Two Fayetteville Police officers—Lem Guinn and D. A. "Slim" Burson—were near Webb's when they heard the shots. They unsuccessfully pursued Williams, both firing their revolvers at the fleeing killer as he ran through the Hollow towards the Baptist Church on South Willow.

Back in the field where the shooting had taken place, Lem McPherson lay still in the grass and weeds. He had been hit by two shotgun blasts, one in the back and side of the head and "between the shoulders by the other." The patrolman left behind a wife, Willie, two sons and a daughter. After two years of keeping order in the Hollow, Lem McPherson was dead and his police revolver was missing.

Dennis A. "Slim" Burson
Fayetteville Police Department

Weekend Manhunt

With the killer at large, Fayetteville Police mounted a full scale dragnet for Williams. Officers on foot combed the crime area while others cruised the narrow, hilly streets in police cars looking for the escaped shooter.

They were looking in the wrong place.

Williams had managed to evade discovery and was reported to have been seen several times on the Square not long after the killing. He was said to have calmly gone into a hardware store and then boldly entered the Farmers Exchange around nine p.m., where witnesses said they saw him "carrying a revolver stuck in his left pocket."

Despite the sightings and the police search, Williams was on the loose for the rest of the weekend. He later testified that he spent Saturday night after the killing by Stone's Bridge near the White River out east of town where he had built a fire to keep himself warm.

The search continued without success all day Sunday—although Major Blackburn's shotgun, the one used in the killing, was found leaning against a post on the path he always traveled to work. On Monday, however, there were signs that the police were onto their man.

Rumors flew that Williams had been seen "fully armed" and "had been surrounded" at one point. It was also said he had actually been close enough to watch Patrolman McPherson's funeral that afternoon in the Twin Oaks (now Oaks) Cemetery on the south side of town. Finally, late Monday evening, the police got a tip that Williams was holed up in the basement of the Phi Mu sorority house on Dickson Street where his sister worked as a cook.

Arrest and Escape Again

Two unnamed policemen (most likely Guinn and Burson again), using a taxi cab for a patrol wagon, captured Williams at the sorority house and brought him to jail. However, the officers had not handcuffed their prisoner and allowed him to sit in front of the cab by the driver while they sat in back. When the taxi came to a stop outside the jail at East Mountain Street and College Avenue, the front door jolted open and Williams rolled out of the vehicle and onto the street "unhampered" in any way.

"Don't shoot," he cried out as he backed away towards the corner of the jail building. "I'll give up."

Then, while the surprised officers were still off guard, Williams bolted around the side of the jail and was gone. The officers fired at him with their pistols but to no avail. Completing yet another daring escape, the killer was once more on the loose, having vanished as he did before into the dark of night.

Lem Guinn
Fayetteville Police Department

More Sightings and Fears

With Williams free a second time, the manhunt resumed. This time Fayetteville Police called in bloodhounds from Ft. Smith and the city was again scoured for signs of the elusive shooter. On Tuesday, Officer Guinn stopped a Ft. Smith-bound car but the black man inside the vehicle was not Williams. Later Williams' sister was trailed because she was carrying "a bundle" with her, but that turned out to be a false lead, as well.

Wednesday morning Williams was reportedly seen near the Sigma

Chi house by the university where another man worked that Williams believed had shown undue attention to his wife. In this case, it was said, he had vowed to "get his man," but once again the lead played out and the killer remained at large.

Williams Surrenders

Around eight o'clock Thursday night, through the intervention of his brother-in-law Duck Macklin and another man, Arco Hall, a tired and hungry—he'd gone three days without food—Everett Williams finally surrendered to police. Macklin and Hall found Deputy Sheriff Bob Day sitting on the jailhouse steps that night and informed him that Williams was ready to give himself up if an officer "would come to him unarmed in 'back of the jail.'"

Without hesitation, Day removed his gun and with Macklin and Hall at Williams' side, the deputy sheriff placed the killer into police custody assuring the worried man that he needn't fear "mobbing"— one of Williams' major concerns during his flight from the law—and that he "would be granted a fair trial."

The Trial

The trial of Everett Williams began in the Washington County Courthouse promptly at nine a.m. on Monday, May 8, 1928, Circuit Court Judge J. S. Maples presiding. Jury selection ran until around ten twenty-five and twelve suitable jurors were duly sworn in—several men had been excused because of their membership in "a secret organization supposed to be prejudiced against the [black] race."

Seventeen witnesses were called for examination in the open session, including Sam and Embrus Young, Patrolman Burson, Patrolman Neal Cruse (later to become chief of police and the subject of corruption charges in the 1930s), Williams' wife Henrietta, and lastly, Williams himself.

The Young brothers testified first, with Embrus stating again that Williams had fired the first shot in the gun battle with Patrolman McPherson. The defense strategy, as presented by court-appointed attorneys J. Wythe Walker and Donald Trumbo (soon to become city attorney), was to present Officer McPherson as a "homespoiler who made love to Williams' wife while the latter was imprisoned and unable to protect his home."

Attorney Walker, taking the defense lead, described Williams as "innocent" and as having "a right to self-defense and defense of his home and fireside." The lawyer attempted to convince the jury that the defendant was "a wronged man."

The prosecution, led by Washington County Prosecuting Attorney J. S. Combs[360] of Rogers, conversely argued that Williams had not only fired the first shot but had been planning to do so all day. McPherson, it was argued, had himself only acted in self-defense.

The prosecution also squeezed out of Williams the admission that he was "angry" at Patrolman McPherson when he first got the shotgun and that he was also looking for a man named Levi Ross[361] who he believed had also been "courting" Mrs. Williams while he was in jail.

At one-thirty p.m. the prosecution rested its case, and began final arguments to the jury at three-thirty. Closing arguments by both the prosecution and the defense were described as "brief." Around six p.m. the jury adjourned to deliberate the case and the multiple charges against Williams: first degree murder, second degree murder, voluntary and involuntary manslaughter. Nearly one hundred people were reported to have lingered in the courtroom in anticipation of the final verdict.

Verdict and Sentencing

The jury deliberated the case against Williams for only three hours, returning to court with their verdict around nine p.m. The twelve white men found him guilty of second degree murder in the death of Patrolman Lem McPherson. Williams did not have to wait long to hear the final disposition of his case.

Immediately after the verdict, Judge Maples sentenced the now convicted killer to a term of twenty-one years imprisonment to be served in the Arkansas State Penitentiary. With the sentencing, one of the most extraordinary shooting episodes in Fayetteville history came to an end.[362]

Epilogue

In the years following the shooting death of Lem McPherson, the incident dropped from public awareness. It is not known what became of Williams, whether he eventually completed his prison term and returned to Fayetteville afterwards or not. However, there was an obituary listing for an Everett Williams in the October 22, 1946 issue of the *Northwest Arkansas Times*. The deceased was 44 years old, which is close to the age Williams would have been then but there is no certainty this is the same man.[363]

As for McPherson, on April 30, 1928, just two days after his death, the Fayetteville City Council unanimously approved "an appropriation of $150.00...to pay for the funeral expenses of Patrolman McPherson, killed in the line of duty."

When the present day Fayetteville Police Department learned of McPherson's sacrifice, they made sure it went unnoticed no further. McPherson's grave was located in Oaks Cemetery, next to his brother Ollie, and a new gravestone was placed there.

In addition, the police department had a monument built and located in front of the Fayetteville police station honoring McPherson and two other local officers who died in the line of duty, William D. Patton and Elmo Ritchie.

And finally, Lem McPherson's name was placed on the National Law Enforcement Officers Memorial in Washington, D. C.[364]—a fitting tribute to a public servant whose story was lost for almost eighty years.

PROFESSOR JOSEPH A. THALHEIMER:
MR. CHIPS AT THE UNIVERSITY OF ARKANSAS

IN THE FALL of 1930, Joseph A. Thalheimer was hired as a professor in the developing journalism department at the University of Arkansas[365] in Fayetteville. Skilled and amiable, Thalheimer would be an integral part of the department for almost thirty years, retiring in 1957[366] as a revered Mr. Chips-style professor. Never one to draw attention to himself or his accomplishments, Thalheimer has now nearly dropped from university and public consciousness.

Teaming with Professor Walter J. Lemke, who had been hired to build the journalism department by university president John C. Futrall in 1928,[367] Thalheimer helped expand the department that now bears the name of the far better known Lemke.[368]

While Lemke certainly deserves the recognition given him—his accomplishments are legion[369]—Thalheimer, who was with Lemke virtually every step of the way, deserves a better historical fate than to be relegated to an afterthought, if even that is afforded him.

Joseph A. Thalheimer was born November 5, 1901 in the little desert town of Phoenix, Arizona. Now one of the largest cities in the desert Southwest, at the time the population of Phoenix was less than six thousand.[370] Thalheimer's early years are not well documented,[371] but after high school he graduated from both Stanford University and Columbia University. He worked as a journalist, including time with "one of the large Chicago dailies"[372] prior to becoming a professor. In 1926, he married Gladys Twedell—also from Phoenix[373]—and four years later the young couple moved to Fayetteville.

When Thalheimer arrived at Arkansas, Walter Lemke had already spent two years building the journalism department. But in the decade prior to their coming to Fayetteville, journalism classes, usually News Writing and News Editing, were offered through the English Department, and had been taught by a number of different professors. Among these were J. Wainwright Evans (1914-1916), Dr. Virgil L. Jones (1916-1917), Norman John Radder (1917-1919), Maurice Eldred Votaw (1919-1920), J. Wymond French (1924-1926), and Victor R. Portmann (1926-1927).

Perhaps the most intriguing of the early journalism teachers and easily the most controversial in the years before Lemke and Thalheimer came to Arkansas was Murray Sheehan. Flamboyant and eccentric, Sheehan (1920-1924)[375] was renowned for riding a horse to class every day and for his frequent conflicts with university president John C. Futrall. A final spat between the two educators sent Sheehan packing from the university.[376]

In 1927, Sheehan's strange, satirical beast fable entitled *Half-Gods* was published by the E. P. Dutton Company of New York City. Set in a fictitious Missouri town and college, the novel was nonetheless a clear and biting condemnation of the socio-economic power structure in Fayetteville and the University of Arkansas at the time. The book, while it drew national attention,[377] did little to endear Sheehan in certain quarters of the local community.

When Joseph Thalheimer, being the polar opposite of Sheehan, brought his brand of amiableness and acumen to Arkansas in 1930 he jumped right in and immediately began teaching the core journalism classes of News Writing, News Editing, Feature Writing and History of American Journalism.[378]

This freed Lemke to teach higher level courses and run the News Bureau, which provided, among other services, publicity for the university sports teams. During his first four years at Arkansas, Thalheimer's teaching load remained the same but in 1934 he began co-teaching Newspaper Problems and Policies with Lemke. That year Thalheimer was also promoted to Assistant Professor.[379]

Joseph A. Thalheimer (left) and Walter J. Lemke (right)
Razorback Annual, University of Arkansas, 1933

Besides the additional classes now offered to aspiring journalism students, the decade of the 1930s was active in other ways as well. In the spring of 1932, for example, a dozen journalism students, under the supervision of Lemke and Thalheimer, were bussed to several towns around the state to write and edit an issue of the local newspapers. Among the recipients of this student invasion were the *Russellville Courier-Democrat, Pine Bluff Commercial, Hope Star,* and *Texarkana Press.*

In Ernie Deane's brief history of the University of Arkansas journalism department, he tells of an amusing—and possibly apocryphal —headline in the Russellville paper regarding the student onslaught. *"UA Journalists Due Tomorrow,"* the headline read, *"Will Edit This Paper/Have Punished Four Papers in State This Year."*[380]

Among the better known students Thalheimer and Lemke instructed during this era, some of whom helped teach classes and all of whom became working journalists, were Johnny Erp, Marvin Hurley, Ernie Deane—the latter two helping out as instructors—and Marguerite Gilstrap.[381]

With Thalheimer carrying a yeoman's load of classes during the

Mystery of the Cortez Emerald
University of Arkansas Libraries, Special Collections

30s, this allowed Lemke time to write columns for the local *Fayette-ville Daily Democrat/Northwest Arkansas Times*—he paper changed its name on July 8, 1937. Among Lemke's columns were "This and That," "Ozark Moon" and "Angel Food."[382]

Busy as he was teaching, Thalheimer still managed to pursue a literary career as well. Although it is not generally known today, Thalheimer, writing under a pseudonym, published what we now call Young Adult novels—adventure stories for boys. Using the name J. A. Lath (Lath are the first four letters of Thalheimer mixed up), his books *The Lost City of the Aztecs* and its follow-on *The Cortez Emerald Mystery,* were published in 1934 and 1935, respectively. Both books were published by Cupples and Leon Company of New York City as part of their 1930s eight-title series: Adventure and Mystery Books for Boys.[383]

Life in the first half of the 1940s was, of course, dominated by news of World War II. One steadying factor during these uncertain times, at least for University of Arkansas journalism students, was the continuing presence of the solid and dependable Thalheimer, who continued to teach the same classes he had for a decade. By the early 1940s, the always popular professor had been dubbed "Smoky Joe" in reference to the ubiquitous pipe he was always smoking or holding in his hand.[384]

He was promoted to Associate Professor by 1942[385] and throughout the war and the years immediately after, he continued to teach, serve on the university Publication Board and worked behind the scenes as an advisor for the *Arkansas Traveler* and the *Razorback* Annual.

The big news out of the journalism department during the war was a series of bulletins written by Lemke which served to connect old UA students, mostly his former students, with others who were in the service. These War Bulletins were considered of such importance in keeping folks in touch with each other and boosting morale that after the war Lemke was honored in a ceremony at Razorback Stadium where, among other gifts, he was presented with a new car.[386] Among the prominent 1940s students, many of whom served in the war, were Floyd Carl, Bill Penix, and Maurice "Footsie" Britt, who lost an arm in the war but came back home to eventually become Lt. Governor of Arkansas.[387]

By the time the 1950s rolled around, Thalheimer and Lemke had been teaching in the University of Arkansas journalism department for two decades plus. They were in the home stretch of their careers. In May of 1952, Lemke announced that he was stepping down from the chairmanship of the department,[388] possibly due to his added workload as founder and driving force of the newly created Washington County Historical Society.[389] As Lemke's heir apparent, Thalheimer would replace him as chairman in July 1952.[390]

Caricature of the University of Arkansas Journalism Group
Joseph A. Thalheimer is at top left, Walter J. Lemke at bottom right
Razorback Annual, University of Arkansas, 1935

During his tenure as chairman of the department, Thalheimer—now elevated to Full Professor[391]—continued teaching the courses he had since the 1930s (News Writing, News Editing, Feature Writing, and Newspaper Problems and Policies). The 1953-1954 university catalog shows he added classes in the Study of Mass Communications and Technical Journalism, reflecting the changing, modernizing world of journalism.[392] He continued to serve on the Publications Board, with long-time Professor Bunn Bell among others, and as always, continued behind the scenes advising the *Razorback* Annual and the *Arkansas Traveler* student newspaper.

As the decade slipped into its second half, Lemke retired from full-time teaching in 1956 and became Professor Emeritus.[393] The long-standing era of journalism at the University of Arkansas led by "Uncle Walt" Lemke and his steady, "well-loved colleague,"[394] the universally liked "Smokey Joe" Thalheimer was coming to a close.

The next year, 1957, Thalheimer himself stepped down as chair of the journalism department and, with little or no fanfare, retired. By that fall, he and his wife Gladys had given up their home at 625 N. Wilson where they had lived for years and left Fayetteville for their original hometown of Phoenix in the desert southwest.[395]

In 1959, with the Thalheimers living the retiree life in Phoenix, Walter John Lemke retired as Professor Emeritus. The *Arkansas Traveler* put out an eight-page special edition honoring the long-time father of University of Arkansas journalism. Besides Lemke's history of the department and his role in that history, the issue had innumerable letters of congratulations and well-wishes from former students and colleagues. One of the most entertaining letters was from one Joseph Thalheimer of Phoenix, Arizona that was printed under the title "Iron Chips."[396]

Lemke had been compared by exuberant supporters to Mr. Chips, the nickname of the lead character in British author James Hilton's novella of the same name and the subject of a well-received 1939 English film, also of the same name. Thalheimer used his good-natured letter to congratulate his old boss but he felt the need to bring a touch of reality into the general congratulatory mood.

Joseph A. Thalheimer
Razorback Annual, University of Arkansas, 1957

"Uncle Walt has sometimes been called the Mr. Chips of the journalism department," Thalheimer wrote, but that "isn't too good a char-
acterization of him. Mr. Chips' sympathy and understanding he does
have, but also there's salt and iron and vinegar. There's a puckish humor and just a touch of irascibility which all add up to a beloved and
unique entity—Uncle Walt Lemke."[397]

Within a year, "Uncle Walt" could have exacted revenge on Thalheimer's tongue-in-cheek comments in person if he'd been so inclined
when his old second-in-command moved back from Phoenix to Fayette-

ville. Taking up residence at 1017 Crest Drive,[398] the Thalheimer's settled into a quiet life up among the hills of the quaint little university town.

While her husband seemed content to live out his retirement in the same calm and unobtrusive manner in which he had taught college students for nearly thirty years, Mrs. Thalheimer remained socially active, participating in various ladies and literary clubs.[399]

Towards the end of the decade, on December 4, 1968, Walter J. Lemke died of a heart attack. Thalheimer's old boss and the prime mover of so many university and local community activities and projects had passed. In 1988, the University of Arkansas honored Lemke by naming its journalism department after him.

Thalheimer himself, the easy-going, kindly professor of journalism, passed away just less than three years later on November 21, 1971. He was buried in Fayetteville's Fairview Cemetery far from his original Arizona home but close to the university where he had devoted the better part of his adult life.

Shortly after his passing, a scholarship was begun in Thalheimer's name and it is still going strong. From 2011-2017 alone, the program provided some $32,000 in financial aid to aspiring University of Arkansas journalism students.[400]

Nearly fourteen years after her husband's passing, on October 8, 1985, Gladys Twedell Thalheimer died. She was buried beside him in Fairview Cemetery.

In summarizing the life of Joseph A. Thalheimer, an unnamed editorialist for the *Northwest Arkansas Times* offered some fine words with which to remember the beloved "Chipsian" professor.

"Smokey Joe, as he was best known to his students, was a happy, academic complement to the wide-ranging enterprise of his colleague...the late W. J. "Uncle Walt" Lemke....Mr. Thalheimer's gifts included enormous loyalty to his students and to his profession and....He understood, better than most, that success is a quality of the spirit. That's a good thing to have in a teacher, and Mr. Thalheimer was, above all else, a fine teacher."[401]

The sentiments expressed in this editorial eulogy and the affection which he engendered among his legion of students stand in testimony to the regard with which he was held. The tributes are evidence that Joseph A. Thalheimer, though never as well-known to outsiders as Walter John Lemke, was in fact a real life Mr. Chips and one of the finest and most highly-regarded professors in the history of the University of Arkansas journalism department.

CABIN ORGY DEATHS:
DECEMBER, 1936

AROUND SEVEN-THIRTY a.m. on the cold morning of December 7, 1936, John Butler, proprietor of Uncle John's Tourist Cabins on North College[402] in Fayetteville, having "failed to get an answer to his call" unlocked the front door to one of his small cabins to discover a grisly scene. Five bodies littered the cabin in various stages of undress. Making his way past the dead, which were described as being "sprawled over the room," he turned off the gas range which was still burning "three to four inches above the stove." The victims had died, authorities would determine just hours after Butler had "immediately telephoned officers," from "asphyxiation following a drinking party."[403]

Cabin Orgy Deaths
Fayettevulle Public Library

The dead were two men and three women. The men were Bert Atkinson of Fayetteville, 41, married with four children, ages eight to fifteen, a veteran of the World War and owner of the White Swan Club,[404] which the city of Fayetteville had recently tried to shut down as a "nuisance"[405]; and William "Bill" Reed of Fayetteville, 28, married (his wife was living in Bentonville) and the operator of a "four for a dime" photography gallery. The women were Mabel "Esther" Todd of Huntsville, 27, married with two small children, ages two and five, but separated from her husband and living in a trailer in Fayetteville; Jewell Hudson of Fayetteville, 20 and single; and Alice Taylor of Springdale, 18 and single.

According to the *Fayetteville Daily Democrat,* the group had started drinking at Atkinson's club the night before and had picked up five bottles of beer along the way to Uncle John's Cabins. Butler told the police "Atkinson rented the cabin between 9:30 and 10 o'clock" the previous evening. He did not check on the group again until they failed to respond to his early morning call.

The paper recounted that Deputy Sheriff Arthur Davidson, who was the "first to reach the scene," found that the "bodies of the victims were only partially clad" and that both men "were lying on the floor." Bert Atkinson, according to the newspaper, "apparently had attempted to reach the door and was lying on his face with head cushioned on his arm next to the door."

William Reed, the article went on, "apparently had tried to turn off the gas, and had fallen across the stove and then to the floor. His legs were badly burned. The Taylor woman had fallen on the floor and bodies of the other two women were on the two beds in the room."

Sheriff Herbert Lewis told the newspaper that all of the victims had died of asphyxiation following a drinking party. They had succumbed, the sheriff added, "due to carbon monoxide gas after a gas stove had burned the oxygen in the tightly closed room."

Coroner Glenn Riggs stated that "carbon monoxide poisoning" was the official cause of death and that all five of the unfortunate revelers "had been dead several hours when the bodies were found." Moisture on the windows of the room, it was determined, "had frozen, sealing the

Sheriff Herb Lewis
Washington County Sheriff's Office

windows air-tight." No coroner's jury had been called, the newspaper reported, because the coroner and three attending physicians had "concurred in the view that asphyxiation had caused the deaths."

In the aftermath of the tragedy, bodies of the victims were removed to Moore's Funeral Home while attempts were made to locate families of the deceased. By the next day, December 8, 1936, a headline in the *Daily Democrat* told that *"Four Bodies In Tragedy Disposed Of."* Only the remains of Jewell Hudson had not as yet been claimed, although it was known that she had relatives living in Fayetteville.

Burial details were given in the paper for each of the other persons. Services for Bert Atkinson were scheduled for Wednesday, December 9, 1936 at Moore's Chapel. As befit a veteran of the World War, he would be buried in the National Cemetery on the south side of town. William Reed was to be buried Tuesday, December 8, in Huntsville.

Mabel Todd had been taken by her parents to Thompson and she was to be buried on Wednesday, December 9 in Pinnacle. Alice Taylor, the paper said, had been taken to Berryville for burial but that no other details were known at this time.

As shocking and scandalous as the "cabin orgy" deaths were—Prohibition had been lifted just three years before and Fayetteville had only begun issuing liquor licenses the previous year (1935)—the story dropped out of the paper until the next summer. Families and representatives of the victims then filed wrongful death lawsuits against both Butler, owner of the tourist cabin, and the Arkansas Western Gas company.

On July 30, 1937, the newspaper (now the *Northwest Arkansas Times*) gave details of a $90,000 lawsuit filed on behalf of three of the

Williams Tourist Cabins
Courtesy of Professor James Chase

"cabin orgy" dead. The lurid nature of the case was revisited by the *Times* in sensational style.

The newspaper article told how pictures "taken of the affair" showed Reed apparently reaching his hand toward the burning gas heater "as though in a final effort to turn off the heat before he had expired." The White Swan, where the party had begun before the night in the cabin, was closed shortly thereafter.

Attorneys for the plaintiffs in the lawsuit were Rex Perkins,[407] Sullins and Sullins,[408] and Carlos B. Hill.[409] They argued that "the deaths were caused by carbon monoxide gas by reason of defective appliances and connections." The case was broken down into three parts.

$60,000 was claimed on behalf of Atkinson, $40,000 for his four minor children and $20,000 for his wife. Plaintiffs were listed as "Robert Atkinson, son, et. al. by Frances Henderson Atkinson, wife, for herself and children." A $10,000 settlement was sought by Georgia Roach, mother of Jewell Hudson, and $20,000 for Alice Taylor by Ward C. Taylor, her adoptive father and estate administrator.

Three months later, the lawsuits were resolved. On November 2, 1937, a front page *Times* headline read *"Ask Court To Instruct Jury For Defendant."* Homer Pearson, representing Arkansas Western Gas and John Butler, entered a motion "for an instructed verdict"[410] on behalf of the defendants. Arguments began at two-twenty p.m. in Circuit Court.

The list of plaintiffs had grown since the case was first introduced back on July 30 and so had the amount of money being sought in damages. The total was now $185,000. The estate of William S. Reed was asking for $75,000 and the estate of Mabel Todd sued for $20,000.

Over a dozen witnesses testified on November 2, including the widows of Atkinson and Reed as well as local plumbers and gas company men. Rex Perkins, arguing for the plaintiffs, contended that "both the gas company and the operator of the tourist camp were negligent."

Homer Pearson countered that "the gas company had nothing to do with" the actual connection of gas lines at the cabins—Butler admitted to doing that work himself and without the gas company's knowledge—and that the "deaths were at the hands of a third party over which neither Uncle John nor the gas company had any control." The "means of preventing the deaths," Pearson added, "were at hand if the victims had used them."

Coroner Riggs reconfirmed that "carbon monoxide poisoning was the cause of the deaths" and he and Sheriff Lewis reiterated that they had been told by Butler that the gas flame "was burning above the top of the stove" when the victims in the "death" cabin had been found.

The next day, November 3, 1937, a final headline concerning the story read *"Take Non-Suit In Damage Case."* According to the *Times,* the "non-suit[411] was taken after attorneys for the defendants had argued for a directed verdict" by the unnamed judge.[412]

Although the plaintiffs had, according to the *Times,* "one year in which to re-file the suits," they do not seem to have done so. Nothing more was found on the case in local records and the case and the scandalous tragedy upon which it was based drifted into the obscurity of distant, forgotten local history.

THE CAR ACCIDENT
THAT CHANGED AMERICAN HISTORY

ON SEPTEMBER 12, 1939, around 5:30 p.m., University of Arkansas President John C. Futrall was driving back to Fayetteville after meeting with medical school officials in Little Rock.[413] As he rounded a sharp curve about two miles south of West Fork on narrow Highway 71, his car suddenly drifted across the road and crashed head-on with a pickup traveling southbound toward Winslow.[414] Futrall was killed instantly, his car a mangled mess. Of five people in the pickup driven by Thomas Bradley, 45, of Winslow, only one, Earl Moore, 25, also of Winslow, suffered serious injuries.[415]

The unexpected death of President Futrall came as a terrible shock both to the university community and to the citizens of Fayetteville.[416] He had been associated with the University of Arkansas as student, teacher, coach, and administrator since his arrival on campus from Marianna, Arkansas in 1888.[417]

After studying in Fayetteville for two years,[418] he attended the University of Virginia, where he graduated with B.A. and M.A. degrees before returning to the University of Arkansas (still called Arkansas Industrial University) in 1894 as a professor of Latin and Greek.[419] In addition to his professorial duties, from 1894 until 1896, he also was the first university football coach. His teams were a collective 5-2 during his tenure.[420]

In 1913, the year after "an open student revolt" may have played a contributing role in the resignation of university president Dr. John N. Tillman[421] and the brief temporary presidency of Dr. John

John C. Futrall Death
Fayettevulle Public Library

Hugh Reynolds, Futrall was selected as the new acting president of the University of Arkansas. On March 6, 1914, the university Board of Trustees, meeting in Little Rock, unanimously selected him as permanent president of the university—the position he held until his untimely death.[422]

During his twenty-five year tenure, the longest in school history, the University of Arkansas experienced an extended period of growth and progress. Several campus landmarks that still stand today, although in sometimes altered forms, were constructed during his administration, including Razorback Stadium, the old men's gymnasium (now the Faulkner Performing Arts Center), Vol Walker Library (now Vol Walker Hall), and the Greek Amphitheatre.[423]

The university experienced unprecedented academic growth under his guidance, as well. Not only did the school gain full accreditation during this time but a number of college divisions also were established. Among these were the College of Education (1916), School of Law (1924), and graduate school (1927).[424]

In the aftermath of Futrall's death, tributes poured in from all quarters. The city of Fayetteville basically shut down for his funeral, with most stores closing at 10 a. m. on Thursday, September 14. All city schools also closed, as did all campus activities, including construction work.[425] Governor Carl Bailey came up from Little Rock to attend the services.

Mrs. Roberta Fulbright, publisher of the *Northwest Arkansas Times* devoted her "As I See It" column completely to his memory, referring to him as an "imposing figure" who had "lived nobly as leader of youth and men."[426] Variously described as being a "reserved"[427] and a "dignified, competent man,"[428] he was also eulogized by several members of the faculty.

Harkening back to Futrall's organization and coaching of the university's first football team, Athletic Director Fred Thomsen called him "a gentleman and a friend." A man who was "an exponent of fair play and good sportsmanship." H. G. Hotz, the Dean of Education, emphasized the late president's "rare and unusual talents," foremost of which was his "loyalty to the ... faculty and teachers" of the university."[429]

Dr. Julian S. Waterman, university vice-president, Dean of the Law School and presumptive heir to the now vacant presidency, said Futrall would be "remembered for his high standards of scholarship" and his "fearless and courageous" adherence "to the finest ideals of the academic world." Martha M. Reid, Dean of Women, simply called him "a great University President."[430]

John C. Futrall
Razorback Annual, University of Arkansas, 1940

Futrall's unexpected death left the university without a permanent leader—Dr. Waterman was acting president—but the search for a successor moved quickly. Governor Bailey, who was chairman of the university board of trustees and had been supported by and was a friend of the Fulbright family,[431] wanted to name a new president "swiftly."[432]

Just six days after Futrall's death, the university board of trustees, chose James William Fulbright, second son of Jay (deceased) and Roberta Fulbright, as the new President of the University of Arkansas. Only 34 years old upon taking office, J. W. Fulbright would be the youngest college president in the country. The trustees proclamation also paid tribute to the late president and his memory by naming the new student union Futrall Memorial Hall, now just known as Memorial Hall.[433]

Fulbright's selection as university president was both surprising and yet well received by many, both on campus and in the city. Most observers believed that Dr. Waterman, acting college president and dean of the Law School, was the obvious choice, but it was reported that he declined Governor Bailey's offer of the president's chair, an act which opened the door for Fulbright's selection.[434]

Although born in Missouri, Fulbright had lived in Fayetteville since he was one-year old. He had attended the University of Arkansas where he was an extremely successful student and athlete. He was President of Associated Students in 1923-1924[435] and a bona fide sports hero.[436]

After graduating from the University of Arkansas in 1925, he was selected—university president and Fulbright family friend John C. Futrall was chairman of the selection committee—for a Rhodes Scholarship to England's prestigious Oxford University.[437] During his three years at Oxford, Fulbright excelled in sports, playing rugby and starring on the varsity lacrosse team,[438] and was well-respected enough by his fellow students to be invited to join several elite clubs including the (Samuel) Johnson Society, of which he was elected president.[439]

He graduated from Oxford in 1928 and, after taking the Grand Tour of Europe, returned to America. In the summer of 1929, while helping an old college mate with legal and financial difficulties in Washington, D. C., he met Elizabeth "Betty" Williams, daughter of a prominent Philadelphia family. After a "prolonged and difficult" courtship, they were married June 15, 1932.[440]

During this time, Fulbright also pursued a law degree from George Washington University, finishing second in his class.[441] In 1936, he returned to Fayetteville to take a part-time faculty member position in the University of Arkansas Law School.[442]

By 1939, he had settled into a comfortable, promising academic life when the unexpected death of Professor Futrall led to his selection as new president of the University of Arkansas. From that moment on, Fulbright was thrust into a public spotlight that would shine on him for the better part of the next forty years.

His tenure as university president was, however, a brief one: just less than two years. He was reportedly quite popular with students and although he had little time to leave much of a legacy, he did focus on scholastic awards and he and English Professor Jobelle Holcombe instituted an Honors Day program, which included presenting Senior Keys to top-rated senior students.[443]

If some people might argue that Fulbright's selection as university president had been political, the result of his mother's support of and friendship with Governor Carl Bailey, his ouster can leave no doubt. Bailey had been in a political power struggle with rival Homer Adkins, either directly or by proxy, since the early 1930s.[444]

In 1940, the two adversaries faced each other directly in the Arkansas gubernatorial campaign. In a factional and fractional battle, Adkins won the election. His doing so guaranteed the shortening of J. W. Fulbright's tenure as university president. For one thing, Adkins wanted to rid the university of ex-Governor Bailey's friends and supporters, which included Fulbright.[445] Adkins also had a fair-sized axe to grind with Mrs. Roberta Fulbright, who had made her opposition to his candidacy quite clear.

True to expectations, by mid-May 1940, Adkins was preparing for a house-cleaning of Bailey adherents at the University of Arkansas—chief among those, Fulbright. On June 9, 1940 the Adkins-stuffed board of trustees voted 6-4 to dismiss Fulbright, who had declined to resign.[447] Arthur M. Harding was selected the next president of the University of Arkansas.

Despite the humiliation of being dismissed from his university position by a family and political enemy, Fulbright did not spend much time feeling sorry for himself. In 1942, family lawyer and friend Clyde T. Ellis chose to step down from his U. S. Congressional seat to run for the U. S. Senate.[448] He recommended Fulbright run to replace him.

Running against Karl Greenhaw, a noted Fayetteville attorney and

J.W. Fulbright
Razorback Annual, University of Arkansas, 1940

Adkins appointee to the Arkansas Supreme Court, and Virgil Willis of Harrison, Fulbright received the most votes in the primary and then defeated Greenhaw in a runoff election.[449]

Although he only served one term as a congressman, Fulbright was an effective legislator—especially so for a junior member of the House. In early April 1943, he had attempted to introduce legislation that would create an international body along the lines of the League of Nations which had failed to gain U. S. support after World War I. American attitudes were different this time, however, and on September 21, 1943, the Fulbright Resolution passed the House by a vote of 360 to 29.[450]

The resolution called for "the creation of appropriate international machinery with power adequate to establish and to maintain a just and lasting peace, among the nations of the world, and as favoring participation by the United States therein through its constitutional processes."[451] The Fulbright Resolution is credited with being a primary impetus leading to the creation of the United Nations.

Buoyed by his success as a congressman, Fulbright was emboldened to challenge incumbent Hattie Caraway in the 1944 Arkansas senatorial campaign. In the race, he would also compete against Col. T. H. Barton of El Dorado, and his long-time nemesis, Governor Homer Adkins. Once again, the election ended with a runoff and once again, Fulbright won, decisively defeating Adkins—in a moment of supreme irony, no doubt—for the senatorial seat.[452]

Over the next thirty years, J. W. Fulbright became one of the most powerful leaders in the nation. Among his significant, enduring accomplishments: early preparations for the establishment of the United Nations, creation of what has become the prestigious Fulbright Scholarships, and opposition to Senator McCarthy and the House Un-American Activities Committee.[453] Senator Fulbright voted against funding for and directly challenged Senator McCarthy's communist witch-hunting campaign during committee meetings.[454]

Many in the United States may consider Senator Fulbright's early and powerful opposition to the War in Viet Nam as perhaps the hallmark of his career. Even though he had signed the Gulf of Tonkin Resolution—which was used to justify U. S. military expansion in Indochina to begin with—he changed his mind on the war and his position against it gave credence and respectability to the movement opposed to the war.

In the end, J. W. Fulbright became one of the most important political figures of the twentieth century in the United States. His contribution has been summed up as follows:

No senator in this century has had greater influence on our foreign policy; his critical dissent in the Cold War and in the Vietnam War…and his sponsorship of the celebrated Fulbright scholarships made an enduring imprint on both foreign policy…and the way the Americans and other nations regard each other.[455]

Senator Fulbright's contribution to and influence on American history came to pass after that tragic car wreck on an out of the way stretch of highway, in an out of the way part of the nation, long ago. The unexpected death of long-time university president John C. Futrall and the sequence of events that followed led to the ascendancy of J. W. Fulbright, university president, congressman, long-serving senator. For decades Fulbright was a central figure on the national scene and left an indelible stamp on American politics for all time.

YOU CAN'T GO HOME AGAIN: CHARLES MORROW WILSON'S UNHAPPY RETURN TO FAYETTEVILLE

IN A MAY 1951 article entitled "Hometown Revisited," author Charles Morrow Wilson—in advance of moving back to Fayetteville after more than two decades away—declared that although he had been a "world traveler for many years" he had also remained a person who believed "in going home to live."[456]

Buoyed by the successful production of his play *Acres of Sky,* partly based upon his 1930 novel of the same name, at the November 1950 opening of the Fine Arts Center on the Fayetteville campus of the University of Arkansas, Wilson believed that he and his family would find "a good life" back in the Ozarks. It would be the ideal place, he thought, where he and his wife Martha could "work and serve the community" and raise their three sons.[457]

Despite experiencing what he called "a great deal of extremely shabby snobbishness"[458] while growing up in Fayetteville and attending the university, he felt that the city and college had changed and that in "the main, greatness is emerging at the University of Arkansas as well as in the town of Fayetteville."[459]

Just three short years later, denouncing friends and foes alike and angrily referring to Fayetteville as "Nastyville,"[460] he removed himself and his family and returned to Putney, Vermont where they had lived for a number of years before the ill-fated attempt to return home. He would call the New England farm home for the rest of his life.

What caused Charles Morrow Wilson, one of the most successful authors Fayetteville has ever produced, to re-embrace his hometown so enthusiastically and then in such a short time grow to despise and vilify it so vehemently? A look back at his life and the events leading up to and occurring after his return to Fayetteville provide some of the answers.

Wilson, whose name is now all but forgotten, was once a highly regarded, well-known writer of national and international status. He penned over forty-five books, mostly non-fiction, and wrote countless magazine articles and short stories during the course of a professional writing career that spanned some fifty years. Beginning as a brilliant, precocious high school and university student writer, he later honed his craft as a journalist traveling extensively in Latin America and Africa to attain a considerable reputation.

Born into a prominent Fayetteville family on June 16, 1905, he was the youngest child of Joseph Dickson and Mattie Morrow Wilson. Joseph Dickson Wilson, the son of A. M. Wilson, one of Fayetteville's founding fathers, was a businessman active in local civic affairs. Charles Morrow referred to his father as a "plain-style backwoods farmer who was a renowned Bible Scholar,"[461] although he simply referred to him as a "suburban farmer"[462] elsewhere in his writings.

Wilson's mother, he wrote, was one of the first three women graduates to receive a degree—back in 1890."[463] Later, however, in the introduction to his story "More Light"—from his collection of Ozark folk tales *Stars Is God's Lanterns*—he modified this statement to say that his mother "became the first woman to receive a bachelor's degree from the then mewling University of Arkansas."[464]

Regardless of where she stood as an early graduate of the University of Arkansas, Wilson's abiding affection for his mother is clearly and notably displayed in his desire, years later, to have Fayetteville's city park named after her—it is officially Wilson Park.

Wilson had two older siblings. Carl, a half-brother, was a graduate of the University of Arkansas and worked as a schoolteacher and administrator, mostly in Oklahoma, before his untimely death in 1948 at age 52.[465] Kate Wilson Ripley was Charles Morrow's full sister. She also attended the University of Arkansas and majored in music. She

(From Left): Charles Morrow, Kate, Joseph Dickson,
Carl, Mattie Morrow
University of Arkansas Libraries, Special Collections, MS W692

married a local boy, Vincent Ripley, an artist and the son of a University of Arkansas professor, and lived all but the last few years of her life in Fayetteville.[466]

By Wilson's own account, his grandfather, Alfred M. Wilson was a public official for over 50 years and was an attorney for the Cherokee Nation as well as a member of the Governor's Commission that helped Oklahoma eventually gain statehood.[467] Alfred M. was elected to the Arkansas State Legislature in 1848 and in 1852 was appointed "United States District Attorney for the western district of Arkansas," by President Franklin Pierce, a position to which he was reappointed in 1856.[468] He also served as mayor of Fayetteville in 1876-1877.[469]

Charles Morrow Wilson's large extended family included his uncle Robert J. Wilson, A. M. Wilson's eldest son. R. J. Wilson served as city attorney and mayor of Fayetteville and was a state senator for 22 years.[470]

Senator R. J.'s son, Charles Morrow's cousin, Allen M. Wilson, was also a mayor of Fayetteville, serving non-consecutive terms in 1917-

1919 and 1921-1929.[471] After his terms as mayor, Allen M. served as Fayetteville Postmaster from 1934 until his early death in 1942.[472]

Nell Wilson Jones, Charles Morrow's aunt, played a key role in her nephew's life as well, particularly in regard to the sale of Wilson's Pasture to the city of Fayetteville which greatly expanded the west side of city park. Aunt Nell was often involved when Charles Morrow and other family members began to sell off Wilson land in the north part of the city during the mid to late 1940s. Some of the sales were at least partially in response to the increased demand for local housing created by the influx of returning veterans just after the end of World War II.

A highly intelligent young man from a fine, old local family, then, Charles Morrow showed early signs of finding his own way in the world beyond that already bestowed upon him by virtue of the Wilson name. A 1922 graduate of Fayetteville High School, he attended the University of Arkansas where he soon began to make a name for himself as a writer.

By his sophomore year, he was described in the annual *Razorback* yearbook as a "young journalist of note" and was listed among the contributors (as "Chas. Wilson") to the university humor magazine *The White Mule*.[473] The following year, as a junior, he became the Military Editor of the 1925 *Razorback* and Rewrite Editor for the student newspaper *The Arkansas Traveler*.[474]

During that junior year, 1925, he also became a regular visitor at the home of celebrated author Charles J. Finger. Finger, a British world-traveler and adventurer, had settled on land west of Fayetteville late in 1920. From the gentleman farmer's compound he called Gayeta, Finger held literary court and put out a nationally-known, well-respected journal entitled *All's Well*. Recognizing Charles Morrow Wilson's budding writing skills, the "picturesque" Finger[475] took the young college student under his wing.

After graduating from Arkansas in 1926, Wilson soon began working steadily on *All's Well* and by late 1926 he was contributing book reviews to the journal.[476] In March 1927, he was listed as Associate

Charles J. Finger
University of Arkansas Libraries, Special Collections, Loc C1328

Editor and that summer he penned an essay "On Cats," perhaps his first professional publication.[477]

In June 1927 he had added Business Manager to his titles and *All's Well* was actually listed as being owned by both Charles J. Finger and Charles Morrow Wilson. Also in June 1927, Wilson published an article entitled "In the Arkansas Backhills."[478] This early interest in local hillbilly color would stand him in good stead as he tilled this fertile soil repeatedly in his subsequent work.

Later in 1927, he became involved with the first major project of his editorial and literary career. With Finger's help and blessing, Wilson compiled and edited a collection of the elder writer's regional stories. This book was *Ozark Fantasia* and it was published locally under the Golden Horseman Press imprint. Thanks to Charles J. Finger, Charles Morrow Wilson's fledgling literary career was ready to soar.

In March 1928, *All's Well* printed his story "The Reeds Go Forth."[479] This was almost certainly Wilson's first published fiction and seemed to confirm Charles J. Finger's earlier assessment of the young writer's ability. "I'm willing to wager the best five books out of my library...," Finger wrote in the afterglow of the release of *Ozark Fantasia,* "that Wilson is a writer in the making."[480]

Finger's encomium was echoed in the spring of 1928 when Wilson was honored by membership in the New York City Writer's Club[481] and then later that fall when an article in the *Fayetteville Daily Democrat* declared Wilson a "genius."[482]

Yet by May of 1928, he was no longer listed in the *All's Well* masthead, although he was listed as Business Manager at the back of the journal. In the August-September issue he was not listed at all and Finger told his readership that "Charles Wilson has severed his connection with the paper."[483]

The reasons for Wilson's leaving *All's Well* are not clear but during this time, according to his own autobiographical material, he was also working as a "stringer" (on-assignment reporter) for newspapers in both New York City and St. Louis.[484] One of his more prominent newspaper assignments came back in 1927 when the *St. Louis Post-Dispatch* sent him to cover the second Jack Dempsey-Gene Tunney heavyweight championship bout held in Chicago on September 22.[485]

Relocating temporarily to New York City, he had also begun to write articles for national magazines by this time and on October 19, 1928 sold the article "Elizabethan America" to the prestigious *Atlantic Monthly* for the tidy sum, in those days, of one hundred dollars.[486]

In 1929, right about the time his life-long Fayetteville friend J. W. "Bill" Fulbright was returning from an extended period of study abroad, Wilson made his own trip overseas. He left in late April for

England where he hoped to study history at Oxford University and observe local rural life in order to write about it for American magazines like *Outlook*. In these heady days, he was virtually exploding upon the journal and magazine scene in the United States, publishing almost everything he wrote in such disparate publications as the *North American Review, New Republic,* and *American Druggist*.[487]

Unfortunately, shortly after he arrived in England he developed appendicitis and had to undergo an emergency appendectomy in a British hospital. Recovering and studying in Winchcombe, Gloucestershire, however, he optimistically wrote home to his mother that "from now on I will enjoy health of a sort which I had never so much as conceived of before."[488]

His restored health also buoyed his youthful hopes and enthusiasm for his chosen profession. "I am going to continue to win at writing," he proclaimed in the same letter, and "I am going to find life interesting and beautiful wherever I may come upon it."[489] Returning to the United States in late August 1929, Wilson returned briefly to Fayetteville then moved back to New York to permanently pursue his literary career.

Despite the Stock Market crash in September 1929 and the subsequent and severe economic downturn of the Great Depression, the decade of the 1930s saw Charles Morrow Wilson rise rapidly as a writer. From 1930 to 1940, he published nine books and innumerable articles and short stories.

His first novel, *Acres of Sky,* an Arkansas backwoods story later to be made into the aforementioned play at the University of Arkansas, was published by Putnam in 1930. *Meriwether Lewis of Lewis and Clark,* a biography of the celebrated explorer, and *Backwoods America*, again mining the cultural ore of rustic America, both appeared in 1934. *Money at the Crossroads,* an early foray into politics and economics, and *Country Living: Plus and Minus,* which was more homespun material, were published in 1937 and 1938, respectively.

His shorter works continued to pile up as well, as he was steadily published in most of the prominent journals of the age such as the *American Spectator, Atlantic Monthly, Saturday Evening Post,* among many others. These article and story sales provided Wilson with a decent flow of income in an era of generally rough financial times. He was paid as much as $400 for an article in the big eastern journals[490]—very good money when average workers were lucky to make one dollar a day doing physical labor.

During the 1930s, he maintained correspondence with a number of well-known people. In addition to his ongoing correspondence with J. W. Fulbright, who would later rapidly move up the national political ladder, he interviewed famous automobile entrepreneur Henry Ford,[491] and his editor at John Day Co. Publishers in 1934 was none other than Pearl Buck, then at the peak of her fame and success.[492]

Another famous acquaintance of his was Theodore Dreiser, the celebrated author of *Sister Carrie* and *An American Tragedy,* masterpieces of early twentieth century American literary naturalism. Dreiser sought out young Wilson as a possible contributor to the novelist's journal *American Spectator.*[493] The two men dined together occasionally in New York, often enough for Wilson to offer an evaluation of the noted novelist. Dreiser was "a likeable old cuss," he wrote to his mother about the great writer, and "in many ways an extremely fine man."[494]

In the mid-1930s, Wilson began working as a publicist for the United Fruit Company and traveled widely as part of his work for the giant banana corporation. He made trips to Cuba, Jamaica, Mexico, and to most of the countries of Central America including Guatemala, Honduras and Costa Rica.

By the late 1930s, he had settled down to a life as noted author and gentleman farmer in Putney, Vermont. In November 1938, he and his wife, professional photographer Iris Woolcock, divorced (they had married in 1935). Remaining on good terms with his ex-wife, Wilson actually purchased his own farm site on land adjacent to where he and Woolcock had lived in the last years of their marriage.

The following year, 1939, he married Martha Starr, daughter of *Northwest Arkansas Times* writer Fred Starr.[495] The Wilson-Starr union produced three boys: Charles Morrow, Jr. (b. 1940), James S. (b. 1941), and J. Mathew (b. 1945).

Iris Woolcock
University of Arkansas Libraries, Special Collections

When the 1940s rolled around, then, Charles Morrow Wilson was firmly established as a writer of note, especially so in New York City, the hub of book and magazine publishing. He knew and had interviewed famous people, was well known by key magazine and book editors, and had continued to pour out articles and books—he averaged about one book a year throughout his long career.

In the summer of 1941, United Fruit asked him to help create the Middle America Information Bureau, a publicity arm, or "bona fide information service" as he deemed it, of the multi-national fruit company.[496] As part of his work, he helped write the Middle America Charter, a document meant to reassure Central American and Caribbean nations of United Fruit's good intentions.

The "paramount goal" of "Pan-American relations" and of United Fruit, the document made clear, was "Inter-American brotherhood" and the "unity of ideals and attainments."[497] Despite United Fruit's creation of hospitals and schools in the banana producing countries, they had had a history of difficult labor relations, including numerous work stoppages.

One of the Middle America Charter's main points was to assure farm workers that United Fruit was not and would "never be in the market for 'coolie' labor."[498] The document also tried to calm jittery and unstable countries in the region by asserting that the company recognized and respected the "just sovereignty of all Middle American governments."[499]

Wilson's work with United Fruit provided the base material for a spate of articles and books and during the first half of the 1940s he would write several books on tropics-related subjects.

Ambassadors in White, a study of several physicians who devoted themselves to tropical medicine, including William Gorgas, Carlos Finley and Walter Reed, came out in 1942 and was one of Wilson's best-selling and highly regarded works. *Challenge and Opportunity: Central America* was published the following year and *Middle America,* a product of his through United Fruit's Middle America Information Bureau, was released in 1944.

Even though Wilson's ever growing success and reputation as an author was a product of his life and contacts in the east and although he continued to maintain his home there in Putney, Vermont, he still visited Fayetteville when he could. As far back as the summer of 1937 he had told his father that he "looked forward to getting home" and was "now working out my life and work so that henceforth I can spend a great deal more time at home."[500]

In early October 1944, with the outcome of World War II swinging steadily towards an Allied victory, Wilson—now out of a short stint in the military (by his own account "brief and undistinguished")[501] and working again in New York City—wrote Mrs. Roberta Fulbright, owner-publisher of the *Northwest Arkansas Times* and mother of soon-to-be U. S. Senator J. W. Fulbright, concerning their shared interest in improving the quality of life in Fayetteville.

Agreeing "wholeheartedly" with Mrs. Fulbright, Wilson said that he felt that an "effort to establish a museum, a park, a really good library and perhaps other so-called cultural institutions is particularly in order at this time.[502] His pursuit of one of these goals—giving Fayetteville the type of park he envisioned it would want—would be a long and arduous one, full of pitfalls and conflicts, but the first step nonetheless in the writer's eventual—if short-lived—return to his hometown.

Less than three weeks later, on October 31, 1944, he again wrote the first lady of Fayetteville journalism to tell her that he had taken out an option from his aunt Nell Wilson Jones for the nearly seventeen acres of land adjoining city park known then as Wilson's Pasture.[503]

He suggested that while the Fayetteville city council debated whether to buy city park from the City Park Company (headed by Dr. Noah Drake of Drake Field airport fame),[504] his purchase of Wilson's Pasture might be "a way to start this park program."[505] The implication was that he would sell the adjoining family property to the city, thereby greatly expanding the current municipal park.

In early January 1945, he wrote his sister Kate that he had "taken steps" to purchase Wilson's Pasture from his Aunt Nell for $8,500.[506] That same day he wrote his Fayetteville attorney, Suzanne "Peggy" Chalfant Lighton, to write a $2,500 check for the down payment on the land and listed the per acre cost of the land at $500.[507]

Mrs. Fulbright, getting wind of the potential sale, mildly prompted him in a letter dated February 26, 1945. "My dear Charlie," she wrote pleasantly, "I keep wondering if you aren't itching to present us a 'Wilson Park." Towards the end of the letter, her tone became more sober: "Seriously," she added, "if you want to give or sell? that park area, let us know."[508]

In late March, Wilson and Fayetteville Mayor George T. Sanders exchanged letters concerning the possible sale of Wilson's Pasture to the city. He told the mayor that, despite his "deep personal affection" for the seventeen acres and the city's "disappointing" record in park maintenance, he would still be "glad to help the city…without any view of profit to myself."[509]

By summer time, Wilson and the city were ready to deal. On July 3, 1945 the *Times* reported his proposal to the city council in which he would sell the sixteen and seven-eighths acres of Wilson's Pasture to Fayetteville, thereby nearly tripling the size of city park. He wanted the new, vastly larger park to be known as Mattie Morrow Wilson Memorial Park, in honor of his mother.

The selling price for the land would be $22,500 (better than $1,300 an acre) but he planned to donate $7,000 to the city as a gift. The selling price to the city would then be $15,500 (a little over $900 per acre). On August 15, 1945 the city council approved the purchase and the next day the sale contract was signed.[510]

Wilson envisioned the new park as a "beautiful and valuable"[511] place for local residents to enjoy an undeveloped natural site in the heart of Fayetteville. Yet, only four days after the contract was signed with the city, Mayor Sanders opened up the entire park, newly acquired Wilson's Pasture and all, as a trailer camp for returning World War II veterans.[512]

Even after signing the contract, Wilson had reservations about the sale of his family's pasture to the city. In a letter to his sister Kate in December of 1945, he wrote that his mind was "pretty definitely made up not to deal with the city of Fayetteville in terms of a park." He was not sure that public interest in the city park expansion was more than "lukewarm."[513]

Despite the lingering concerns on Wilson's part, the sale officially went through on August 21, 1946.[514] Fayetteville City Park was officially and finally the size that it still is today. And it is so thanks to Charles Morrow Wilson.

Like many situations in his life, however, the conclusion of the park sale didn't bring the matter to a close. In March 1948, a local group (including his lawyer "Peggie" Lighton) tried to purchase part of city park to build a Boy's Club. During the following months, opposition to the Boy's Club plan grew and late in the year Wilson himself entered the fray.

In letters to the *Times* printed December 23 and 29, 1948, he called the proposed plan a "sly sharper's trick" and a violation of the "gentleman's agreement" he had made with the city when he sold them Wilson's Pasture. The land purchased by the city, he maintained, was to be "used as a wooded park."

The controversy continued into 1949, even bringing Mrs. Fulbright to editorialize that while she supported the idea of a Boy's Club for the youth of Fayetteville, her respect for Charles Morrow Wilson and his family led her to think the park was not "adequate for anything more than a park."[515] For his part, Wilson offered to end the controversy by buying the Wilson's Pasture land back.[516]

Arguments continued on both sides of the issue until November 3, 1950 when Fayetteville Mayor M. Powell Rhea (he succeeded George T. Sanders in 1949) wrote Wilson to let him know that the idea of a Boy's Club using part of city park "has been well erased from the public's mind."[517]

The new mayor wished to ease Wilson's concern about how the park was being used as well. As noted earlier, Rhea's predecessor, George T. Sanders, had allowed city park, including the land "donated" by Wilson, to be used as a trailer camp for university student housing. Rhea assured Wilson that this practice would be eliminated and that "everything now is towards getting rid of the trailers ... not later than June, 1951."[518]

At about the same time he was involved in the different controversies surrounding his city park "gift," Wilson also was actively engaged in two projects that would enhance his international reputation and, in one case, create a bit more controversy as well.

The somewhat controversial project was an archaeological mission to Mexico sponsored by United Fruit and the Carnegie Institute. This

National Geographic
Ellen Compton

mission was to the Mayan ruins at Bonampak in the jungles of Chiapas, a Mexican state bordering Guatemala.

Early in 1946, adventurer-photographer Giles Greville Healy was led by a Lacandone Indian, descendants of the Mayans, to the ruins of an ancient temple near their village. What Healy was shown inside the temple were the remains of murals painted some 1200 years earlier. The murals were doubly significant: first, they revealed a level of Mayan artistic skill not yet suspected at the time; and second, they provided a window to the Mayan peoples and their highly evolved but nearly forgotten culture.[519]

Later commentators remarked that the find at Bonampak "shattered illusions that the Maya were a totally peaceful people and shed light on the sophistication of their arts, culture, and economy."[520]

From his office at the Middle America Information Bureau in New York City, Wilson supervised (he referred to himself as "General Manager and Coordinator")[521] the exploration of Bonampak and the documentary that was to be made from Healey's film of the adventure. Wilson wrote several articles about the expedition and also worked closely in producing the film. Herein lay the source of the controversy.

In early articles like "Backwards a Dozen Centuries"[522] and "Bonampak,"[523] Wilson gave credit to Healey but in later pieces such as "Nature's Own Children"[524] he wrote as if it had been he who had lived among the Lacandone Indians and not Healey. As work on the documentary film about the Maya stretched into 1947, a rift developed between writer and adventurer.

"I am fully aware of the value of this Lacandone work," Wilson wrote noted Hollywood producer Kenneth MacGowan, "but I have frankly been somewhat peeved by Giles' reiteration that ... he was in the jungle bleeding for me." He added that he had been "in the jungles of New York City doing considerable suffering for him (Healey) ... and by suffering I mean heavy specific financial sacrifices." He did allow that Healey, like he himself in earlier trips to the tropics for United Fruit, had "repeatedly ... risked life and health."[525]

The feud with Healey grew to the point that on September 4, 1947, Wilson wrote MacGowan to complain that Healey was acting like "a very spoiled brat." More seriously, he told the Hollywood executive that Healey had accused him of having "hyphenated my name with the project," a charge Wilson vehemently denied.[526]

"I am getting awfully annoyed at all the friction between you and Giles," MacGowan responded to Wilson's letter of September 4. As for article credits relating to the Bonampak-Lacandone expedition, he wondered why Wilson couldn't "recast a few sentences" from third to first person and put "Giles' name on it?" Or better: "leave it alone and use the byline" by "Giles Greville Healey, as told to Charles Morrow Wilson." However it could be done, MacGowan wanted the problem resolved because he was "getting sick to death of the tediousness of trying to keep you and Giles in the same stable."[527]

After MacGowan's dressing down, Wilson was conciliatory. He made it clear that he wanted Healey "to get the money" from a proposed article for *National Geographic* just as Wilson had for "Backwards a Dozen Centuries," an article published in *Natural History*.[528]

With the feud under control, *Maya Through the Ages* was finally completed and released in 1949. It was the last film Kenneth MacGowan ever made. Choosing the perhaps less contentious world of academia, he left Hollywood in order to "found the first theatre and film school at UCLA."[529]

In addition to the Mayan project and his other work with United Fruit, in the mid-1940s Wilson was hired by Firestone Plantations Company to travel to the African nations of Liberia—where in 1946 he was appointed Special Consultant to President William S. Tubman, [530]and Equatorial West Africa.

Firestone Plantations, a part of automobile tire magnate Harvey Firestone's economic empire, was involved in the production of rubber for the United States war effort. Wilson's work for Firestone was primarily in, as he described it, the field of "subsistence farming,"[531] concerned with producing crops to feed native workers.

Still, as he always did, Wilson managed to harvest enough material to produce books and articles based on his experiences. In 1943, he published *Trees and Test Tubes: The Story of Rubber,* a history of Charles Goodyear and the production of rubber around the world. The book featured photographs by his ex-wife Iris Woolcock.

In 1945, he pursued his new and ongoing interest in food and farming with the publication of *New Crops for the New World. Liberia,* based on his African work, was published in 1947.

In that same year, with twenty books and dozens of articles and stories to his credit, Wilson's national and international success was recognized by his alma mater. On June 9, 1947, the University of Arkansas presented him with one of its highest honors: the Distinguished Alumni Citation. Wilson was cited in particular for his tropical medicine work in nations like Liberia and for his involvement in the agriculture of Central American nations such as Honduras.[532]

At the beginning of the 1950s, then, Charles Morrow Wilson was being tugged back toward Fayetteville, his hometown. He had sold the city his family's land to treble the size of its city park. He had become a renowned author with ties around the globe. He had come home to receive the Distinguished Alumni award at the University of Arkansas, from which he had graduated in 1926. What more could happen to make the homeward tug even stronger? The answer was given in the first year of the new decade.

That year, 1950, the University of Arkansas planned to open a brand new Fine Arts Center designed by architect Edward Durell Stone of New York City, who was himself a native of Fayetteville[533] and had for a while attended the University of Arkansas. The center consisted of three interconnected structures: a classroom and studio building, a music recital hall, and a theatre. University officials were looking for a special program to celebrate the grand opening of the center and they chose a musical, dramatic adaptation of Wilson's book *Acres of Sky* as the opening show.[534]

Material from *Acres of Sky*, his first published novel, and from *Rabble Rouser*, also fiction and making use of historical material from the life of Arkansas and Fayetteville legend Archibald Yell, was combined to make an Ozarks "song-dance show."[535]

The university agreed to pay up to $8,000 dollars towards the total cost of the production.[536] With finances settled and Virgil L. Baker, head of the Arkansas Department of Speech and Dramatic Art, serving as his liaison, Wilson hired New York City friends Arthur Kreutz and Zoe Schiller to provide words and music for the play. By summer 1950, the production was on.

Throughout the fall, excited preparations continued as Wilson, Kreutz and Schiller (the musical couple would later marry) came to Fayetteville to direct the play. After selecting actors, mostly locals from the University of Arkansas, and completing other pre-production tasks, *Acres of Sky* was scheduled to open Thursday night, November 16, 1950.

Two nights before the opening, Mrs. Fulbright and her former longtime *Fayetteville Daily Democrat/Northwest Arkansas Times* Editor Lessie Stringfellow Read held a dinner at the Washington Hotel on the Fayetteville Square honoring Wilson and the other prime movers of the play.[537]

On the day of the opening, the paper listed a number of out of town guests arriving in Fayetteville for the play. Among these were Governor and Mrs. Sid McMath, E. S. Whitman of United Fruit, Edmond Burks of Firestone, and George Freedley, theatre writer for the New York City Public Library.

"Critics Praise Production," the Friday, November 17 *Times* heralded its opinion of the premiere of *Acres of Sky.* The music was deemed to be "a clever combination of folk tunes" arranged using "contemporary harmonic devices."

Mrs. Fulbright, in the same issue, was more effusive. "We are now in the stream to produce," she enthused, "great products, great actors and actresses, drama and song artists and dancers." She concluded that Edward Durell Stone and Charles Morrow Wilson "should be pensioned and treated like royalty."[538]

With such praise, *Acres of Sky,* easily and successfully completed its schedule of ten performances at the university. The final show was presented Sunday afternoon, November 26, 1950.[539]

In the afterglow of the reception given *Acres of Sky,* with the Distinguished Alumni award from the University of Arkansas evidence of his acclaim as an author and the "gift" of his family pasture greatly expanding Fayetteville's city park, it is no wonder Wilson believed the time was right to come back home.

The next spring, 1951, he published his somewhat qualified encomium of Fayetteville in the journal *Tomorrow.* Yet, the article also

Acres of Sky
Fayetteville Public Library

included occasionally enthusiastic descriptions of the reasons for his return: "We," he wrote, "my wife and I and our three young sons–are going home to work and live."[540]

While conceding that life growing up in Fayetteville wasn't always perfect—"I learned not to expect to be spoken to by the self-indicated 'better people'" Wilson wrote[541]—he concluded his article with a highly optimistic tone. "We feel and believe," he said, "that our home town stands for springtime, robust, sensitive, self-perpetuating, with bird songs, south winds, brave new leaves and invincible hope."[542]

Given his status and all that had happened of late, he was certain he would be well received upon returning to Fayetteville. He even quoted Mrs. Fulbright as saying he would be "welcomed with open arms."[543]

In June 1951, while still retaining his farm in Vermont, Wilson purchased a farm off Highway 45, east of Fayetteville. He and his wife settled in with the reasonable hope of making the farm a success, raising their three sons in a positive environment, and reentering local society. It didn't take long for reality to alter that hope.

Back in Vermont and especially when he was in New York City, he had become accustomed to having something of a social life. The previously mentioned dinners with Theodore Dreiser, get togethers with his friends Arthur Kreutz and Zoe Schiller, as well as other engagements enriched his and his family's eastern experience. In this regard, Fayetteville severely disappointed.

"We asked people whom we hoped were our friends out to our place," he wrote, and "gave party after party which were never reciprocated." Those friends, he bemoaned, "did not phone and did not call."[544] Yet, as will be shown, part of the reason for the lack of a social life in Fayetteville may have been his own penchant for feuding, both with foe and friend alike.

In June 1950, a year before purchasing the farm outside Fayetteville and while he was preparing for the staging of *Acres of Sky*, Wilson became convinced that he had been offered a teaching job in the English Department at the University of Arkansas.

Feeling that he could "be of tremendous service to Arkansas," he wrote that he had told Howard Carter, Chairman of the English Department, he would "make every effort to join the university faculty starting in the fall of 1951."[545] The only problem was that no one from the University of Arkansas had officially offered him this faculty position. What ensued was a vitriolic three-year conflict with the university.

In letters to Herbert L. Thomas, a member of the University of Arkansas Board of Regents, Wilson insisted that back in 1950 he had been invited to join the faculty by none other than Chairman Carter. When this position was not forthcoming during his relocation to Fayetteville, Wilson later wrote that a contract between himself and the university had been "wilfully (sic) violated"—although he admitted the position was just "part-time." The contract, he said, had been "lied and skunked out of" by no less a personage than former University of Arkansas President Lewis Webster Jones.[546]

Jones' replacement as president of the university, John Tyler Caldwell was besieged by angry letters from Wilson as well, which rehashed the writer's claim on the faculty job. Wilson informed Caldwell that the "welched" out of agreement had done "very serious injury … to my family, my professional integrity, my financial facilities, and my … works in behalf of the University of Arkansas."[547]

After several more exchanges of a similar nature, Dr. Caldwell had had enough of the topic and told Wilson that you "will properly drop the whole matter."[548] When Wilson continued to write him about the presumed faculty job offer, Caldwell finally excused himself from the argument by simply saying "I bow out."[549]

While the flap over the University of Arkansas teaching job was going on, other incidents occurred that supported Wilson's feeling that he and his family were not only being left out of local society but were openly being ostracized, even outright attacked. He felt obliged to defend himself on two separate fronts.

For one, some people in town had from the beginning accused him of making a profit on the Wilson's Pasture deal with the city. He was also accused of using this sale as an income tax dodge. Naturally, he strongly defended himself in letters to prominent Fayetteville citizens.

He maintained flatly, for example, that his reduction of $7,000 from the selling price of Wilson's Pasture was "the largest donation ever made in Fayetteville civic history."[552] He did acknowledge that

Dr. Noah Drake, who gave $3,500 in 1929 for the creation of the Fayetteville Airport that would later bear his name, had also made a large gift to the city.[553]

He was also quick to point out that he could have sold Wilson's Pasture for "approximately $22,000, more than the amount paid by the City" for the land. He also labeled the income tax evasion accusation as "absolutely false and eminently libelous."[554]

During this time, he also had a falling out with influential Professor Walter Lemke, head of the University of Arkansas Department[555] of Journalism, who had been an early friend and booster of Wilson in the young man's formative stage as an author. Wilson now claimed that "for years" Lemke had been the perpetrator of "the completely untruthful and completely vicious gossip" that most of his books and articles had been "subsidized or ... bribed by ...Interests,"[556] meaning his employers like United Fruit and Firestone.

Addressing a letter to his old friend as *"Herr* Lemke," he directly accused the professor of lying. Wilson insisted that he held "in hand" *bona fide* contracts for all twenty-three of his books and demanded that Lemke "issue in writing an apology and explanation of your conduct as performed behind the figurative breastworks of the University of Arkansas."[557]

Worse than his own treatment, he also accused Lemke of having the "unpardonable insolence" to insult Mrs. Wilson "in an University office" when she had tried "in good faith and kindness to intervene and seek to re-establish pleasant relations" between the feuding men.[558]

As for his boys, he later wrote that they had been "cruelly snobbed, insulted and snotted on."[559] The youngsters had been "grievously hurt" when they instead should have had every "right to grow up in my homeland without being so victimized."[560]

With things deteriorating rapidly in Fayetteville—his attempt at farming had even failed, primarily due to an extended drought that hit the region during the early 1950s—he was already considering moving back to Vermont by December 1952.[561] The following March he wrote that "1953 is my final year in home pastures."[562] By July 21, 1953 he was back in Putney temporarily, although he made it clear that it was where "I shall presently return to live."[563]

Even though it hadn't taken him long to decide that coming home was a mistake he had to correct, he didn't let that stand in the way of his writing productivity while he was living in Fayetteville. He was out of town frequently, mostly going back to New York City or traveling down to New Orleans to interview Samuel Zemurray, the former president of United Fruit, about whom he was writing a biography.

Early in 1952, his play *Acres of Sky* was again performed. This time it was produced in New York City at the Brander Mathews Theatre as part of the American Music Festival at Columbia University. Wilson had always harbored hopes his play would make it on Broadway and after the Columbia performances, there was also some talk of *Acres* being produced in Paris.[565] Neither scenario came to pass; however, and eventually interest in the play died out.

He did get two books published during his short stay in Fayetteville. *The Tropics: World of Tomorrow*, one of his more forgettable efforts, was published by Harper in 1951. His juvenile (young reader) book *Butterscotch and the Happy Barnyard* came out from Caxton in 1953, although it appears to have been a "subsidy" published work.[566] He also continued magazine work, placing articles in such diverse journals as *Science Digest, Nature Magazine, Think* and *Progressive Farmer.*

By mid-summer 1954, Wilson had had enough of his old hometown and he and his family returned to their farm in Putney, Vermont. Early in January 1955, he sold his Fayetteville farm and the prodigal son permanently removed himself from his ancestral home.

In a letter, he once described himself as "a notorious sourpuss and conservative."[567] Based on the tone of much of his personal correspondence through the years, that is putting it mildly. In fact, as shown earlier, he could be plainly vitriolic and vengeful—excessively so, even when he had a legitimate gripe. Frequently, his was a "caustic and demanding personality."[568]

He also tended to hold on to grudges, slights, and disagreements for a long time. Thus, he was still fretting about the contentious sale and renaming of Wilson Park, the phantom University of Arkansas faculty position, and the treatment of his family upon their return to Fayetteville many years after these events were long past.

Nowhere in his correspondence is he so fierce in his condemnation of Fayetteville than in a late December, 1954 letter to Lessie Stringfellow Read. In this letter, Wilson condenses all the anger he felt towards his hometown and its less than welcoming response to his return.

"At fifty," he wrote, "I am trying to start again in authorship and recover from the nastiness and viciousness of Fayetteville, Arkansas." Despite Mrs. Fulbright's belief that he and his family would be "welcomed with open arms," they were "not welcomed at all." The Wilsons endured "the snobbing and nastiness and stenches for three years" and they "lost terribly by trying to come home" where they were "thoroughly and despicably betrayed." Fayetteville, he concluded, would be better off if it changed its name to "Nastyville."[569]

In Wilson's defense concerning these feuds, it needs to be said that he suffered from considerable health issues, lung problems and diabetes in particular, which no doubt contributed to his "cranky" personality. His wife Martha also had health problems from time to time and this added stress to the already stressful world of the free-lance writer. Oftentimes he *did* have legitimate points of conflict with colleagues and others in his feuds—such as the use of Wilson's Pasture for student trailer housing. Moreover, as a man, he seems to have been a truly caring husband and a protective father.

Personal conflicts and arguments aside, it must be remembered that Charles Morrow Wilson was a highly successful, nationally and internationally respected author. And although his work never quite made the big leap to Broadway, Paris or Hollywood, as he hoped it would, many of his books are quite good and still well worth the trouble to find and read today.

In addition to the aforementioned *Ambassadors in White,* which presents biographies of several famous medical men devoted to tropical medicine, his history of the banana industry in *Empires in Green and Gold* is particularly interesting and well done. This book showcases

Charles Morrow Wilson, 1960
University of Arkansas Libraries Special Collections, MS W692

his ability to blend information from multiple sources into a readable, cohesive whole.

For local color, there are *The Bodacious Ozarks: True Tales of the Backwoods* and *Stars Is God's Lanterns*. Both books provide a wealth of Arkansas back country stories. Wilson also wrote biographies, notably *Meriwether Lewis of Lewis and Clark, Rudolph Diesel: Pioneer of the Age of Power*, and *The Commoner: William Jennings Bryan*.

Beginning with *Ginger Blue* in 1940, he published several juvenile books as well. Other titles in this genre were: *The Great Turkey*

Drive, Dow Baker and the Great Banana Fleet, and *Butterscotch and the Happy Barnyard.*

In addition to the large number of books, stories and articles he wrote, Wilson's work, including large amounts of his correspondence and other professional and private material, has been collected in three library holdings in various locations around the country. The most extensive collection is in the Special Collections Department at the University of Arkansas. The University of Vermont in Burlington and the University of Oregon Library in Eugene, Oregon also have Charles Morrow Wilson Collections.

In the end, all personal feuds and enmity aside, Charles Morrow Wilson was a prolific author of great skill, able to rapidly marshal vast and disparate sources of information into coherent, readable prose. He was a tireless worker and like many successful writers always looking for a follow-up project, always moving on to the next assignment. When it was all said and done he left behind an enormous writing legacy.

Even though much of his work was topical and hasn't perhaps aged well, it's unfortunate that an author of his once considerable stature is hardly remembered today in the town where he was born and raised. He may have grown up in Fayetteville and he may have developed his genius for writing here as well, but in the end he simply could not come back home to live. Perhaps he had changed too much after all those decades in the east and maybe Fayetteville had changed a lot, too.

In either case, the title of famed southern writer Thomas Wolfe's groundbreaking 1940 novel *You Can't Go Home Again* provides an appropriately pithy aphorism for the case of Charles Morrow Wilson and his failed return to Fayetteville. He, like many another small town success, found that after too many miles and too many years away, you really can't go home again.

On Tuesday, March 1, 1977, Charles Morrow Wilson died in Putney, Vermont at age 71. The child prodigy, the youthful genius, the man of conflict and ambition was gone—gone a long way from home.

A MOST UNUSUAL
SHOOTING

IN THE MID-1950s, the house at 350 South Combs Street (now Avenue) where my family lived—it was razed long ago and the area is now part of the Church of Christ parking lot—was at the far southern end of what was at the time an unremarkable dirt road. The Craftsman-style wood house faced north and had small yards on the sides and back that were bounded by a large, fenced-in, L-shaped field leased by Otis Parker, well-known horseman and one of Fayetteville's most respected black citizens.

For low-income people—my mother Phydella Hogan raised four children as a single, working woman—who had almost no public profile in the small town Fayetteville of those days, my family nonetheless had a close connection to several remarkable local events that occurred during that time. One of the most unusual was the case of Charles Friddle, a man who visited our home on Combs Street and who later would be involved in surely one of the most unusual shootings to ever take place in Fayetteville.

Friddle was a thin-faced, balding man and I recall him coming to our house to visit Bertha Terry, our great-aunt. Aunt Bertha, as we called her, was our Uncle Bob Fultz' mother, and she was popular with men, especially single or divorced ones like Charles Friddle.

Aunt Bertha had come into town from my uncle's farm in Mayfield to make a better living than she could out in the country. Although she was not a particularly handsome woman, she had a winning personality and always had gentleman callers and suitors. Friddle was one of them.

Charles Friddle
Fayetteville Public Library

Not more than a year from the time Friddle had sat quietly visiting Aunt Bertha in our family living room on Combs Street, on Sunday morning, December 4, 1955, he took a .22 caliber pistol from his home on Wood Street in southeast Fayetteville, not far from where we lived, and walked uptown to the Bus Station on College Avenue. By chance or design, he saw Yellow Cab dispatcher Chester Goss in the station's café.

Following Goss and a friend out of the café, Friddle tailed them to the corner of Dickson Street and College Avenue where they parted and Goss crossed the street to go home. Suddenly and inexplicably, Friddle shot and mortally wounded the unsuspecting taxi man. The reasons behind this terrible event were as peculiar as they were deadly.

For Goss, the morning had started normally enough. After finishing his night shift at Yellow Cab, located then just below the Square at 44 N. Block Street, he walked the short distance to the Bus Station. At that time it was situated on the northwest corner of Meadow and College. The station's café was one of the few places in town that a man could get a cup of coffee early on a Sunday morning.

Goss met his friend Ed Wilcox at the café where the two men had a casual chat while enjoying their coffee. Neither of them could have suspected that within a half hour Goss would lie on a Fayetteville sidewalk, mortally wounded.

The only hint of potential trouble, though it was not recognized as such by either Goss or Wilcox at the time, was that Charles Friddle came into the café while the men were having their coffee. Friddle did nothing in particular to draw attention to himself and as Goss would describe later, the soon to be assailant simply made a "pass through the restaurant."

According to accounts in the *Northwest Arkansas Times*, a little before nine-thirty, Goss and Wilcox paid for their coffee and left the Bus Station café. Outside, they turned left, walking north on the sidewalk beside busy College Avenue. College was particularly busy at this time of day on Sundays as local worshipers arrived in droves to attend one of three churches in the near vicinity of College and Dickson. Apparently unaware that Friddle was now walking on the sidewalk behind them, Goss and Wilcox made their way up to the corner.

At the southwest corner of the intersection in front of Maeder's Lion Service Station (in later years the longtime location of Jerry's Restaurant), the two men parted company. Wilcox headed west down Dickson, while Goss waited for a chance to cross the intersection to the east. The dispatcher, a bachelor, lived a short distance away, at 229 E. Dickson Street, with his mother.

Having just completed a night shift, the fifty-six year old man was surely looking forward to getting some rest. There was still no indication that he knew Friddle had been stalking him and that the sixty-six year old "unemployed restaurant worker" was close behind, a .22 caliber revolver in hand.

Right at 9:30 a.m., with church services imminent, Friddle raised the revolver and fired one shot, hitting Goss square in the back. Due to the noise of automobile traffic, witnesses did not seem to hear the report of the small caliber weapon. Across the street from Friddle, however, Goss fell in a heap just as his foot touched the other sidewalk. As he dropped, he looked back to see Friddle across the street "with a smoking pistol in his hand."

Church-goers at the First Baptist Church, diagonally across College from where Goss fell, thought the cab dispatcher must have taken ill, perhaps had a heart attack. Rushing to the injured man's side, the witnesses quickly ascertained the real nature of the man's wounds and

Bloody Corner Today
J.B. Hogan

called police. While attention was thus centered on the stricken man, Friddle calmly walked away—heading west, towards the nearby home of his divorced wife.

Within minutes, the fallen Goss was whisked away from the scene and, as a veteran of World War I, taken to the Veterans Administration Hospital on North College. Doctors there soon realized the gravity of his wound. Even though the respected member of the Veterans of Foreign Wars and American Legion had been shot with a light caliber pistol, the bullet had been more destructive than might have been expected.

The .22 round that entered his back, the doctors discovered, had damaged his spinal column before coming to rest lodged in his abdomen. As a result of the spinal injury, he was, at least temporarily, paralyzed from the waist down. Additionally, the taxi dispatcher suffered a collapsed lung and other unspecified "internal injuries."

Back in town, just moments after the shooting, Friddle arrived at the nearby home of his ex-wife, Mrs. Mabel Villines, a cook at the University of Arkansas, and their two daughters. Friddle had one of his daughters, Miss Thelma Friddle, a 1953 graduate of Fayetteville High School and a clerk at the Scott Five and Ten Cent Store on the East Side of the Square, call a cab for him and shocked the young woman by telling her that he had "just shot a man."

Miss Friddle tried to get a Checker Cab for her father but when the line was busy she called for a Yellow Cab. In one of the extreme ironies of the case, Friddle was driven home—to the house he shared on Wood Street with a man named Bill Gibson—in a cab owned by the company that employed the man he had shot down not a quarter of an hour before. When he left his ex-wife's house, Mrs. Villines reported his behavior and conversation to the police.

By 9:45 a.m, the *Times* reported, Friddle was back home where, to Gibson, he appeared agitated and confessed for the second time in a quarter of an hour that he had "just shot a man." He also took the extraordinary measure of warning Gibson "not to be nervous" if the police arrived. At this time, Friddle apparently hid the discharged pistol beneath the mattress of his own bed.

For the next few hours, while VA doctors treated the gunshot victim, Friddle kept out of sight. But around one p.m., Washington County Sheriff Bruce Crider, accompanied by unnamed deputies and members of the Fayetteville Police Department, descended upon the Gibson-Friddle residence at, in those days, the edge of town.

Sheriff Crider found both men at home and after a search of the house discovered a .recently fired .22 caliber revolver, with one round missing from its cylinder, under the suspect's bed. Friddle offered no resistance when Sheriff Crider put him under arrest but denied shooting Goss. The authorities took a signed statement from Gibson at this time and then booked Friddle into jail.

Later in the afternoon, Sheriff Crider and Police Chief Pearl Watts went to the VA Hospital where they interviewed Chester Goss. At that time, the severely wounded man identified Friddle as his assailant, indicating that he knew him only by sight, but was unable to think of any logical reason for the attack.

The December 5, 1955 issue of the *Times* reported two significant events in the case. In the afternoon, Deputy Prosecutor Leonard Greenhaw filed a charge of assault with intent to kill in circuit court against Friddle. Earlier, the paper noted, doctors at the VA Hospital had operated on Goss to both repair his gunshot wound and to relieve the pressure on his spinal column which was believed to be the cause of his paralysis. After the surgery, he was said to be "showing continued improvement."

The following day, the *Times* reported that Friddle still denied shooting Goss but nonetheless told Sheriff Crider and Deputy Prosecutor Greenhaw that he "would have shot Goss five years ago" if he'd been able to obtain a permit to carry a pistol. The *Times* noted that at the time Arkansas had "no law relative to pistol permits."

Sheriff Crider added that, despite the continued denial of wrongdoing, Friddle gave what amounted to his motive for doing so. While indicating, as Goss had before, that he knew the victim "only by sight," Friddle explained that people had been "shooting holes in his house" with "television rays." He apparently believed, Crider noted, that Goss was the head of a "gang" shooting these rays at him.

Sheriff Bruce Crider
Washington County Sheriff's Office

Two days after Friddle's conversation with authorities, on Thursday, December 8, 1955, his defense attorney, John W. Murphy, entered a plea of not guilty by reason of insanity. Circuit Court Judge Maupin Cummings accepted the plea and after briefly questioning Friddle set his bond at $5,000. The judge also tentatively set a trial date for January 17, 1956, and ordered Friddle sent to the "state Mental Hospital at Little Rock" for a thirty-day period of observation.

One can only imagine how Friddle's comments were received at the time. His reasons for the shooting seem oddly contemporary, though the

Murder Charge Filed Against Charles Friddle

Count Issued After Chester Lee Goss Dies At VA Hospital

Friddle Murder Charge
Fayetteville Public Library

events occurred over sixty years ago. They do so because the crime, as was pointed out at the time, made no sense whatsoever. It was not done for revenge, nor passion. It wasn't even committed for economic gain. While subsequent evaluations would label Friddle insane, his long ago crime has a strange, surreal quality of dissociation, alienation, and separation from reality that is a hallmark of much of the crime of our post-modern, urban society.

A week passed before the *Times* updated the story. On Thursday, December 15, 1955, Goss was reported to be making "fair progress" at the VA Hospital. It would be the last good news in the case. The following Tuesday, December 20, 1955, after lingering sixteen long days, Chester Goss died. The next day, first degree murder charges were filed against Charles Friddle, who was described as "undergoing" a thirty-day period of observation at the "state Hospital for Mental Diseases at Little Rock."

Funeral services for Goss, conducted by Reverend Marius J. Lindloff, were held in the chapel of Nelson's Funeral Home at 10:00 a.m. on Friday, December 23, 1955. Goss, as a war veteran, was buried in the National Cemetery in south Fayetteville. His obituary appeared in the Times on Monday, December 26, 1955. Chester Lee Goss had been born in Fayetteville on July 29, 1899. He was survived by his mother, a brother, and three nephews.

As for the man who killed him, there was no word until January 11, 1956, when the *Times* ran the headline "*Charles Friddle Reported To Be 'With Psychosis.'*" According to the story, he had been "found insane by a State Hospital examining board."

"Normally," the story went on, "persons charged with murder and later found to be insane, are committed to the State Hospital by order of the Circuit Court. They must remain in the hospital until they recover, which frequently means for life." Friddle was, as reported by Dr. W. P. Kolb in a letter to Judge Cummings, unequivocally insane.

Friddle's condition was diagnosed, the report concluded as "schizophrenic reaction, paranoid type." The board recommended that he "be committed to the hospital under the terms of Act 241 of 1943."[570] Judge Cummings himself was quoted as saying that Friddle would "probably be committed permanently."

Charles Friddle, the unobtrusive man who once sat calmly in my family's living room and who later shot and killed the unsuspecting Chester Goss for reasons considered completely "insane," may well have spent the rest of his life at the state mental hospital. No obituary was found for him in local records and no other mention of him has surfaced. After more than six decades, this case, so strange and yet compelling, has nearly been lost in the unending passage of time.[571]

KIRBY L. ESTES:
FAYETTEVILLE'S FIRST POET LAUREATE

ON APRIL 3, 2006, in conjunction with National Poetry Month, William R. "Bill" Mayo, owner of Delta House Publishing, Indian Bay Press and its poetry journal *Poesia,* selected long-time Fayetteville resident Kirby L. Estes to be the city's first poet laureate.[572] Mayo, who had long lobbied for the city to create a poet laureate position, made it clear that Estes' position, while fully deserved, was an honorary one and would last for one year or until the City of Fayetteville established a permanent, official post.

As a poet the 68-year-old Estes was a legitimate selection for the honorary position. While still a student at Fayetteville High School in the mid-1950s, his poem "The Concert of the Stars" was accepted for two different high school poetry anthologies: *Songs of Youth*[573] and *Young America Sings.*[574]

After serving in the U. S. Navy, he attained Bachelor of Arts and Bachelor of Architecture and Landscape Architecture degrees from the University of Arkansas. He continued writing poetry during his years as an architect, publishing poems in the independent newspaper *Grapevine*[575] and the *Northwest Arkansas Times.*[576] Upon his retirement in 2001, Estes focused on pursuing a second career as an author and poet.

From 2003 on, he regularly published poetry and non-fiction and held several readings in Fayetteville. His poetry appeared in such journals as *Slant,*[577] the *Arkansas Literary Forum,*[578] *Megaera,*[579] and the *Istanbul Literary Review*[580] and he read his work at local venues like GoodFolk House, Nightbird Books, and Arsaga's Coffeehouse.

Bill Mayo
Courtesy of William Mayo

Toward the end of 2005, his poem "Development Will Discourage Shanty Building: A Left-Handed Protest from the Non-Right" was published in the journal *Paradoxism* and garnered him a Certificate for Distinguished Achievement in Paradoxism. His poem "Nothing of What You Say" then went on to win second place in the 2005 Oliver W. Browning Poetry Competition sponsored by Indian Bay Press. With these latter successes, Bill Mayo was moved to select Estes as his choice for the honorary position of Fayetteville's first Poet Laureate.

Kirby L. Estes
Courtesy of Martha Hogan Estes

Estes took to his new position with energy and enthusiasm, and from his selection in April 2006 until his untimely death in January 2008, he penned some ten articles on the subject of poetry for *Poesia* and published almost the same number of poems in journals like *Red Owl*,[584] *Respiro*,[585] *Word Catalyst*,[586] and *Asbestos*.[587] In April 2007, Lost Creek Press published his poetry chapbook entitled *Backroad*.

Backroad is a powerful, allusive—and sometimes elusive—poetic journey in search of meaning both personal and public. At its best, as in the ultimate long poem in the collection, "Fealty Unbound," *Back-*

road leads to a discovery of the self and an understanding that we are like "angels on the head of a pin," at once "nothing and everything."[588]

In addition to the general promotion of poetry, one of Estes' tasks as Fayetteville's first Poet Laureate was to help the new editor of Indian Bay Press, Jay Ross, lobby the city to turn this honorary designation into an official, permanent position. To that end, Ross laid out the case for Mayor Dan Coody in a long e-mail.[589] Mayor Coody was receptive to the idea and at the City's September 13, 2006 agenda session he named a Poet Laureate Task Force comprised of Ross, Mayo, and Estes.[590]

By the fall of 2006, the Task Force had selected and formed the Poet Laureate Selection and Advisory Committee. This committee consisted of renowned poet Miller Williams (since deceased), co-founder of the University of Arkansas Creative Writing Program; Molly Giles, then head of the University of Arkansas Creative Writing Program; Becky Cox, Faculty Advisor and Coordinator at the time for the Fayetteville High School journal *Connotations;* Bill Herring, computer engineer and poet; and Steve Holst, poet and board member of the Ozark Poets and Writers Collective.[591]

The committee, with Poet Laureate Estes also in attendance, met during the fall and winter of 2006 to consider possible candidates for the position. Among the writers considered were Mohja Kahf, Rebecca Newth, Bob Haslam, Brenda Moosy and popular local slam poet Clayton Scott.[592]

All of the nominees submitted several poems for consideration by the committee. Based upon the strength of a resume as well as samples of their written poetry, a selection was made.[593] In a highly competitive vote, Scott won to become the city's first elected Poet Laureate.

On Saturday, April 7, 2007 at the GoodFolk House in Fayetteville, Mayor Coody proclaimed Scott the next, and first official, Poet Laureate of Fayetteville.[594] Mayor Coody and outgoing Poet Laureate Estes gave short addresses and Scott delivered some of his poetry in the contemporary "Slam" style.

Scott, a Magna Cum Laude honors graduate from Southwestern

Clayton Scott
Courtesy of Clayton Scott

Oklahoma University with a Bachelor of Science degree in Education and a minor in Language Arts, had been a teacher, television producer, actor and comedian prior to gaining the Poet Laureate position. His varied background also included time as a youth minister, detention counselor, and arts educator.[595]

During his four year stint as Fayetteville's Poet Laureate, which he considered a "high honor," Scott traveled around the state teaching and being, in his words, "an ambassador for my community." He saw himself as "a representative" of the city and always promoted it as an "artistic" and "poetic" place. "Because poetry is such a misunderstood literary art," he said, "it was a joy to heighten awareness and to generate the passion and joy of poetry for four years."[596]

During National Poetry Month in April 2011, at a Town Hall Meeting, Mayor Lioneld Jordan, who succeeded Coody, announced the next official Poet Laureate of Fayetteville. The choice was Miller

Miller Williams
City of Fayetteville

Williams, described by Jordan as "one of the foremost American poets of the post-World War II era."[597]

Williams' literary, academic, and poetic background was impeccable. He had helped found the University of Arkansas Press in 1980[598] and was its director for some two decades. He had been a professor of English, foreign languages, and comparative literature at Arkansas for over thirty years, as well.[599]

He had published over twenty-five books and won numerous prizes including the Amy Lowell Traveling Fellowship in Poetry. He was selected by President Clinton to deliver his poem "Of History and Hope" at Clinton's second inauguration in 1997 and the president later honored Williams with the National Arts Award for the poet's life-time contribution to American arts.[600]

With Miller Williams'[601] selection as Fayetteville's Poet Laureate, and Clayton Scott before him, the continuity and legitimacy of the now established position had been achieved. The once uncertain hope of Bill Mayo, Jay Ross, and Kirby L. Estes that Fayetteville would have a permanent Poet Laureate finally had come true.

Less than a year after Scott's selection, on January 3, 2008, Estes passed away, but his poetry is still available and his final efforts live on in the now official position of Fayetteville Poet Laureate.

END NOTES

Early Historians of Fayetteville and Washington County

1. The Colonel James P. Neal material was researched and written by Susan Parks-Spencer, who also helped edit the article.

2. "The Story of Alfred W. Arrington," Ted R. Worley, *The Arkansas Historical Quarterly,* Volume XIV, Number 4, Winter 1955, p. 315.

3. Ibid.

4. Ibid, p. 317.

5. *Biographical and Pictorial History of Arkansas,* John B. Hallum, Albany: Weed, Parsons and Company, Printers, 1887, p. 281.

6. *Flashback,* Volume VI, Number 1, January 1956, p. 3.

7. *Goodspeed's Washington County History, Washington County, Arkansas,* Goodspeed Publishing Company, Chicago, Illinois, 1889, p. 201.

8. *Flashback,* Volume VI, Number 1, January 1956, p. 2.

9. For fully detailed accounts of these 1839 bloody incidents, see Walter J. Lemke, "Violent History or Historical Violence," *Flashback*, Volume VI, Number 1, January 1956; and David Malone, "The Cane Hill Murders, Part I," *Flashback*, Volume 47, Number 4, November 1997, pp. 4-23, "The Cane Hill Murders, Part II, *Flashback*, Volume 48, Number 1, February 1998, pp. 2-13, and "The Gazette Reports on the 'Fuss at Fayetteville,'" *Flashback*, Volume 48, Number 2, May 1998, pp. 2-22.

10. "The Desperado as Hero," Phillip Durham, *The Arkansas Historical Quarterly,* Volume XIV, Number 4, Winter 1955, pp. 340-341.

11. "The Story of Alfred W. Arrington," Ted R. Worley, *The Arkansas Historical Quarterly*, Volume XIV, Number 4, Winter 1955, pp. 326-327.

12. Ibid., p. 316.

13. Ibid., p. 328.

14. *Goodspeed's Washington County History, Washington County, Arkansas,* Goodspeed Publishing Company, Chicago, Illinois, 1889, p. 159.

15. *Biographical and Pictorial History of Arkansas,* John B. Hallum, Albany: Weed, Parsons and Company, Printers, 1887, p. 281

16. Ibid.

17. Ibid., p. 282.

18. Ibid.

19. "The Story of Alfred W. Arrington," Ted R. Worley, *The Arkansas Historical Quarterly*, Volume XIV, Number 4, Winter 1955, p. 337.

20. Memorial of Alfred W. Arrington, *Chicago Bar,* Chicago, Illinois, 1868, p. 12. The memorial, 70 pages long, includes a 24-page biography with Arrington's temperance sketch "Apostrophe to Water" and his poem "Flora." The remainder of the document is made up of tributes from Arrington's colleagues in law and politics.

21. Van Hoose's obituary in the *Fayetteville Democrat,* May 8, 1899, says the family arrived in Arkansas on June 1, 1839.

22. *Goodspeed's Washington County History, Washington County, Arkansas,* Goodspeed Publishing Company, Chicago, Illinois, 1889, p. 1030.

23. Mt. Comfort is, today, a part of Fayetteville.

24. *Goodspeed's Washington County History, Washington County, Arkansas,* Goodspeed Publishing Company, Chicago, Illinois, 1889, p. 1030.

25. Some accounts give 1850 as the date Van Hoose moved to Fayetteville and others say 1853. He gave the date himself as March 8, 1852 in an article on page 1 of the *Fayetteville Sentinel,* March 15, 1882. The 1852 date was repeated in the 1889 *Goodspeed's History of Washington County, Washington County, Arkansas,* Goodspeed Publishing Company, Chicago, Illinois, 1889, p. 1030.

26. *The Square Book: An Illustrated History of the Fayetteville Square*

1828-2016, Anthony J. Wappel with J. B. Hogan, Fayetteville, Arkansas, 2017, pp. 157-158.

27. *Goodspeed's Washington County History, Washington County, Arkansas,* Goodspeed Publishing Company, Chicago, Illinois, 1889, p. 1030.

28. Obituary of James Hayden Van Hoose, *Fayetteville Democrat,* May 8, 1899.

29. Ibid.

30. Ibid.

31. Ibid.

32. "Albert Pike (1809-1891)," entry in the *Encyclopedia of Arkansas,* Carl Moneyhon, http:// www.encyclopediaofarkansas.net/ encyclopedia/entry-detail.aspx?entryID=1737 (accessed June 24, 2018).

33. *Flashback,* Vol. XI, No. 4, November 1961, p. 29.

34. Ibid., p. 33.

35. *Goodspeed's Washington County History, Washington County, Arkansas,* Goodspeed Publishing Company, Chicago, Illinois, 1889, p. 1030.

36. *Flashback,* Vol. XI, No. 4, November 1961, p. 30.

37. "A Fayetteville Man, on an Unusual Errand, Meets Abraham Lincoln," Mildred Mayhill Crawford, *Flashback,* Vol. XIII, No. 4, October, 1963, p. 3.

38. Ibid., pp. 7, 10.

39. Ibid., p. 3.

40. *Goodspeed's Washington County History, Washington County, Arkansas,* Goodspeed Publishing Company, Chicago, Illinois, 1889, p. 245.

41. "Fayetteville Thirty Years Ago," James H. Van Hoose, *Fayetteville Sentinel,* March 15, 1882, p. 1.

42. Ibid.

43. "Early History," James H. Van Hoose, *Fayetteville Democrat,* May 25, 1882, p. 3.

44. "1849," James H. Van Hoose, *Fayetteville Democrat,* April 19, 1889, p. 3.

45. Ibid.

46. Obituary of James Hayden Van Hoose, *Fayetteville Democrat,* May 8, 1899.

47. Ibid.

48. *Flashback*, Vol XI, No. 4, November 1961, p. 30.

49. *Fayetteville Democrat,* December 9, 1871, p. 3.

50. *Fayetteville Daily Democrat,* January 30, 1928, p. 1.

51. Ibid.

52. *Once Upon Dickson,* Anthony J. Wappel, Fayetteville, Arkansas, 2008, p. 67.

53. Ibid., p. 70.

54. Ibid., p. 214.

55. *Fayetteville Daily Democrat,* January 30, 1928, p. 1.

56. *Flashback,* Vol. X, No. 1, January 1960, pp. 9-13.

57. *Flashback,* Vol. X, No. 2, April 1960, pp. 35-36.

58. *Flashback,* Vol. X, No. 3, July 1960, pp. 15-20.

59. *Once Upon Dickson,* Anthony J. Wappel, Fayetteville, Arkansas, 2008, pp. 233-234.

60. "Migration and Settlement of My Stepfather and Family; My First Day and First Ramble in the Valley", Col. James Preston Neal, Sr., *Flashback* Volume V, Number 3, June 1955, pp. 8-9. This was the first installment of a three-part series in *Flashback* that was edited by Tom Feathers. The second and third installments were both titled "The Memoirs of Col. J.P. Neal" and were in the August and December 1955 editions of *Flashback*.

61. Ibid.

62. Her first name is also spelled as "Adeline" in other documents.

63. "The Prairie Grove Valley and Its Communities; Part One," Willard B. Gatewood, *Flashback* Volume 53, Number 1, Winter 2003, p. 20.

64. Ibid.

65. "James Preston Neal," Luginbuel Funeral Home, accessed June 18, 2018, http://www.luginbuel.com/genealogy/person/i47310, and "Death of Col. J.P. Neal," p. 2.

66. Ibid.

67. "Prairie Grove," *Fayetteville Democrat,* August 14, 1884, p. 3.

68. Advertisement, *Fayetteville Democrat,* September 26, 1868, p. 1.

69. "James Preston Neal," and "Death of Col. J.P. Neal," p. 2.

70. *History of Benton, Washington, Carroll, Madison, Crawford, Franklin, and Sebastian Counties, Arkansas,* Chicago: The Goodspeed Publishing Co., 1889, p. 265.

71. "Prairie Grove Items," *Fayetteville Democrat,* February 9, 1878, p.2.

72. "Personal Items," *Fayetteville Democrat*, June 15, 1872, p. 5.

73. "Death of Col. J.P. Neal," p. 2, and "Directory; Township Officers," *Fayetteville Democrat*, May 4, 1872, p. 4, and "Directory; Township Officers," *Fayetteville Democrat*, October 30, 1875, p. 8.

74. "Local Affairs," *Fayetteville Democrat*, February 14, 1880, p. 3.

75. Plat of Prairie Grove, Surveyed by J.A. Buchanan, September 24, 1877.

76. Ibid, and James P. Neal, p. 10. The 1833 Leonid meteor shower was seen by many people in North America who observed thousands of meteors falling from the sky. "Leonid Meteor Shower 1833," Eleanor Imster, earthsky.org, November 16, 2018, accessed June 10, 2018, http://earthsky.org/?p=209177.

77. "The Memoirs of Col. J.P. Neal," Tom Feathers, ed., *Flashback* Volume V, Number 6, December 1955, pp. 5-6. These letters and documents from Andrew Jackson may have dealt with early plans regarding independence efforts for the Mexican territory of Texas from the Mexican Government. In 1836, some of this land became the Republic of Texas and Sam Houston was elected its President.

78. "Prairie Grove Battle," J.P. Neal, *Fayetteville Democrat*, December 14, 1888, p. 2.

79. Ibid.

80. "Prairie Grove Items," p. 2.

81. "James Preston Neal."

Fletcher Family History

82. Fletcher family genealogical records.

83. The Fletcher men have served in the military throughout the family's history. From 1957-1966, Jimmy Fletcher served in the U. S. Army Reserve, the U. S. Army (Active Duty) and the Arkansas National Guard.

84. National Archives search, May 23, 1947, Mrs. O. L. Fletcher, Temple, Texas, and online ancestor search of Daughters of the American Revolution (DAR) website (www.dar.org), Mickey Clements, Reference Librarian, Grace Keith Genealogy Collection, Fayetteville, Arkansas Public Library, April 27, 2011.

85. Fletcher family genealogical records and online ancestor search of Daughters of the American Revolution (DAR) website (www.

dar.org), Mickey Clements, Reference Librarian, Grace Keith Genealogy Collection, Fayetteville, Arkansas Public Library, April 27, 2011.

86. Fletcher family genealogical records.

87. Ibid.

88. Ibid.

89. Ibid.

90. Department of Military Affairs, Commonwealth of Kentucky, Statement of Service, War of 1812, 24 August 1964. Robert Fletcher, Jr.'s service in the War of 1812 is also corroborated by the listing of his wife Mary "Polly" Wilson in the Widows of 1812 Veterans Pension roster, *Flashback*, publication of the Washington Country (AR) Historical Society, Vol. VII, No. 4, July 1957, p. 9.

91. This places the Fletcher family in Arkansas only 5-6 after it had become a Territory.

92. The children of Robert Fletcher, Jr. and Mary "Polly" Wilson are listed in the 1840 and 1850 Federal Census of Washington County, Arkansas.

93. Arkansas History Commission Certification of Confederate Service, Old State House, Little Rock, Arkansas, February 8, 1966. Private Robert Fletcher is listed in the roll of Company E, First Battalion, Arkansas Confederate Cavalry. This unit was organized in Fayetteville, Arkansas, October 9, 1861.

94. Campbell, William S., *One Hundred Years of Fayetteville 1828-1928*, Fayetteville, Arkansas, 1928, pp. 26, 45, and 98.

95. Arkansas History Commission Certification of Confederate Service, Old State House, Little Rock, Arkansas, February 8, 1966.

96. Ibid.

97. Ibid.

98. In the 1850 Federal Census of Washington County, Arkansas, only three children were as yet listed for the Jobe and Sarah Ann Williford Fletcher family.

99. Fletcher family genealogical records.

100. Fletcher family genealogical records indicate that Lou Emma Eacret Fletcher's father, George Eacret (1855-1932) was of French and Osage descent.

101. Fletcher family genealogical records indicate that Audra Phillips Fletcher, Jimmy Fletcher's mother, was of Cherokee de-

137. City Clerk, Fayetteville, Arkansas, "Mayors of the City of Fayetteville, Arkansas," 2008.

138. City Clerk, Fayetteville, Arkansas, Resolutions, Ordinances and Minutes of the Fayetteville City Council, February 14, 1966 to March 12, 1969.

139. City Clerk, Fayetteville, Arkansas, "Mayors of the City of Fayetteville, Arkansas," 2008.

140. Ibid.

141. Campbell, p. 26.

142. *Fayetteville Democrat* (Weekly), January 9, 1869.

143. Ibid., December 3, 1870.

144. Ibid., March 14, 21, and 28, 1874.

145. Ibid., April 3, 1875.

146. Ibid., July 7, 1881.

147. Ibid., March 3, 1904 and April 12, 1906.

148. Ibid., April 8, 1908.

149. City Clerk, Fayetteville, Arkansas, Minutes, Resolutions, and Ordinances of the Fayetteville City Council, 1909.

150. Ibid., 1939.

151. Ibid., 1941.

152. Ibid., 1941 and 1944.

153. Ibid., 1945.

154. City Clerk, Fayetteville, Arkansas records.

155. Campbell, p. 30.

156. *Fayetteville Democrat* (Weekly), December 4, 1869, August 24, 1872, and January 17, 1874.

157. Ibid., March 31, 1877, and May 29, 1880.

158. Campbell, p. 30.

159. City Clerk, Fayetteville, Arkansas, Minutes, Resolutions, and Ordinances of the Fayetteville City Council, 1934 and 1939.

160. Ibid., 1941.

161. Ibid., 1949.

162. City Clerk, Fayetteville, Arkansas records.

Fayetteville's Old Schools

163. Flashback, Number 6, November

164. City of Fayetteville website, https://www.fayetteville-ar.gov/CivicSend/ViewMessage/Message/89154, accessed July 8, 2019.

165. Ibid., p. 56.

166. *Fayetteville Daily Democrat* (FDD), February 16, 1931.

167. *FDD,* February 19, 1931.

168. *FDD,* September 3, 1936.

169. Ballard and his poetry will be discussed in a subsequent section.

170. Washington County Retired Teacher's Association, School Days, *School Days, The History of Education in Washington County, 1830-1950,* Fayetteville, AR, 1986.

171. Sanborn Fire Insurance Map of Fayetteville, AR, July 1913.

172. Anthony J. Wappel, "College Cemetery: A Second Look," *Flashback*, Vol. 38, No. 3, August 1988, pp. 6-12. See also, Cemetery Records of Washington County, Arkansas, Volume 1 (unpaginated), published by Washington County Historical Society, Fayetteville, Arkansas (undated). The College Cemetery was created in the 1870s and was at the Maple and Garland location until the 1920s when the graves were moved to other cemeteries.

173. *FDD,* September 4, 1939.

174. *Northwest Arkansas Times* (NWAT), September 10, 1951.

175. Campbell, p. 56.

176. *NWAT,* September 12, 1955.

177. *NWAT,* September 18 1959.

178. *NWAT,* August 16, 1966.

179. *NWAT,* June 13 and 19, 1969.

From the Lyric to the UArk: Fayetteville's Old Movie Houses

180. Campbell, William S., *One Hundred Years of Fayetteville, 1828-1928,* Fayetteville, AR, 1928, p. 90.

181. Ibid.

182. Sanborn Fire Insurance Map of Fayetteville, AR, July 1908.

183. *Fayetteville Daily* (FD), Fayetteville, AR, June 4, 1907. Subsequent references to Fayetteville newspapers, including the *Fayetteville Democrat* (weekly—FDW), the *Fayetteville Daily Democrat* (FDD), and the *Northwest Arkansas Times* (NWAT), will be made in the text.

184. "History of Edison Motion Pictures: Origins of Motion Pictures—the Kinetoscope," online article, http://memory.loc.gov/ammem/edhtml/edmvhist.html.

185. Campbell, p. 90.

186. Valentine, Maggie, *The Show Starts on the Sidewalk: An Architectural History of the Theatre,* Yale University Press, New Haven, Connecticut, 1994, p.23.

187. Sanborn Fire Insurance Map, July 1908.

188. Campbell, p. 90.

189. Ibid.

190. Sonneman, Emil H., Ozarks Regional Library, Oral History Project, Mullins Library, Special Collections, University of Arkansas, Fayetteville, p.1.

191. Many will recall that the popular, African American country duo of Sarge and Shirley West often performed at the post-movie Palace Theatre.

History of Wilson (City) Park

192. The ballfield in City Park opened in 1955 as home to the Sherman Lollar Little League, as well as other youth baseball leagues. With the opening of Walker Park on the city's south side in 1961, Fayetteville Little Leaguers alternated play at both locations. City Park field was phased out of youth baseball and turned into a softball field in 1968.

193. Campbell, William S., *One Hundred Years of Fayetteville, 1828-1928,* Fayetteville, AR, 1928, pp. 17 and 78. Trent's obituary in the *Northwest Arkansas Times,* Thursday, May 2, 1940 refers to him as a "prominent realtor."

194. Campbell, pp. 70 and 87.

195. As early as 1904, A. L. Trent was selling home lots in the recently platted City Park Addition.

196. *Fayetteville Daily* (FD), October 21, 1916.

197. Trent's Pond, a small, spring-fed lake used for boating and swimming in City Park, was located just north of the current swimming pool, basically covering what is now the softball field. The 1908 Plat Map of Fayetteville clearly shows where the lake was located.

198. FD, April 8, 1908.

199. Ibid, June 27, 1917.

200. Ibid.

201. *Fayetteville Daily Democrat* (FDD), April 23, 1923.

202. Ibid.

203. Ibid. Although difficult to see today because it is covered with buildings and thick undergrowth and trees, the natural amphitheatre is located along the ridge and in the small valley to the north of Trenton Boulevard in the area approximately bounded by Park and Lollar Avenues on the west and east, respectively, and by Prospect Street to the north.

204. Ibid., January 4, 1924.

205. Ibid., April 2, 1924.

206. Ibid., April 11, 1924.

207. Ibid., April 29, 1924.

208. Ibid., March 1, 1926.

209. Ibid., March 25, 1926.

210. Ibid., March 31, 1926.

211. Ibid., August 6, 1926.

212. Trent's Pond was used again, for boating only, in 1927 but by 1928 it had been drained and the paper reported there were plans to put a sunken garden in its place (*FDD,* April 25, 1928). In later stories in the *Northwest Arkansas Times,* the location of the pond was described as "directly north of ... current swimming pool" (November 6, 1982) and as lying "beneath park's softball field" (June 22, 1985).

213. One stone cottage remains today in the park. It is located north of the swimming pool, facing the tennis courts.

214. FDD, April 25, 1927.

215. Ibid., September 7, 1928.

216. Ibid., October 23, 1933.

217. Ibid., May 5, 1942.

218. Ibid., December 12, 1944. The official date of sale was January 15, 1945.

219. Ibid., July 3, 1945.

220. *NWAT,* August 16, 1946.

221. Ibid.

222. Ibid., August 17, 1946.

223. For more detailed information about the controversial and oftentimes acrimonious sale of Wilson's Pasture, see Hogan, J. B., "You Can't Go Home Again: Charles Morrow Wilson's Unhappy Return to Fayetteville," *Flashback*, Washington County (AR) Historical Society, Winter 2010, Vol. 60, No. 4, pp. 115-145.

224. Ibid., October 17, 1946.

257. Germany signed the armistice ending World War I on November 11, 1918.

258. Spring Valley is located east of Springdale where Highway 303 and Highway 68 (412) intersect.

259. War Eagle Mills is located east and north of Springdale, to the west of Spring Valley.

260. Huston Jasper Peter Edward Scott, 1891-1972. Buck Gilbert's uncle on his mother's side. In the early 1900s, Huston Scott journeyed to California to work. Excerpts of his letters from this period, compiled and edited by Martha Hogan Estes can be found in her article in *Flashback*, Vol. 56, No. 2, Spring 2006, pp. 37-54. Huston Scott is buried in the Goshen, Arkansas Cemetery.

261. Mayfield is about five miles northeast of Goshen, Arkansas just off Highway 45 where it intersects with Highway 303.

262. Almedia Phydellia Stringfield Scott, 1861-1940. Mother of Huston Scott and Sophia Elizabeth Scott Gilbert, Buck's mother. Almedia was born in Pea Ridge, Arkansas. She died in Mayfield and is buried in the Goshen, Arkansas Cemetery.

263. Vaughn Branch is a small stream running near Whitener, Arkansas.

264. Melvin Clyde Gilbert, 1885-1938. The brother of Joseph and Richard "Dick" Gilbert, and Buck's uncle. He was born in Dekalb County, Missouri and died in Madison County, Arkansas. He is buried in Farmer's Cemetery, Huntsville, Arkansas.

265. Habberton is about 2 miles north of Highway 45 at the bottom of Slaughter Mountain which is about 1 mile east of Son's Chapel on the far east side of Fayetteville.

266. Stinkbase was an involved version of tag with two teams of children facing each other across a playfield; Blackman was another tag game but it was more individual and is like the game "Tag, You're It" where one child at a time is tagged; Crack the Whip was a line of children holding hands and running around until the leader, usually a big kid at one end of the line, stopped abruptly and whipped the line as hard as possible. This normally resulted in the farthest out child flying wildly and sometimes dangerously away from the line; Scrub Up Baseball is like Work Up Baseball: each player moves through all positions in the field until it is his or her turn to bat.

267. Zion is located east of Fayetteville just south of the intersection of Zion Road and Old Wire (Butterfield Coach) Road.

268. The highway being built was Highway 68.

269. A Fresno scraper is a machine pulled by horses and used for constructing canals and ditches in sandy soil. The American Society of Mechanical Engineers website, https://www.asme.org/ about-asme/who-we-are/engineering-history/landmarks/158-fresno-scraper, accessed November 2, 2018.

270. Fishback was located along the Butterfield Coach Road between Zion and Springdale.

Early History of Drake Field

271. Co-written with the late Kirby L. Estes who did much of the initial research and a portion of the first draft before he passed in January of 2008.

272. Glenn L. Martin Papers, Glenn L. Martin Aviation Museum, Middle River, Maryland.

273. Campbell, William S., *One Hundred Years of Fayetteville, 1828-1928*, Fayetteville, AR, 1928, p. 35.

274. *Fayetteville Daily*, Monday, August 21, 1911. Further references to Fayetteville papers will be noted in the text.

275. *Springdale News*, Friday, October 6, 1911. Further references to Springdale papers will be noted in the text.

276. Campbell, p. 50.

277. Ibid., p. 51.

278. Jordan, Thomas E., *Jerome Zerbe, Early Aviation Pioneer*, internet article (http:// www.geocities.com/Cape Canaveral/2905/airsedan.htm).

279. "Zerbe Air Sedan," http://www.aerofiles.com/yz.html.

280. Jordan, *Jerome Zerbe, Early Aviation Pioneer*.

281. Eckels, Michael V., "80 Years of Aviation in Fayetteville (1911-1991)," Arkansas Air Museum, Aviation Historian.

282. Newberg, Ronald E., SWAviator Online Edition, April/May 2000, internet article (http:// www.swaviator.com/html/issueAM00/eaglerockAM00.html). The Alexander Eagle Rock biplane was built in the early 1920s by the Alexander Aircraft Company of Englewood and Colorado Springs Colorado.

283. Wings of History Museum article, internet article (http://www.

wingsofhistory.org). The single wing Waco 10 was built in 1927 by the Advance Aircraft Co. of Troy, Ohio.

284. McCullom Mountain is west of Highway 71 South, across from the current airstrip at Drake Field. McCullom runs north to near where the original airport was.

285. Fayetteville City Council Minutes, Resolutions & Ordinances: 10-03-1927—12-30-1929, p. 384.

286. Ibid., p. 386.

287. Ibid., p. 384.

288. Ibid., p. 412.

289. Ibid., p. 412.

290. Ibid., pp. 413-414.

291. Ibid., p. 422.

292. Ibid., p. 444.

293. "American Experience" (PBS): *Timeline: A selected Wall Street chronology*, internet article (http://www.pbs.org/wgbh/amex/crash/timeline/index.html)

294. Fayetteville City Council Minutes, p. 462.

295. No known relation to Dr. Noah F. Drake.

296. Ibid., p. 463.

297. Ibid., p. 464.

298. Federal Aviation Administration, "A Brief History of the Federal Aviation Administration," internet article (http://www.faa.gov/about/history/brief_history).

299. Co-Operative *Advertiser*, Fayetteville, AR, No. 18, Friday, July 27, 1934.

300. Eckels, Mike, The Fayetteville Experience, The Story of the Fayetteville, Arkansas Civilian Pilot Training Program, War Training Service, and the 305th College Training Detachment (1939-1944), pp. 18-20, publisher unknown (undated).

301. Fayetteville City Council Minutes, Resolutions & Ordinances: 1-7-1935—8-12-1944, p. 576.

302. The White Hangar is the only structure in Fayetteville designated a local ordinance district.

303. Online Arkansas Register of Historic Places (Arkansas Historic Preservation Program) document located at the following URL: http://www.arkansaspreservation.com/arkansas-register-listings/fayetteville-municipal-airport-hangar-quot-white-hangar-quot (accessed July 30, 2018).

History of Collier Drug Store

304. "Change in Management of Red Cross April 1," *Fayetteville Democrat* (Daily), March 5, 1917, reported that M. M. Collier was to become manager/owner of the Red Cross Drug Store. This article also said that Collier had "purchased an interest in the Red Cross drug store."

305. W. S. Campbell, in his *100 Years of Fayetteville: 1828-1928,* and local newspaper accounts both say that the Red Cross Drug Store opened in 1904 but the first reference in the *Fayetteville Democrat* (Daily) to "The Red Cross Store" is in an ad for the Hight-Carnahan Co. dated March 30, 1906 (the first ad for just Hight-Carnahan by itself appeared in early February 1906). On May 3, 1906 the first ad for just the Red Cross Store appears.

306. "Change in Management of Red Cross April 1," *Fayetteville Democrat* (Daily), March 5, 1917.

307. Collier Drug Store web site (www.collierdrug.com).

308. Collier Drug Store web site (www.collierdrug.com).

309. Morris Collier had actually begun working in his dad's store as a delivery boy back in 1919, *NWAT,* November 2, 1949.

310. *Fayetteville Daily Democrat,* April 27, 1932.

311. *NWAT,* November 2, 1949.

312. *NWAT,* September 1, 1948.

313. *NWAT,* November 2, 1949.

314. Ibid.

315. Local residents will recall that during this era the two establishments with the coldest and most effective air-conditioning in town were the Ozark Theatre and Collier Drug Store.

316. Ibid., July 25, 1949.

317. Ibid., July 26, 1949.

318. Ibid.

319. Anthony J. Wappel, with Ethel C. Simpson, *Once Upon Dickson* (Fayetteville, Arkansas: Board of Trustees of the University of Arkansas, published in cooperation with the University of Arkansas Libraries Special Collections Department, 2008), p. 110.

320. Ibid., pp. 106-107.

321. In 1958, the "Collier family donated the soda fountain from the Fayetteville Store to the Fayetteville Youth Center, where it was

enjoyed for several years." Collier Drug Store web site (www. collierdrug.com).

322. *NWAT,* April 24, 1950.

323. Ibid., January 5, 1953.

324. Collier Drug Store web site (www.collierdrug.com).

325. Ibid.

326. *Once Upon Dickson,* p. 112.

327. *NWAT,* June 20, 1969.

328. Collier Drug Store web site (www.collierdrug.com).

329. *NWAT,* January 19, 1995.

330. Interview with Mel Collier, October 30. 2009.

331. *Once Upon Dickson,* p. 112.

332. Collier Drug Store web site (www.collierdrug.com).

333. *Once Upon Dickson,* p. 112.

334. Ibid.

George Ballard: Forgotten Poet of the Hollow

335. "Remembering an Arkansas Poet," Joe Neal, *Grapevine,* Vol. VIII, No. 26, March 16, 1977, pp. 5-7. Information about Ballard's life is sketchy at best but this article is one of the best sources for details of his life.

336. *Fayetteville Daily Democrat* (FDD), February 19, 1928.

337. Ibid, February 16, 1924.

338. Ibid.

339. Ibid., February 28, 1924.

340. *Ozark Ballards,* George Ballard, Democrat Publishing Company, Fayetteville, AR, 1928, p. 28.

341. Ibid., p. 17.

342. *FDD,* July 2, 1928 and Neal, p. 6.

343. *Ozark Ballards,* unpaginated front matter dedication page.

344. Ibid., unpaginated front matter acknowledgement page.

345. Ibid., pp. 13-14. Paul Laurence Dunbar was a highly regarded African-American poet of the late nineteenth and early twentieth centuries.

346. Ibid., unpaginated front matter introduction page.

347. Ibid., p. 23.

348. Ibid., p. 31.

349. Ibid., p. 38.

350. Ibid., p. 48.
351. Ibid., p. 52. Ballard is here most likely referring to United States interventions in Nicaragua and Haiti that occurred during this era.
352. Ibid., p. 61.
353. *FDD*, April 15, 1929.
354. Ibid., February 10, 1930.
355. Henderson School was later incorporated into a home dwelling which still stands today. Lincoln lasted until all the schools in Fayetteville were integrated, closing its doors in 1965. It was demolished in the 1970s. See J. B. Hogan, "Fayetteville's Old Schools," *Flashback*, Vol. 59, No. 2, Summer 2009, p. 46.
356. *FDD*, May 21, 1936.
357. In an earlier news story in the *FDD*, March 4, 1936, some 78 books had been donated to the new Ballard Library. Ballard himself said that he was trying to collect as many books for the library as he could find about successful African-Americans.
358. Neal, p. 7.
359. *Ozark Ballards*, p. 53.

Death of Patrolmen Lem McPherson

360. Washington County Records, Book Y, Page 319.
361. Levi Ross may have been the man Williams was looking for when he, Williams, was reportedly seen in the vicinity of the Sigma Chi fraternity.
362. *Fayetteville Daily Democrat,* April 30, May 1, 2, 4, 7, and 8, 1928. Quotations and details of the case are from the newspaper, chronological sequencing, summary, and narrative by the author.
363. Fayetteville City Council Minutes, Resolutions & Ordinances: January 3, 1927 to December 30, 1929, p. 278.
364. http://support.nleomf.org/Individual%20Panels/Builds/West%20Tours/05-West/build.html Lem McPherson's name appears on the NLEO Memorial on Panel W-05, Line 28 (next to last line on the panel, second name in from the left).

Professor Joseph A. Thalheimer:
Mr. Chips at the University of Arkansas

365. *Fayetteville (AR) Daily Democrat*, September 16, 1930.

366. *University of Arkansas Catalog*, Fayetteville, 1957-1958. Thalheimer was such a low-key individual that when he retired neither the *Northwest Arkansas Times* nor the University of Arkansas student newspaper, the *Arkansas Traveler*, seemed to take notice as no stories about his retirement were found.

367. "Fifty Years of Journalism at the University of Arkansas," Ernie Deane, the Bob Sanders Memorial Laboratory, Fayetteville, Arkansas, April 1981, p. 1. Journalism was then part of the English Department and Lemke also headed up campus publicity, which included sports promotion.

368. The University of Arkansas journalism department is now known as the School of Journalism and Strategic Media, founded 1930, Walter J. Lemke. Email correspondence from School chair Professor Larry Foley, University of Arkansas, Fayetteville, received by the author on January 9, 2018.

369. Besides his university work, Lemke founded the Arkansas High School Press Association and the Washington County Historical Society, among many other accomplishments.

370. A Glimpse of Growth: Metropolitan Phoenix Area Population, 1900-1999 Census Chart, Arizona Geographic Alliance, 1910 Census figures, Internet document, https:// geoalliance.asu. edu/sites/default/files/LessonFiles/Sepp/SeppGlimpseS.pdf., accessed January 2, 2018.

371. We do know that his brother Walter J. Thalheimer (same first name and middle initial of Joseph's Arkansas boss Lemke) served as Mayor of Phoenix, Arizona from 1938-1940, so the family had some prominence in the area. Internet document, "List of Phoenix Mayors:" Internet file, https://www.revolvy.com/main/ index.php?s=List%20of%20mayors%20of%20Phoenix, accessed January 2, 2018.

372. *Northwest Arkansas Times* obituary for Mr. Thalheimer, November 22, 1971.

373. Ibid., obituary for Mrs. Thalheimer, October 10, 1985.

374. *University of Arkansas Catalog, Fayetteville, 1914-1920, 1924-1926*. The dates given are the beginning and ending academic year dates in which these professors are listed by name in the catalogs.

375. Ibid., 1920-1924.
376. "An Instructor Arrives," *History of The Arkansas Traveler: Profiles,* Internet document, arkansastraveler.typepad.com, accessed January 3, 2018.
377. *Fayetteville Daily Democrat,* April 12, 1927.
378. *University of Arkansas Catalog,* 1930-1931.
379. Ibid., 1934-1935.
380. Deane, p. 4.
381. "15 Years in the Basement of Old Main," Walter J. Lemke, *University of Arkansas, Fayetteville, 1943,* unpaginated.
382. "Angel Food" was a frequently humorous column dedicated to the local Class D professional minor league baseball team the Fayetteville Angels. The column ran from 1937 into 1940.
383. "The Cupples and Leon Adventure and Mystery Books for Boys," Jennifer's Series Books, Internet document, http://series-books.com/cupples/adventure.html, accessed January 2, 2018.
384. *Razorback* Annual, University of Arkansas, 1942, p. 110.
385. *University of Arkansas Catalog, Fayetteville, 1942-1943.*
386. *NWAT,* April 15, 1946.
387. "15 Years in the Basement of Old Main," Lemke.
388. *NWAT,* May 28, 1952.
389. The Washington County Historical Society was founded in late 1950 into early 1951 with the first meeting of the organization occurring on February 18, 1951. Among the attendees were Mr. and Mrs. Joseph A. Thalheimer. *Flashback,* journal of the WCHS, Number 1, March 1951, p. 1.
390. *Arkansas Traveler,* student newspaper, University of Arkansas, May 27, 1952, p. 1.
391. *University of Arkansas Catalog, Fayetteville, 1952-1953.*
392. Ibid., 1953-1954.
393. *Arkansas Traveler,* March 28, 1956, p. 4.
394. *The First 100 Years: Centennial History of the University of Arkansas,* Robert Leflar, University of Arkansas Foundation, Fayetteville, Arkansas, 1972, p. 144.
395. *NWAT,* September 9, 1957.
396. *Arkansas Traveler,* June 1, 1959, p. 4.
397. Ibid.
398. Fayetteville (AR) Telephone Directory, 1960.
399. *NWAT,* October 10, 1985.

400. Email correspondence from Professor Dale Carpenter, University of Arkansas, Fayetteville, received by the author on November 29, 2017.

401. *NWAT,* November 23, 1971.

Cabin Orgy Deaths: December 1936

402. Uncle John's Tourist Cabins stood near where the Walgreen's is now on the northwest corner of the intersection of Township and North College.

403. *Fayetteville Daily Democrat,* December 7, 1936. Subsequent quotations, details, and dates of the case are from the newspaper. Chronological sequencing, summary, and narrative by the author.

404. The White Swan Café was located at 11 East Mountain Street just off the Fayetteville Square.

405. The City of Fayetteville had brought a chancery suit against the White Swan in August of 1936 to shut the club down. The suit failed when it was declared "there had not been enough evidence produced in court to have the café declared a nuisance and closed." *FDD,* December 7, 1936.

406. The *Fayetteville Daily Democrat* became the *Northwest Arkansas Times* on July 8, 1937.

407. Rex Perkins was one of Fayetteville's best known defense lawyers for many decades.

408. G. T. "Tom" Sullins and his son Paul had a law partnership from about 1935 until 1940. When Paul Sullins moved his practice to Crossett, Arkansas, Tom partnered with Rex Perkins.

409. Carlos Hill, like Tom Sullins and Rex Perkins, practiced law in Fayetteville for many decades.

410. An instructed or directed verdict is usually made when a judge concludes that a plaintiff "has failed to offer" a "minimum amount of evidence" to prove his or her case. It amounts to an acquittal of the defendant. See internet website http://www.nolo.com for a full definition of this term.

411. A non-suit ruling can be given when a judge believes "there is no evidence to prove the plaintiff's case." After this ruling, the trial is terminated and results in "a dismissal of the plaintiff's case and judgment for the defendant." See internet website http://www.

legal- dictionary.thefreedictionary.com for the full definition of this term.

412. John S. Combs was Circuit Court Judge in November of 1937.

The Car Accident That Changed American History

413. *The Arkansas Traveler,* University of Arkansas, Fayetteville, September 22, 1939, p. 3.

414. Among the theories as to why Dr. Futrall's vehicle swerved into the oncoming lane, it was suggested that he "suffered a heart attack just before the accident." *Arkansas Gazette,* September 14, 1939 and Leflar, Robert A., *The First 100 Years: Centennial History of the University of Arkansas,* University of Arkansas Foundation Inc., Fayetteville, Arkansas, p. 101.

415. *Northwest Arkansas Times* (NWAT), Fayetteville, Arkansas, September 13, 1939. Mr. Moore sustained a broken collarbone, shock, as well as cuts and bruises. He was taken to City Hospital where he recovered from his injuries. The other passengers in the pickup were W. R. Sealey, his four-year old son, and Clifton Mills, all of Winslow.

416. In her "As I See It" column for the September 13, 1939 *Northwest Arkansas Times,* p. 2, Mrs. Roberta Fulbright said Futrall's unexpected death "stunned" people "into abject silence and dismay."

417. The Arkansas Traveler, University of Arkansas, Fayetteville, September 22, 1939, p. 3.

418. Leflar, Robert A., *The First 100 Years: Centennial History of the University of Arkansas,* University of Arkansas Foundation Inc., Fayetteville, Arkansas, p. 30. Leflar states that Futrall transferred from Arkansas because of "some disciplinary difficulties."

419. Ibid.

420. Henry, Orville and Bailey, Jim, *The Razorbacks: A Story of Arkansas Football,* The Strode Publishers, Huntsville, Alabama, 1973; new edition, The University of Arkansas Press, Fayetteville, Arkansas, 1996, pp. 427.

421. Leflar, p. 79. The student revolt, known as the X-Ray Incident, occurred in February 1912 in reaction to, among other grievances, student opposition to book costs and President Tillman's administration. The *X-Ray* was an "unauthorized" student newspaper printed in Fort Smith. All 36 contributors to the *X-Ray*

were expelled but were reinstated after a March 1912 meeting of the university Board of Trustees and a seven-man committee representing the dissident students.

422. Leflar, p. 87.
423. *Southwest-Times Record,* Fort Smith, Arkansas, June 5, 1938, p. 6.
424. Ibid.
425. *NWAT,* September 14, 1939, p.1.
426. Ibid., September 13, 1939, p. 2.
427. Leflar, p. 88.
428. Woods, Randall Bennett, *Fulbright: A Biography,* Cambridge University Press, 1995, p. 54.
429. *The Arkansas Traveler,* University of Arkansas, Fayetteville, September 22, 1939, p. 3.
430. Ibid.
431. Mrs. Fulbright had been a "vocal supporter" of Bailey in his 1938 gubernatorial campaign. Stuck, Dorothy D. and Snow, Nan, Roberta: *A Most Remarkable Fulbright,* The University of Arkansas Press, Fayetteville, 1997, p. 145.
432. Leflar, p. 173.
433. *NWAT,* September 18, 1939.
434. There are various reasons as to why Dr. Waterman declined the presidency. One version says he "turned down the offer" because he had "grave doubts that Arkansas was ready for a Jewish University chief executive." Stuck and Snow, p. 135, which is a direct quotation taken from, Gilbert, Allan, *A Fulbright Chronicle,* Fulbright Investment Co., Fayetteville, AR, 1980, p. 137. Another version says that Mrs. Waterman did not believe the job had been actually offered to her husband. She was "quite disappointed" it was said, and Dean Waterman was "crushed." Woods, p. 56.
435. Leflar, p. 388.
436. Woods, p. 14. In the 1922 Homecoming game against Southern Methodist University, Fulbright accounted for all points in a 9-0 Razorback victory. He passed for one score and kicked a field goal for the last three points.
437. Woods, pp. 19-20.
438. Ibid., pp. 25, 29-30.
439. Ibid., p. 32.

440. Ibid., p. 40.

441. Ibid., pp. 40-41.

442. Ibid., pp. 50-51.

443. Leflar, p. 175.

444. Stuck and Snow, p. 144.

445. Ibid., p. 148.

446. Ibid., pp. 144-148.

447. Leflar, p. 178.

448. Woods, p. 65. Ellis would lose the election to John. L. McClellan, who went on to serve thirty- six years in the U. S. Senate.

449. Ibid., p. 70. It should also be noted that in Arkansas politics of the time, winning the Democratic primary was tantamount to winning the general election as there was only token Republican opposition in those days.

450. Ibid., pp. 80, 83.

451. Internet document, http://www.ibiblio.org/pha/policy/1943/1943-09-21a.html

452. Woods, p. 98. The runoff election results were: 117,121 for Fulbright to 85,121 for Adkins.

453. Blumenthal, Sidney, "Fulbright's Legacy," *The New Yorker,* March 6, 1995, p. 90. Blumenthal points out that Fulbright was "the sole senator to vote against funding" McCarthy's committee and that he "instigated the Senate's condemnation of McCarthy."

454. Woods, p. 178.

455. Powell, Lee Riley, *J. William Fulbright and His Time,* Guild Bindery Press, Memphis, Tennessee, 1996, p. v

You Can't Go Home Again: Charles Morrow Wilson's Short-Lived Return to Fayetteville

456. Wilson, Charles Morrow (CMW), "Hometown Revisited," Tomorrow, May 1951, p. 21.

457. Ibid.

458. Ibid., p. 18.

459. Ibid., p. 20.

460. CMW to Lessie (Stringfellow Read), December 28, 1954. Charles Morrow Wilson Papers, Location C1271, Box 7, Folder 10. Special Collections, University of Arkansas Libraries, Fayetteville.

461. CMW, "Farmers Will Stop Communism," *The Progressive Farmer*, May 1951, reprint (unpaginated folio). C1346 OV Box 1.

462. "Hometown Revisited," p. 18.

463. Ibid., p. 19. Mattie Morrow did receive her degree from the Arkansas Industrial University in 1890 but she was not among the first three female graduates of the school. A check of Senior Walk outside Old Main reveals that between 1876 (the first graduating class) and 1889 some twenty-five women graduated prior to Mattie Morrow.

464. CMW, "More Lights," in *Stars Is God's Lanterns,* University of Oklahoma Press, 1969, p. 176.

465. *Northwest Arkansas Times* (NWAT), May 10, 1948.

466. *NWAT,* September 10, 1993.

467. CMW, detailed resume, undated (ca. 1975). Charles Morrow Wilson Papers, Location C1318, Box 37, Folder 1. Special Collections, University of Arkansas Libraries, Fayetteville.

468. Campbell, William S., *One Hundred Years of Fayetteville, 1828-1928,* Fayetteville, AR, 1928, p. 92.

469. Hogan, J. B., "Fayetteville City Officials," *Flashback*, Summer 2007, Vol. 57, No. 3, 70.

470. Campbell, p. 98.

471. Hogan, pp. 68-69, 71.

472. *NWAT*, December 17, 1942.

473. *Razorback* Annual, University of Arkansas, 1924, pp. 88, 117.

474. Ibid., 1925, pp. 123 and 125.

475. Campbell, p. 108.

476. *All's Well,* Vol. 6, No. 8, December 1926, p. 17.

477. Ibid., Vol. VI, No. XII, April-May 1927, pp. 18-19.

478. Ibid., Vol. VII, No. I, June 1927, pp. 14-15.

479. Ibid., Vol. VII, No. VII, March 1928, pp. 7-10.

480. Ibid., Vol. VII, No. III, September-October 1927, p. 3.

481. *Fayetteville Daily Democrat* (FDD), April 3, 1928.

482. *FDD,* October 16, 1928.

483. *All's Well,* Vol. 7, No. 10, August-September 1928, p. 10.

484. CMW, detailed resume, April 27, 1961. The newspapers were the *St. Louis Post-Dispatch* and the *New York World.* C1318, Box 37, Folder 1.

485. *FDD*, September 16, 1927. This bout is famous for the referee's "long count" given to Tunney who went on to defeat Dempsey

again and bring to an end the ex-champion's former dominance as a heavyweight fighter.

486. *Atlantic Monthly* to CMW (Payment Form), October 19, 1928. C1274, Box 10, Folder 1.

487. *FDD*, April 4, 1929.

488. CMW to Mattie Morrow Wilson, May 24, 1929. C1265, Box 1, Folder 2.

489. Ibid.

490. Ben Hibbs (Editor, Country Gentleman) to CMW, June 14, 1937. C1274, Box 10, Folder 5.

491. CMW to Joseph Dickson Wilson, April 1, 1938. C1267, Box 3, Folder 14.

492. Pearl S. Buck to CMW, September 10, 1934. C1274, Box 10, Folder 3.

493. CMW to Mattie Morrow Wilson, November 23, 1933. C1265, Box 1, Folder 7.

494. CMW to Mattie Morrow Wilson, February 17, 1937. C1267, Box 3, Folder 13.

495. Fred Starr wrote the Ozarks column "Hillside Adventures" for many years in the *Northwest Arkansas Times.* He was the author of nine books, perhaps the best known of which is *Of These Hills and Us* published in 1958. Fred Starr died in 1973 aged 77.

496. CMW, detailed resume, April 27, 1961. C1318, Box 37, Folder 1.

497. "A Charter for Middle America," Middle America Information Bureau, United Fruit Company, 1941, p. 2.

498. Ibid., p. 3.

499. Ibid., p. 2. A somewhat ironic position, given the well-documented involvement of United Fruit in the overthrow of the Guatemalan government in 1954.

500. CMW to Joseph Dickson Wilson, June 15, 1937. C1267, Box 3, Folder 13.

501. CMW, detailed resume, April 27, 1961. C1318, Box 37, Folder 1. According to other biographical materials, Wilson indicates he served in the Navy procurement "of strategic supplies" (C1318, Box 37, Folder 2).

502. CMW to Mrs. Roberta Fulbright, October 11, 1944. C1270, Box 6, Folder 4.

503. CMW to Mrs. Roberta Fulbright, October 31, 1944. C1270, Box 6, Folder 4.

504. Dr. Drake and the City Park Company had purchased the city park grounds from A. L. Trent in 1926.

505. Ibid.

506. CMW to Kate Wilson Ripley., January 2, 1945. C1268, Box 4, Folder 20.

507. CMW to Suzanne "Peg" Chalfant Lighton, January 2, 1945. C1270, Box 6, Folder 4.

508. Mrs. Roberta Fulbright to CMW, February 26, 1945. C1270, Box 6, Folder 4.

509. CMW to George T. Sanders., March 29, 1945. C1270, Box 6, Folder 4.

510. *NWAT,* August 16, 1946.

511. Ibid.

512. Ibid., August 20, 1945.

513. CMW to Kate Wilson Ripley, December 14, 1945. C1268, Box 4, Folder 20.

514. Warranty Deed, Book 370, Page 207, Washington County Records, Fayetteville, Arkansas, August 26, 1946.

515. *NWAT,* January 5, 1949.

516. Ibid., January 6, 1949.

517. Powell M. Rhea to CMW, November 3, 1950. C1270, Box 6, Folder 7.

518. Ibid.

519. CMW, "Backwards a Dozen Centuries," *Natural History,* 56:370-378, October 1947.

520. Branch, Mark Alden, "Secrets of the Temple," *Yale Alumni Magazine,* internet document, URL http://www.yalealumnimagazine.com/issues/02_11/maya.html, November 2002.

521. CMW, detailed resume, April 27, 1961. C1318, Box 37, Folder 1.

522. CMW, "Backwards a Dozen Centuries," *Natural History,* 56:370-378, October 1947.

523. CMW, "Bonampak," St. Louis Post-Dispatch, July 27, 1947.

524. CMW, "Nature's Own Children," *Nature Magazine,* February 1951, pp. 65-70.

525. CMW to Kenneth MacGowan, August 5, 1947. C1275, Box 11, Folder 13.

526. CMW to Kenneth MacGowan, September 4, 1947. C1275, Box 11, Folder 13.

527. Kenneth MacGowan to CMW, September 8, 1947. C1275, Box

11, Folder 13.

528. CMW to Kenneth MacGowan, October 31, 1947. C1275, Box 11, Folder 13.

529. "Biography for Kenneth MacGowan," undated internet document, Internet Movie Database, URL http://www.imdb.com/name/nm0532284/bio.

530. Compton, Ellen, "Charles Morrow Wilson," entry in *The Encyclopedia of Arkansas History and Culture,* April 21, 2007.

531. CMW, detailed resume, April 27, 1961. C1318, Box 37, Folder 1.

532. NWAT, May 17, 1947.

533. Edward Durell Stone was the grandson of Stephen K. Stone. In his autobiography Evolution of an Architect (Horizon Press, New York, 1962), Edward Durell described his grandfather as "one of the earliest settlers of northwest Arkansas and one of the founders of Fayetteville" (p. 16). In addition to buildings throughout the world, Edward Durell Stone designed the Windham College campus in Putney, Vermont, Charles Morrow Wilson's long-time hometown.

534. Ibid., September 12, 1950.

535. CMW, personal correspondence, undated (ca. 1951). C1316, Box 35, Sub-series 242, Folder 1.

536. Joe E. Covington to CMW, July 27, 1950. C1270, Box 6, Folder 7.

537. NWAT, November 15, 1950.

538. Ibid., November 27, 1950.

539. Ibid., November 25, 1950.

540. "Hometown Revisited," p. 16.

541. Ibid., p. 18.

542. Ibid., p. 21.

543. CMW to Kate Wilson Ripley, December 28, 1954. C1271, Box 7, Folder 10.

544. Ibid.

545. CMW to Dudley Dowell, June 16, 1950. C1270, Box 6, Folder 7.

546. CMW to Herbert L. Thomas., July 6 and July 21, 1953. C1271, Box 7, Folder 9.

547. CMW to John T. Caldwell, November 2, 1954. C1271, Box 7, Folder 10.

548. John T. Caldwell to CMW, September 21, 1954.

549. John T. Caldwell to CMW, November 1, 1954.

550. CMW to J. K. Gregory, January 31, 1949. C1270, Box 6, Folder 6.

551. CMW to W. C. Whitfield, June 30, 1950. C1270, Box 6, Folder 7.

552. CMW to W. C. Whitfield, August 4, 1949. C1270, Box 6, Folder 6.

553. CMW to George T. Sanders, December 23, 1948. C1270, Box 6, Folder 6.

554. CMW to W. C. Whitfield, June 30, 1950. C1270, Box 6, Folder 7.

555. Professor Lemke was then head of the University of Arkansas Journalism Department and was one of the organizers of the Washington County Historical Society.

556. CMW to Walter J. Lemke, July 21, 1953. C1271, Box 7, Folder 9.

557. Ibid.

558. CMW to John T. Caldwell, November 2, 1954. C1271, Box 7, Folder 10.

559. CMW to Donald Trumbo, Jr., August 8, 1967. C1272, Box 8, Folder 16.

560. CMW to Donald Trumbo, Jr., August 10, 1967. C1272, Box 8, Folder 16.

561. CMW to Edward I. Salisbury, December 28, 1952. C1276, Box 12, Folder 19.

562. CMW to Merle Thorpe, March 30, 1953. C1277, Box 13, Folder 20.

563. CMW to Herbert L. Thomas, July 21, 1953. C1271, Box 7, Folder 9.

564. CMW, personal correspondence, undated (ca. 1951). C1316, Box 35, Sub-series 242, Folder 1

565. NWAT, February 16, 1952.

566. Subsidy or Vanity Publishing requires the author to finance his or her own work for a percentage of the book's sales. Subsidy publishing is typically a writer's last resort for work not accepted by full-service publishing houses.

567. CMW to Virgil Baker, September 27, 1950. C1270, Box 6, Folder 7.

568. Compton, Ellen, "Wilson, Charles Morrow" entry in *Arkansas Biography: A Collection of Notable Lives,* edited by Nancy A. Williams, University of Arkansas Press, Fayetteville, 2000, p. 309.

569. CMW to Kate Wilson Ripley, December 28, 1954. C1271, Box 7, Folder 10.

A Most Unusual Shooting

570. Arkansas Act 241, 1943, dealt with the maintenance of mental health patients and how the state hospital would be reimbursed for the treatment of those patients by the counties from which they came.

571. *Northwest Arkansas Times,* December 5, 6, 8, 15, 20, 21, 22, and 26, 1955 and January 11, 1956. Quotations and details of the case are from the newspaper, chronological sequencing, summary, and narrative by the author.

Kirby L. Estes:
Fayetteville's First Poet Laureate

572. Internet e-mail between William R. Mayo and Kirby L. Estes, April 3, 2006.

573. Estes, Kirby L., in *Songs of Youth* (anthology), American Poetry Society, 1955, p. 56.

574. Estes, Kirby L., in *Young America Sings* (anthology), National High School Poetry Association, Los Angeles, 1956, p. 79.

575. "The M. C. Escher Memorial Tone Poem" and "In Eliot's Usk," *Grapevine,* ca. 1972.

576. "Tune-In" and "Dark Rain," *Northwest Arkansas Times,* May 14, 1997.

577. "Crystal Adagio: In Memoriam," *Slant,* Vol. XVII, Summer 2003.

578. "Off the Ozarks Tawny Shore," *Arkansas Literary Forum,* October 2005, No. 7.

579. "Remember Me to Herald Square," *Megaera,* December 1, 2005.

580. "The Reunification of Troilus and Cressida," *Istanbul Literary Review,* September 2007.

581. Estes appeared at GoodFolk House, April 7, 2007.

582. Estes appeared at Nightbird Books, April 21, 2007.

583. Estes appeared at Arsaga's Coffeehouse, July 13, 2007.

584. *Red Owl,* Autumn 2006, Vol. XXIII.

585. *Respiro,* November 2007.

586. *Word Catalyst,* Fall 2007.

587. *Asbestos,* Spring 2008.

588. Review of *Backroad,* J. B. Hogan, 2007. Quotations from Backroad, Kirby Estes, Lost Creek Press, Fayetteville, Arkansas, 2007, p.33.

285

589. Internet e-mail, Jay Ross to Dan Coody, June 21, 2006.
590. Indian Bay Press Newsletter, October 24, 2006.
591. Fayetteville Arkansas Cultural Arts District Initiative, internet press release, April 6, 2007.
592. Internet e-mail, Molly Giles to J. B. Hogan, February 16, 2012.
593. Internet e-mail, Clayton Scott to J. B. Hogan, January 2, 2013.
594. Fayetteville Arkansas Cultural Arts District Initiative, internet press release, April 13, 2007.
595. Ibid.
596. Internet e-mail, Clayton Scott to J. B. Hogan, January 2, 2013.
597. "Miller Williams Honored as Poet Laureate of Fayetteville 2011," City of Fayetteville, Arkansas News Release, April 21, 2011.
598. Fayetteville (AR) Mayor Lioneld Jordan speech, University of Arkansas, April 20, 2011.
599. *Northwest Arkansas Times,* archived online article, April 4, 2011.
600. Fayetteville (AR) Mayor Lioneld Jordan speech, University of Arkansas, April 20, 2011.
601. Williams passed away January 1, 2015.

INDEX

294

J.B. HOGAN is a prolific and award-winning author. He grew up in Fayetteville, Arkansas, but moved to Southern California in 1961 before entering the U. S. Air Force in 1964. After the military, he went back to college, receiving a Ph.D. in English from Arizona State University in 1979.

J.B. has published over 300 stories and poems. His novels, *The Apostate, Living Behind Time, Losing Cotton,* and *Tin Hollow,* two short story collections entitled *Fallen* and *Bar Harbor,* and his book of poetry, *The Rubicon*—are available at Amazon, iBooks, Barnes & Noble, Books-A-Million, and Walmart.

Printed in the USA
CPSIA information can be obtained
at www.ICGtesting.com
LVHW061228071023
760363LV00002B/204